AMERICAN BUDDHA

AMERICAN BUDDHA

HOW A
CHRISTIAN MINISTER
DISCOVERED HER
SPIRITUAL DESTINY

Mary Ann McGuire

In honor of my soul brother, Lama Gyatso,
the ancient Tibetan Nyingma lineage tradition,
and its Enlightened Masters.

*This book is dedicated to the great Maha Siddha,
His Holiness the Fourth Dodrupchen Rinpoche,
revered for his complete mastery over his subtle
psychic—spiritual energies and numerous enlightened
yogic activities, whose mere presence conveys the
epic mass of both the sun and moon.*

CONTENTS

PROLOGUE

It sometimes happens that the Angel of Forgetfulness himself forgets to remove from our memories the records of the former world; and then our senses are haunted by fragmentary recollections of another life. They drift like torn clouds above the hills and valleys of the mind, and weave themselves into the incidents of our current existence.

—SHOLEM ASCH, *The Nazarene*

ONE NIGHT, WHEN I WAS FIVE, I saw myself float up from my bed, rise through the roof, and fly into the starry sky. Consumed with curiosity, knowing I would eventually come to the end of the universe, I shot like a comet across the radiant cosmos. When finally I arrived at the edge of the abyss, I hesitated. A vast void, black and opaque, stretched out before me. Sensing that if I went farther I would never return, I retreated and flew home with breathtaking speed.

I had no way of knowing then that this vision held the very story of my life. Forty years later, when I was a mother of three, an aspiring Christian minister, and a community activist, my dreams, my hopes, and many years of hard work dissolved into chaos and uncertainty. My marriage ended in a painful, protracted divorce, and my thriving, self-made ministry faltered under the pressure of petty power dynamics and misogyny. As life unraveled around me, I found myself at that distant place in my vision: the black edge of the sky, facing the unknown. At precisely this moment, I encountered one of the world's greatest Tibetan Buddhist teachers, His Eminence Chagdud Tulku Rinpoche.

Affectionately known among his Western students simply as Rinpoche, HE Chagdud Tulku Rinpoche was a luminary of the Nyingma sect, the oldest of the four major branches of Tibetan Buddhism (along with the Kagyu, Sakya, and Gelugpa sects). *Nyingma* means "ancient" and refers to the carefully preserved lineage that connects the Nyingmas to the founders of Tibetan Buddhism: Padmasambhava, Yeshe Tsogyal, King Trisong Detsen, and other eighth-century luminaries. Nyingma spiritual leaders are therefore known as the "Ancient Ones."

I first saw Chagdud Tulku Rinpoche Rinpoche while he was teaching students in a wooded grove overlooking California's Napa Valley. Although I was a practicing Christian minister, his magnetizing voice and charismatic presence felt remarkably familiar and drew me to him. I was concerned that my Christian faith might eliminate me as a suitable vessel for his teachings. Rinpoche did not share my concern. "Truth the same. Same for Christian, same for Buddhist," he said. "Same truth all over the world. I teach you truth we call *dharma*." Thus reassured, I became his student within hours of meeting him.

For many years to come, I would receive teachings from Rinpoche and his fellow Nyingma masters, who guided me on an extraordinary spiritual journey into an expansive world of compassion, mystery, magic, and wonder. I experienced a profound resonance with the teachings, with Rinpoche, and with his senior student, the Venerable Lama Chödak Gyatso Nubpa Rinpoche, whom I hosted for a few years while he established a Nyingma center in the United States.

During this time, a shattering knowledge began to awaken within me. Not long after I met Lama Gyatso, he asked if I was familiar with Yeshe Tsogyal, revered as the "Mother of All Tibet" and the sacred consort of Padmasambhava, who many practitioners of Tibetan Buddhism consider the second incarnation of Buddha. Yeshe Tsogyal was a fierce and brilliant woman who stands as a rare historical figure of female spiritual accomplishment and authority. Her fundamental mission was to embrace the Buddhist teachings, known as *dharma*, and to foster happiness among all sentient beings. At the time I knew little about this legendary figure, but something about Lama Gyatso's seemingly casual inquiry stirred in me a sense that I might be connected to her. Thus began the delicate process of solving a timeless puzzle that, as it slowly assembled, awakened soul memories extending far beyond what I had experienced in this lifetime.

Yeshe (unending primordial wisdom) Tsogyal (vast ocean) was born a princess of Karchan, in eighth-century Tibet, near a lovely canyon village filled with silver-leafed willow trees and ancient meditation caves that are still in use today. Stories of her birth are mythic: skies filled with rainbows, the miraculous appearance of a small lake near her home. Upon entering the world, she declared herself a *yogini nirmanakaya*, a female embodiment of Buddha who incarnates to offer spiritual teachings and to liberate all beings from suffering.

Legend holds that Yeshe Tsogyal was unusually beautiful, and though her parents isolated her until she was sixteen, word of her exquisite presence had spread. Many kings sought her hand in marriage, but she refused, believing that matrimony was the quickest road to the prison of suffering called *samsara*. Brushing aside her pleas for a spiritual life devoted to the *dharma*, her parents insisted that she marry for political gain. They could not decide among her suitors, so they dressed her in silks and expelled her from the palace accompanied by a caravan of animals laden with gifts and personal items—the first suitor to capture her would win her as his bride. Two rivals raced to the princess, and the victor claimed her by grabbing her hair and dragging her toward his entourage. When she struggled, he beat her into submission, but on the journey to his kingdom, the princess escaped and hid in a ravine. The second suitor received word of her whereabouts and sent a team of warriors, who successfully retrieved her. He kept her in chains. When King Trisong Detsen, the ruler of Tibet, heard news of the contest for Yeshe Tsogyal, he sent word to her father requesting that she marry him instead. And so it was that Yeshe Tsogyal became the Queen of Tibet.

Trisong Detsen, as it happened, played a pivotal role in introducing Buddhism to Tibet and in establishing the Nyingma tradition. He also allowed his young bride to study the teachings of Buddhism, although at the time it was not the primary religion in the land. He even provided teachers for her, most notably the enlightened *siddha* Padmasambhava, who at the time was traveling through Tibet to spread Buddhist wisdom. Trisong Detsen offered Padmasambhava many riches, including his kingdom, in exchange for his most esoteric teachings. Padmasambhava refused these material offerings, but accepted Yeshe Tsogyal as his spiritual consort and student. She accompanied him for eight years, undergoing strenuous spiritual initiations into the higher mysteries, and ultimately attained Buddhahood. She was celebrated for her yogic abilities, or *siddhis*—resurrecting the dead, feeding the hungry masses, and healing the sick. Because of Yeshe Tsogyal's unparalleled spiritual accomplishments, she has come to be known as the Mother of Tibet, the most highly revered woman in the Nyingma lineage.

Among her numerous accomplishments, Yeshe Tsogyal memorized, translated, and transcribed all of Padmasambhava's spiritual teachings onto scrolls of colored paper, then traveled the world with him to hide the scrolls in myriad places, including caves, rivers, trees, and mountains. Padmasambhava had foreseen a world plagued by disease and disaster, a time when hunger for and commitment to spiritual accomplishment would diminish. He predicted that after many generations of spiritual depletion highly realized *tertöns*, masters adept at discovering esoteric teachings, would find these hidden, revelatory treasures, known as *termas*.

According to my mentor Tulku Thondup Rinpoche, who was an esteemed Buddhist scholar at Harvard, pure wisdom *termas* have indeed been directly transmitted to *tertöns* for centuries and constitute a significant part of the Nyingma tradition. They appear in many forms. Tarthang Tulku Rinpoche, a Tibetan lama who helped bring the Nyingma tradition to the United States, notes in *Mother of Knowledge*,

> *Thousands of [tertöns] have discovered "symbolic scripts" written on pieces of paper as well as full texts and religious materials miraculously imprinted on the earth, on rocks, in lakes or in the sky, awakening memories of whole ranges of wisdom and teachings from the enlightened nature of their minds.... [Other tertöns have] discovered such wisdom and teachings solely through the power of their own wisdom-mind. Such discovered teachings are called "mind treasures" since the [tertöns] discovered them from their own memory banks of wisdom-power without relying on any earthly or physical objects as the keys.*

Termas are valued because, having been preserved in their original forms, they have retained their pure meaning and can thus serve as direct guides to enlightenment. The *tertön* serves as an intermediary who brings to light a specific *terma* in ways that refresh its wisdom for the time in which it surfaces; they deliver pure and timeless wisdom in the voice of the moment.

Within the Nyingma lineage is another centuries-old tradition that allows essential, treasured teachings to be carried forward through time. Highly realized masters take rebirth so that they may continue their work to bring benefit to all living beings, and there is an elaborate system of finding, recognizing, educating, and revering reborn masters. In *Incarnation: The History and Mysticism of the Tulku Tradition in Tibet*, Tulku Thondup Rinpoche, himself "recognized" at age four as the reincarnation of a celebrated Tibetan scholar and saint, describes how *tulkus* are discovered—sometimes a realized teacher will foretell where he will take rebirth; some awakened beings, like Yeshe Tsogyal, are born and announce who they are as soon as they are old enough to speak; others will demonstrate accumulated wisdom from their previous lives; yet others are recognized by living lamas who find them by way of clairvoyance, dreams, or recognition of specific qualities; and some reveal themselves by discovering *termas*.

HE Chagdud Tulku Rinpoche describes being recognized at the age of three in his autobiography, *Lord of the Dance*, and details his deep connection to his mother, Dawa Drolma, who was revered as a woman of extraordinary spiritual attainment. She was widely known as a *delog*, one who has crossed the threshold of death, traveled to unseen realms, and returned to tell of what they have discovered. During her lifetime, she enthralled huge audiences with vivid tales of her journeys of consciousness and the revelations she found in these other realms.

Dawa Drolma was also recognized as a living incarnation of Yeshe Tsogyal—and it was her son, HE Chagdud Tulku Rinpoche who recognized me as a *tertön* and the current living incarnation of Yeshe Tsogyal. I was unaware of this recognition at the time, but I *was* aware in myself of a strange and unprecedented resonance in Rinpoche's presence. Mesmerized by stories of his homeland and his mother, I could perfectly visualize Tibet's wild rivers and sacred snow mountains. I could picture, as though I were there, Dawa Drolma teaching under the family's black yak-hair tent, which held up to four hundred people, while her young son observed. "Seeing" like this was an experience that I can describe only as harmonic memory, whereby Rinpoche's memories evoked visions so lucid and so familiar that they felt like my own memories, much in the way an A string played on one violin will cause the A string on another violin to vibrate in unison.

Despite having recognized me as Yeshe Tsogyal, Rinpoche chose to keep his own counsel—after all, this is not the sort of thing that you casually announce to a Western, middle-aged woman who also happens to be a Christian minister. While there is a long-standing tradition for recognizing Tibetans as reincarnated masters and for schooling them in the Nyingma teachings, this process remains nebulous for those born in the West, where religious and cultural beliefs deny the possibility of rebirth. Therefore, Rinpoche charged Lama Gyatso with guiding me gently into understanding Yeshe Tsogyal's legacy and the ancient practices of the Nyingmas. With his help, I undertook a slow, delicate journey, for many years dancing around intimations that I might be Yeshe Tsogyal, until, at last, I was able to stand fully in the knowledge that she and I are One.

PART 1

WHEN THE STUDENT IS READY

Chapter 1

THE AGE OF REASON

But deep within her the antenatal thing that lay here had a dream. In those eyes that had never seen the day, in that half-shaped brain was a sensation of light! Light—that it had never seen. Light—that perhaps it never should see. Light—that existed somewhere!

And already it had its reward: the Ideal was real to it.

— OLIVE SCHREINER, "A Dream of Wild Bees"

I WAS BORN UNDER a waxing gibbous moon on May 1, 1939, a date that sat at the midpoint between the greening hopes of spring and summer and at the outset of humanity's darkest chapter. Three months prior to my birth, Adolf Hitler had proclaimed to the German Parliament his plan to exterminate the Jewish population and other "undesirables" throughout Europe. Later that year he invaded Czechoslovakia and Poland. Thus, I was ushered into the world just as the Second World War commenced.

Life in Piedmont, California, however, was far removed from the European and Pacific battlefields. Steep streets were illuminated at night by tall lamps that carved across the picturesque hills of our small city, which overlooked Oakland and San Francisco Bay. Our street, Scenic Avenue, set high in a new section of the Piedmont Hills, had few houses, and they were separated by undeveloped lots that provided open space for walking and, depending on your age, for building forts and rigging basketball courts. A gabled roof covered our modest three-bedroom home, which my parents been able to purchase with the help of my maternal grandparents. My two sisters and I shared two upstairs bedrooms that featured dormer windows and window seats designed by Mother.

Daddy disappeared several nights a week, dressed in a smart Coast Guard uniform with a jaunty military cap angled over his dark hair and handsome, fair, Irish face. The California, Oregon, and Washington coasts were destination points for Japanese submarines, and a few had been found washed up on our shores. It was the Coast Guard's job to patrol these waters, and Daddy volunteered to help. Some nights when he was gone, we were forbidden to use lights. During these blackouts, my older sister, Aline, and I sat on the couch on either side of our tearful mother while my younger sister, Cecilia, hid under the pink blanket. Thick curtains darkened the living room. The tall wooden Philco radio stood silent, and Daddy's armchair, where he read the evening paper, sat empty.

In the lot next to ours, Daddy planted a victory garden. It was beyond the realm of my five-year-old understanding to know what lettuce, tomatoes, and spinach had to do with air-raid sirens and blackout curtains, and I wondered if victories looked like tomatoes. Once I asked my father to plant lamb chops. He wiped sweat from his brow, leaned against his tall hoe, and laughed.

"Lamb chops don't grow in victory gardens," he said, looking down at me. "But if I could, I would plant a lamb-chop tree for you, Mary Ann. I'm afraid that's just not how it works."

My parents dreamed of achieving business, social, and financial success after the war. Aspiring to personify the model family of the

1940s, they began each day with an air of confidence, even bravado. Mother cooked breakfast wearing nylons, heels, and starched dresses, occasionally patting her well-coiffed hair and pursing her painted lips. She spoke affectionately to my father as she served freshly squeezed orange juice, oatmeal, toast, and eggs. My maternal grandfather was a founder of the Sunkist orange label, so we never lacked for oranges, and Daddy would hold up his glass of golden juice to remind us how fortunate we were. "Your grandfather is a self-made man," he liked to point out. "He quit school after the seventh grade to support his mother, but spent his evenings reading every book of the Encyclopedia Britannica. He is the most educated man I know!" My parents would worry aloud about how frost and drought might affect the citrus crop before Daddy finally opened the newspaper and read the news.

Mother's fantasies did not include wartime shortages or household duties such as canning tomatoes, washing dishes, or ironing sheets on the back porch. She read a steady stream of romantic novels, visited the beauty parlor weekly, knew the British royal lineage going back centuries, and was convinced that she, like the Duchess of Windsor, should have married a royal. She took afternoon naps. Nonetheless, she met all her daily responsibilities and greeted my father each evening in a smart dress and high heels, her nose freshly powdered. This suited my father well. As a young man with a promising future in the insurance industry, he needed an attractive, socially adept, well-dressed wife (who could serve well-appointed meals), model children (who would remain silent), and immaculate flowerbeds (with no sign of weeds)—all of which he had.

Yet our quiet life on Scenic Avenue was troubled by alcohol. Alcoholism wasn't talked about much in those days—the term was reserved for Skid Row bums—and I never learned to anticipate the

terrifying chaos that ensued when evening cocktails stirred up my
mother's emotional instability and my father's volatile temper. Mother
never demonstrated anger at me and my sisters; she let my father do that
for her. After a few drinks, he was helpless if she complained about us,
his temper flaring quickly at the thought that we might have caused her
distress, and he would lash out verbally and physically, breaking wooden
coat hangers over our outstretched hands. Mother sat by, saying, "Oh,
Tom, don't hurt them too much. I can't stand to see anyone hurting."

Daddy's rage passed quickly, but Mother's air of resentment
never cleared. She did not forget a thing. Slights, real or imagined,
lingered in her mind. If she was excluded from a social event, she would
remember that affront fifteen years later, when drafting her own
invitation list. But both parents were inextricable in the dynamic of
these outbursts. Daddy seemed to need the physical release of anger,
and Mother seemed to need the adrenaline rush produced by these
episodes of violence.

Although our family rarely discussed religion, we faithfully attended
the Roman Catholic Mass, said grace before meals, and ate fish on
Fridays. I would sit next to Mother during Mass at St. Leo's Cathedral
and hold her hand when she cried, trying to console her. When the
priest lifted the Host, Mother would remove her hand from mine and
dab at her eyes while I prayed for a way to ease the mysterious suffering
that hovered around her like a cloud. She would also cry during our
occasional Saturday afternoon visits to the confessional. Afterward, we
would cross the street to Dreyer's Ice Cream Shop. Mother would order
one scoop of chocolate ice cream and one scoop of orange sherbet,
which were served in a fluted glass dish, and I would have a chocolate
soda with vanilla ice cream. This ritual seemed to lift her mood.

Back home she would dress up for the evening cocktail hour, but by dinner her sorrow, her cynicism, her cruelty would have reappeared, seeming to have entered her like spirits from another realm. She'd share with Daddy her routine woes about the terrible sins her girls had committed during the day—I had turned somersaults on the lawn in my dress, staining my skirt; my older sister had spoken rudely and disrespectfully; my younger sister had sucked her thumb. Despite her depression, Mother was actually far kinder, smarter, and more beautiful than any of her daughters. I knew this because my father and grandparents persistently reinforced this message. I understood that she needed me to help her survive the demands of motherhood, so I constantly reminded her of her goodness and beauty. She would weep and shake her head in denial, which I knew only made it more important for me to help her feel better. Though it was plain to me that she was just pretending to be drunk or unkind, I couldn't figure out why she kept up the ruse.

As a child, I could have never explained my choices, but I believe that we do things instinctively, like bees making honey or foxes dipping their paws into stream water to fool the dogs. It was instinct that drove me to take it upon myself to remedy the violence, contentiousness, and tension that gripped our home. While I was often able to momentarily ease what I saw as the ongoing battle between the forces of light and dark in which my family was trapped, I was unable to prevent in any permanent sense the behaviors in which they engaged. My parents and my sister continued to fight, and Mother's sorrow and coldness grew more pronounced.

Yet I remained convinced that such a steady state of rage and suffering didn't belong in the beautiful home Mother had created. It was wrong and unnecessary. Even when I was subjected to spankings,

I had a deep sense that Daddy's punishment had nothing to do with me, that my parents' true anger didn't stem from anything my sisters or I had done. I could not deny, curse, or hate this reality since I had been taught that this was how loving parents raised their children. I learned to stand quietly and accept the punishments, dry-eyed.

I was the strange one. I wanted to be a nun, I was eager to go to church, I prayed my novenas. Outwardly, I was obedient; I fashioned a passive exterior as I dared not violate the boundaries set by parents, culture, and church, which were like invisible electrical fences. But I harbored a rich, secret inner life, where I found solace and silence. I had access to a deep reservoir of peace, awe, and wonder, which I dipped into frequently, sometimes for moments, sometimes for hours. This inner space comforted, guided, and held me in ways the world around me did not. I experienced this sense of deeper connection continually and believed everyone else did the same.

Catholics reach the "age of reason" on their seventh birthday. And so it was that on May 1, 1946, I was eligible to receive my First Holy Communion. It couldn't have come soon enough. During the war years, our grammar school held regularly scheduled air-raid drills, teaching us to use blankets to ward off radiation and our desks as protection from atomic blasts. I would squeeze myself in a tight ball under both blanket and desk, worrying that I might die without the protection of the priest and his Eucharist and thus be vulnerable to the whims of a wrathful God and an unfriendly universe. I prayed that if the bomb were to actually drop, it would happen while the Communion host was in my mouth, for that wafer on my tongue was the difference between Heaven and the fires of an eternal Hell.

In preparation for the auspicious event of First Communion, the nuns, who were of the Holy Names Order, taught catechism class every Thursday afternoon at a large, brown-shingled, turn-of-the-century home that served as a convent. On the first Thursday of catechism class, a kind, soft-spoken young nun sat in front of fifteen squirming seven year olds seated in a half circle on worn wooden dining-room chairs. Sister Mary Angelica called our attention to a painting that depicted an angel of cosmic size with vast white wings protecting a happy, carefree girl and boy playing dangerously close to a cliff.

"She is your guardian angel, who is always with you, day and night, even when you sleep." Sister's voice was soft and musical. "You cannot see your guardian angel now, but she is there, and we will learn a prayer you can say to her every night before you go to sleep."

And so I memorized one of my first prayers, which, along with the two-thousand-year-old Lord's Prayer and the Hail Mary prayer, were woven into my nighttime ritual of kneeling next to my bed with Mother and my sisters.

> Angel dear, my guardian near
> To whom God's love commits me here—
> Ever this day, be at my side
> To light, to love, to rule, to guide
> AMEN

Along with talk of angels, Sister gave us thin blue-and-white catechisms to study and required us to memorize certain questions—*Who is God? Who made God? Who made me? Who am I? Why did God make me?*—and their answers. We took each question one by one and repeated the answers after her.

Every night, Mother and I sat in the kitchen memorizing the catechism. I burned with curiosity and bombarded her with questions that she did her best to answer. My vocabulary expanded. I learned my first multisyllabic words: God is *omnipresent, omnipotent,* and *omniscient.*

"Mommy, what does *omnipresent* mean?"

"It means that God is always everywhere."

My mind stretched outward and upward. "You mean everywhere, like right here and outside and at school, just like Santa Claus?"

"Well, yes, in a way," she replied uncertainly.

"How can one man be everywhere at the same time?"

"Because He isn't just a man," she said. "He is God! Now say the word after me until you have memorized it."

And so I said *omnipresent* over and over. That word was relatively easy to learn, but the next two required some effort.

"What does *omnipotent* mean, Mommy?"

"Mary Ann, even I don't understand who God is or how He knows everything, but He does. He *is* omnipotent. Now say that ten times, along with *omnipresent.*'"

We met at the kitchen table every night that week. There was so much that I wanted to know: Did God have a mother? And if God was the Father, then who was the Mother? I already knew that Mary is our Mother in Heaven as well as the Mother of God, but I thought that was strange because Mary wasn't mentioned in my catechism, nor was she a part of the Eucharistic meal for which I was being prepared. I didn't worry about that, though, because Our Lady the Blessed Virgin Mary and I knew each other quite well by then.

On the last night of my study program, I memorized that I was a child of God and that God made me so that I should know God, love God, and serve God. That's why I was created. It was this last answer, outlining the dictates of knowledge, service, and love that seemed to brand my soul and commission my spirit.

St. Leo's Cathedral was intimidating to a seven year old. The center aisle led directly to the distant railing that protected the High Altar, draped in embroidered white linen, which sat atop three marble steps and was flanked by two tall gold candlesticks. On the altar sat a radiant gold tabernacle that housed the elements of the Eucharist—the bread, water, and wine that the priest would magically transform into the Body and Blood of Christ.

On the morning of my First Communion, I wore a fluffy white dress with a white sash and a capped veil of white tulle, as did the other girls. The boys wore dark pants and white cotton shirts. I concentrated on perfect behavior and on all the priests and altar boys, while also being very aware of my veil, white dress, and shining black Mary Janes. The organ thundered above us and the choir sang the Latin processional hymn as we walked with care, two by two, down the long aisle to our respective pews. Sister's clacker alerted us when to sit, stand, or kneel.

As the Mass proceeded, the priest, vested in an ornate gold and white chasuble, opened the shining tabernacle of mystery. I tried to see beyond the boys sitting in front of me, but Sister wouldn't let me stand on the kneeler to watch the priest perform the magic of turning the elements into the Body and Blood of Christ. I slumped back into the large pew until Sister clacked the signal to kneel. Just as we had practiced the day before, we lined up next to the pews, walked slowly to the altar, and knelt. In the priest's hands were a gold chalice and a small round white wafer called the host. An altar boy garbed in a red under-robe and long white surplice held a gold paten under each person's chin to catch the host should it fall or break.

When the priest reached me, I stuck my tongue out and received the Body of Christ. Prior to this momentous occasion, I believed, I would not have gone to heaven if I died. Sister said that I would have gone to a good place, but not to heaven. So I tasted this bread of heaven on my tongue and was relieved. It stuck to the top of my mouth, which was good because maybe it would last longer that way. Even then, at age seven, with thundering vibrations descending from the organ loft, I knew that like the priest who turned the elements into Jesus Christ himself, I wanted to "do magic" too.

Chapter 2

Blue and the Blessed Virgin Mary

And now here is my secret, a very simple secret: It is only with the heart that one can see rightly; what is essential is invisible to the eye.

—Antoine de Saint-Exupéry, *The Little Prince*

Aunt Edith presented my sisters and me an *Illustrated Children's Bible*, which often lay forgotten in our jumbled playroom. I liked to retreat there to sit alone on the dimly lit floor amid our cast-off dolls, Christmas toys, and puzzles and study the biblical picture stories. There were long-bearded patriarchs like Moses, Abraham, and Jacob, and the beautiful young shepherd boy, David. Most of all, I was mesmerized by the radically different Marys I met in those pages, intrigued by the fact that they shared my name.

The most captivating, confusing, and frightening Mary was called Magdalene. Even though my own sexuality lay dormant until junior high, I understood as an eight year old that Mary Magdalene was disgraced for reasons of sexuality. In Church traditions, women have been depicted in stark terms, as virgins or whores, as saints or sinners. Although Pope Francis has recently taken measures to refute the characterization of Mary Magdalene as a prostitute, for centuries Catholic women have perceived their sexuality, even their very bodies, as sinful. Of course, as a child, I didn't really know what a prostitute was, nor did I ever ask an adult to explain how this beautiful woman dressed in red, adorned with shining bracelets and long gold earrings, could have been so sinful. I didn't know that it was to Mary Magdalene that Jesus came in his spirit body, that it was to her, a woman, that he transmitted the secret spiritual teachings of Christianity. All I knew was that if I wanted to get married and not be a "prostitute," I had to be very good and follow the rules.

In another story, another woman named Mary who remains a figure of some mystery anointed Jesus with fragrant oils from a lovely alabaster jar before his crucifixion. She washed His feet with her tears and dried them with her lush red hair. Though the reasons for this Mary's painful humility were unclear, I concluded that her sins must have been as shameful as those of Mary Magdalene. I often found myself turning the pages of this poignant story, transfixed by the forgiveness Jesus bestowed upon her regardless of her sins.

Then there was Mary of Bethany, who appeared alongside her long-suffering sibling, Martha. Both women were sisters of Lazarus, whom Jesus raised from the dead. Martha, finding herself stuck with the drudgery of housework, complained to Jesus that while she herself worked so diligently, Mary did nothing but sit at his feet listening. Jesus responded, "Martha, Martha, you are worried about many things, but few things are needed—indeed only one. Mary has chosen what is better, and it will not be taken away from her" (Luke 10:38–42). I dismissed this story straight away: I knew that successful women like Mother were loved and rewarded by God (and by husbands) because they kept up their appearance, cooked breakfast, and hired help to keep the house clean; women who did nothing but sit at the feet of their teachers had no role in life on Scenic Avenue. Years later, however, Martha's conflict became mine when, as a young married woman, I came to feel like an unpaid servant imprisoned in a relationship that I could never escape, despite the fact that being a wife was precisely the role I'd sought and bound myself to. This conflict would take me as close to despair as I would ever come. In fact, at different times in my life I eventually identified with each one of those cast-out, confused, unhappy Marys.

My own flesh-and-blood mother Mary had limited loving attention to focus on me, but thankfully she placed images of Our Lady around the house. The celestial Queen of Heaven, the Blessed Virgin Mary, was my own personal Mary, and I studied her on the holy cards that I collected. Draped in a beautiful blue shawl and surrounded by silver stars, she emanated an aura of light while seeming to float above billowing clouds, one dainty foot resting on the crescent of a moon. I often turned to this unconditionally loving and always-present Virgin Mary for guidance and solace. Our private "conversations" helped me navigate whatever I faced, confounding or otherwise, especially when it came to my family, and usually gave me a profound sense of comfort. I would explain to the Virgin Mother that my parent's unhappiness and anger didn't reflect who they really were: *They don't understand, Lady Mary. Please talk to God and tell him not to hurt them. I'm afraid of God, so you talk to him for me.*

Sometimes I would hear a clear, spontaneous voice speak to me. One day, for example, my sisters and I were at a photographer's studio, preparing for a family portrait. Our hair was neatly parted, our satin ribbons artfully tied, but we were restless as the photographer attempted to situate our squirming bodies for the perfect picture. Suddenly a commanding voice spoke to me: *Sit up straight. Very straight!* As I obeyed, a rush of joyful lightness passed through me. Mother kept the framed photograph in her bedroom, where it continued to remind me of that voice. The joy I experienced was much like the rush one feels when unexpectedly encountering a beloved old friend. And, in fact, the feeling was already familiar to me, for I often had mystical experiences, whether clairaudient or clairvoyant. But I knew that I had to keep them to myself.

When I was nine, over the course of a month, I came down with the red measles, then the German measles, then the black measles. Mother and my physician, Dr. Bowman, also suspected a mild case of polio. This fever-filled period of illness changed my life in mysterious and unexpected ways.

On the day I first became sick, I arrived home from school in the late afternoon. My parents were hosting a cocktail party, and Mother, holding an iced drink, reached for me as I walked in the front door. She was laughing and happy. Then she looked at me more closely and noticed how unwell I looked.

"Can't I, just for once, have some fun without you having to ruin everything?" she said.

But she saw to it that I was well cared for in an atmosphere of quiet, rest, and solitude. Trays of healthy food appeared and then were removed. Twice, Mother attempted to read aloud to me. Moving a chair next to my bed, she would open a book and, visibly uncomfortable, begin to read, the sound of her voice disappearing into the curling smoke of her cigarette. I did not interrupt, nor did I complain about the acrid fumes. Mutual relief would sweep through the room when she finally closed the book, smiled, and excused herself, taking the ashtray and leaving me to a beautiful silence.

On the window seat next to my bed was Aunt Edith's birthday gift to me, my first *Jack and Jill* children's magazine, which arrived sometime between Dr. Bowman's house calls during those long days of sleep. The cover featured a mother lion and two cubs under an electric blue sky. I was captivated by that blue, and gazed at it for days on end. At the end of *The Wizard of Oz*, Auntie Em has no way of knowing the journey that Dorothy has taken in her dream. To her, Dorothy's words "There's no place like home" sound like simple delirious rambling. Similarly, had I tried to explain my fixation upon that blue, my words would likely have seemed nonsensical, for in the solitude of the sickroom what I experienced was more like a voyage to a state of being than a simple fascination with the color.

Blue had no past, present, or future, yet as I became absorbed in it, I felt as though I were in a land of remembering and understanding, a wish-fulfilling realm where I felt a deep sense of belonging and love. In one dreamlike vision, I climbed a wall with ladder-like pegs. The ascent was fun, quick, easy. When I arrived at the top, I encountered an expanse of rich azure more electric even than the blue my physical eyes were seeing. White islands floated in a luminosity that radiated in all directions. Exuberance, well-being, and profound peace permeated me. Afterward, I basked in a delightful sense of love and awe. In this way, I believe, *Blue* healed me, and would continue to do so for decades to come.

I returned to school a changed child. Much of my guilt and anxiety—about my family, about the constant challenges of school (I am somewhat dyslexic)—had vanished. Above all, I no longer harbored the wish that another family would adopt me. Though my best efforts to create the peaceful home of my dreams had not succeeded, I somehow now understood that I was right where I was supposed to be, with my family high in the Piedmont Hills at 416 Scenic Ave. With this new sense of inner security, I felt free to explore. I learned to use the mass-transit system by myself and traveled to the neighboring cities of Oakland and Berkeley. I found new libraries and registered for more library cards. As my world expanded, my shyness dissolved.

When I was eleven, we moved from Piedmont to a larger home in Happy Valley, with extensive gardens, apple trees, and a walnut grove. Here my sense of comfort and confidence continued to enlarge. I played baseball, was voted student-body president, and discovered a lifelong passion for the land. The walnut trees in their groves and the apple trees along the driveway followed delightful seasonal patterns that I'd been unaware of in Piedmont. Country smells and the sound of tractors marked specific times in the natural flow of the seasons. Nature's presence surrounded and filled our home with a vitality I enjoyed for many years. I found happiness in the presence of growing things, bird songs, ripening crops, and harvest activities. I reached puberty in Happy Valley, and when I worked outdoors or was away from home, I was able to set aside family struggles.

However, life in Happy Valley seemed only to exacerbate my parent's anxiety, which they continued to manage with alcohol. Moving into America's upper middle class greatly increased the burden on my mother, who now understood how much time, labor, and money it took to care for a place measured in acres rather than square feet. Family tensions intensified, and fights became more volatile. My older sister turned her rage on me until finally, much to my relief, she was sent to boarding school.

By the time I was fifteen, I needed to escape my family, too. My parents were having their nightly scotch and bourbon in the kitchen before dinner when I broached the subject. If I went to a Catholic boarding school, I explained, I could get better grades, the sort of grades that I would need to gain entrance to the University of California at Berkeley. Though I leveraged academic aspirations to sell my parents on the idea, in truth I was hoping that a kinder, gentler environment might exist behind a convent's cloistered walls. I was surprised by my parent's smiles of interest, their obvious relief, and by how quickly I found myself sitting on a horsehair Victorian settee in one of the stately reception rooms at the Sacred Heart Convent boarding school. The small, elderly Reverend Mother Williams sat in front of Mother and me on an upright antique chair during the interview. Preoccupied with taking up less space on the narrow settee, I pushed down on my light-blue cotton skirt, which floated above hidden layers of crinoline. But I must have answered Reverend Mother's questions correctly, because I was admitted to the convent shortly thereafter.

Thus began my formal initiation onto the spiritual path.

Chapter 3

ADMITTANCE
TO HEAVEN

In offering an understanding of human life which transcends our temporary physical existence, religion gives hope and strength to those facing adversity. For all its benefits, however, . . . I do not think that religion is indispensable to the spiritual life.

—HIS HOLINESS THE 14TH DALAI LAMA, *Beyond Religion*

THE CONVENT, AN IMPOSING Edwardian mansion built in a horseshoe shape, was an architectural byproduct of California's Gold Rush era. Central hallways divided each of the three floors: classrooms bordered the third-floor hallway, student dormitory rooms populated the second floor, and public rooms were found on the ground floor. The nuns' quarters and an infirmary occupied a secluded wing of the building.

The partially cloistered nuns of Sacred Heart lived under vows of poverty, celibacy, and silence. They were addressed as Mother Welch or Mother Perch. Part of their ministry was to educate the daughters of wealthy Catholic families. Each morning Mother Perch, covered head-to-toe in a faded black habit, face framed in a delicately pleated wimple of pure, gleaming-white linen, glided like an ice skater on invisible, silent feet through the convent's majestic halls, ushering in dawn's first audible sounds with her little bell and soft prayers.

Hearing the bell's silver voice, I tumbled out of bed and dressed quickly in a shapeless blue skirt, white cotton blouse, ill-fitting blue bolero, and ugly but sturdy brown oxfords. In the dimly lit grand hallway outside our rooms, the girls drowsily "formed ranks" and curtsied to Reverend Mother. I'd clench my black missal between my sixteen-year-old knees and hold my short white gloves between my teeth as I pinned a virginal, white-tulle veil into my hair. Then I'd pull on my gloves and slip my black prayer book under one arm to join the student body as we marched in ranks to Mass. Garbed to enter into the Holiest of the Holy, two lines of Vestal Virgins advanced noiselessly at the muffled sound of Mother Perch's handheld clacker, hidden within her deep black pocket. Down the grand oak staircase we marched, followed first by elementary-school girls and then by yawning kindergarteners with their attendant nun.

We lived by the nun's rule of silence, broken only as the double hand-carved doors opened to the convent's gilded chapel. Angelic melodies, chanted and sung by the community of nuns, escorted us into the early morning Latin Service. Gentle voices sang, lifted, then soared on delicate wings toward heaven before descending and reentering the human realm. Higher and lower ranges of beautifully haunting Gregorian-like chants glided about our heads and shoulders like gold and silver swallows as we reverently entered the chapel's candlelit shadows. The nuns, ensconced in polished prayer stalls, knelt beneath sky-darkened, stained-glass windows like otherworldly statues. Silver stars radiating from a cerulean blue ceiling showered us with cosmic blessings and benedictions while animated flames danced atop beeswax altar candles.

We stood on either side of the narrow center aisle and waited for Mother Perch's wooden clicks before genuflecting and entering the narrow wood pews with military precision. Our rigid spines dared not touch the backs of our benches. I emulated the nuns' disciplined posture and restrained movements as I strived toward advanced levels of holiness and acceptance before a distant Almighty Father God. The chanting ceased as the tall, dignified, white-haired bishop entered and the Latin Mass began: *In nomine Patris et Filii et Spiritus Sancti....*

Morning after morning, as the sun climbed to the horizon, kneeling girls and nuns recited prayers and liturgical responses memorized from black missals. Outside, beyond our hearing, dawn's earliest birds ruffled their feathers, shaking away the morning dew in the ether of our prayers.

As a teenaged convent student, I experienced with ever increasing power the inner, luminous sphere I had known since childhood, whose essence was impossible to capture in words. I was aware of being nurtured, touched, and protected by Our Lady and by certain saints—St. Christopher protected me as I traveled, and St. Jude helped me find lost items. I became deeply immersed in a pervasive feeling of adoration for an invisible but all-encompassing presence at the convent, a presence that also seemed also to stand at an open door beckoning me into the outside world.

Following Mass and breakfast, we were allowed to walk on our own from the elegant dining hall on the first floor to our study hall, where I sat at an assigned wooden desk. With pen in hand, I would mark my carefully handcrafted calendar with yearning, tallying the days to vacation and then to graduation. Although the early morning Latin Masses filled me with a majestic sense of mystery, eternal and powerful, they did not alleviate my sense of isolation or my desire for graduation, independence, and adventure.

I envisioned sustained happiness in the journey toward and fulfillment of my goals, which in the long term included admittance to heaven; in the short term, enrollment in the University of California. I foresaw laughter, freedom, marriage, motherhood, joy. To become a successful woman of the 1950s, I would need to find a husband at college, marry before the age of twenty-one, bear children, and create a perfect home to support my husband's aspirations. I wanted my future husband to worship me as my father worshipped my mother and my grandfather worshipped my grandmother. In those quiet, naïve convent days, I believed a glorious domestic life awaited me if I could just meet Berkeley's academic entry requirements.

My academic devotion seemed to pay off. I was accepted at Berkeley in 1957, and while rushing for a sorority, met my future first husband, George, who would be the only boy I dated during my collegiate years. He was persistent in his attentions, and we spent weekends together, either at his home or mine, for the next two years. He was a quiet boy, which suited me quite well, as it gave me the opportunity to speak freely without being censored or ridiculed, and he seemed to enjoy my chatter.

George also happened to be the scion of a wealthy and well-known family, and Mother was ecstatic. For the first time in my life, she focused sustained positive attention on me, seeing to it that I was fashionably dressed and otherwise equipped for society. Caught up in coed life, in the competitive worlds of academia and dating, I enacted the roles of perfect student and future wife. It was easy. Social rules dictated behavior, and I excelled at playing by the rules. But, in truth, I had no idea what "perfect" meant, much less what I wanted from those experiences. I could not understand why this life left me with a profound feeling of emptiness, which no amount of busyness or success seemed to quell.

One day, while driving alone in my car, I found myself exclaiming aloud, "Don't leave me! Don't ever, ever leave me!" The ache in the center of my heart and my desperate words felt radically incompatible with the rush and thrill of my new life. Yet, as I wept and called out, I became aware that I feared losing my profoundly intimate experience with the loving inner essence within me. How was I to reconcile the requirements of navigating this new world with my desire to remain connected to the soothing, uplifting spiritual connections that had always been with me. I could not bear the thought of losing these precious bonds, and given the whirlwind of my life at the time, such a loss felt possible. This utterly terrified me. It would be another twenty-five years before I understood that one is *never* separate from this divine connection.

George returned from serving summer duty in the Army Reserves after my sophomore year and unexpectedly proposed. Caught off guard, I said that I wasn't sure if I was ready. But it was 1959. Women had few opportunities outside of marriage, which, in any case, had always been my life's goal. In those days, men took care of money, keeping that power close to their chests, so finances had never been discussed in my presence. Although some personal instinct had driven me to set myself up as a babysitter and set aside every dollar I earned, I knew nothing about paying bills or managing bank accounts. Now George pledged to take care of me, and in my family, wealth determined status, love, and security. With George, I'd be financially secure, and my parents would be thrilled. I didn't have any real reason *not* to marry. Marriage seemed inevitable, and I loved George, so after a fifteen-minute discussion, I accepted his proposal. Thus, I'd barely begun to experience the excitement of philosophical and political coffee-house debates before he and I walked down the Roman Catholic aisle of everlasting marriage. He took vows as a man, and I took vows as a wife to obey him. I changed my name to his.

George's dream was to take over the management of his family's cattle-ranching business. After our ten-day honeymoon in Jamaica, George and I moved to a remote cattle ranch, where we had neither neighbors nor telephone, taking up residence in cowboy quarters that hadn't been cleaned in ten years. The ranch hands laughingly said, "Ma'am, these here lands are hell on horses and women, but heaven for cows and men." It was my plan to disprove this myth. I stored wedding presents of crystal glasses, monogrammed linen, and silver in an empty closet and scrubbed fly-specked walls in an unfamiliar world of dense silence.

Within two months, it was evident that our marriage was a terrible mistake. George's silence, a gift when we were at Berkeley, meant days and weeks passed without conversation. He rose early and stayed away until sundown. When I asked my young husband what I could do to make him happy, he gave me a sewing machine—for hemming dishtowels. I had never done such a thing, so I put the machine in the closet with the gold and white boxes of wedding gifts. I had no one to turn to with my uncertainties. Mother had made it clear that should I have any marital problems, she would not discuss them with me; instead, she would talk to George, because if a husband was unhappy, it had to be the wife's fault. Thus isolated from relatives, friends, paved roads, stores, and community, I forgot the sound of my own voice.

The sole moments of togetherness George and I shared were in front of the TV show *Bonanza*, about a California ranching family. The show gave me clues about how to create a home that would please George and offered a romantic alternative to my own upbringing, demonstrating how family codes of honor, harmony, respect, and justice could prevail. Although there were no women on the show, I naively believed it might be possible that a house full of cowboys could engender marital happiness and that I could find fulfillment in cooking for my equivalent of Little Joe, Hoss, and their siblings. I was determined to make my new home life the exact opposite of the one that my parents had created. Rather than drift about in daydreams, in a euphoria of fake love, or in thrall to negative ideas that might recreate the combative environment of my childhood, I filled my mind with thoughts of generosity, kindness, and contentment. Yet Mother's imprint persisted—every evening, I put on a skirt, curled my hair, and applied fresh lipstick before serving our silent suppers—and despite my will to set aside sentiment and wishful thinking, I drifted into a state of profound denial about the true state of my marriage. Eventually, I ended up enacting in the external world all the roles I was internally guarding myself from.

Living an isolated life under such vast, often intimidating skies was not a gentle experience. But it forced a certain discipline on me. I turned to the rituals that had governed my convent days: silence, meditation, comfort in solitude, and strict routines. Silent prayer emerged as my secret but most powerful tool.

On Sunday mornings, I attended Mass and received the Eucharist. To get to the church, I drove well over the speed limit, screeching along curved country roads that ran through pastures fenced off with leaning, moss-covered posts and sagging barbwire. I was headed toward a small, handcrafted chapel hidden among acres of flowing vineyards in Napa Valley. There the priest recounted the biblical parables that I'd heard throughout my childhood. These astounding stories now inflamed my imagination and kept me company during the week, as I tried to emulate their teachings.

Back at the ranch, the wind whipped dusty debris around our little wooden house, and the kitchen thermometer soared to 118 degrees for days on end. Outside, the smell of the septic tank was strong behind the house and clouds blew across an unsettled sky, never staying in one place, always changing color from white to shades of gray, from dark to light, but unfailingly empty of moisture. I listened inward as Jesus, dressed in his white robes, responded compassionately and with great authority to the complaints of the Pharisees: "Which one of you having one hundred sheep and losing one of them does not leave the ninety-nine in the wilderness and go after the one who is lost until he finds it?"

My favorite part was next: "And when he has found the lost sheep, he lays it on his shoulders and rejoices, and when he comes home he calls his neighbor and friends, saying to them, 'Rejoice with me, for I have found the sheep that was lost.'" I envisioned feasts where joy and laughter celebrated the rescue of the one lost sheep, for it was clear to me that in that first year of marriage that I was indeed a lost sheep. I longed to be found, I prayed to be found, I believed I would be found.

In the meantime, my marriage continued to founder. As it turned out, my husband's childhood had been similar to mine—alcohol, volatility, an abusive mother—and he responded by treating me as though nothing I did was good enough, no matter how hard I tried. I blamed myself.

A miracle came in the guise of motherhood. We had a son, Tom, who loved us with a purity neither of us had ever known. Even as an infant, he laughed and gurgled when he looked at me, eyes adoring, his raw joy at being alive suffusing our house with light. Love continued to open my heart ever wider with the arrival of my second son, Jim, who was strong, focused, determined, self-contained, and kind from the moment he was born. And when the doctor delivered my third child, I didn't believe him when he said I had a beautiful daughter—until he laid Aimee on my belly. I immediately sensed that she and I had always known each other. I held my babies as much as I could. The sensual pleasure of stroking their little hands, of rocking them to sleep, of such lovely human physical connections awakened in me a profound maternal joy. My children were the jewels of my world.

Eventually, we moved into a Napa Valley farmhouse, to be closer to schools, hospitals, and community, commuting to the ranch house only as necessary. We began to socialize with a heavy-drinking group of George's fraternity friends, and I made women friends at the children's school and through the church. George was gone much of the time despite my efforts to entice him to stay home. Though my dream of a whole and happy family was not to be, my children and I formed an extremely close, loving unit.

It was during this time that I first entertained the thought of becoming a priest. I was at Mass in my favorite chapel among the vines, with only a handful of others also in attendance. Deeply immersed in the spirit of the service, I felt a stab of passion for a brief but poignant moment and thought, *I want to be a priest!* In the next moment, however, I reprimanded myself: *That is impossible—you are a woman.* Momentary sorrow swept through me, but I quickly buried it.

Little did I know how much was about to change.

Chapter 4

THE CENTER CANNOT HOLD

Turning and turning in the widening gyre
The falcon cannot hear the falconer;
Things fall apart; the centre cannot hold.

—WILLIAM BUTLER YEATS,
"The Second Coming"

THE 1960S AND 1970S ushered in a new wave of moral and ethical ideas that redefined the cultural and religious codes that had governed America's behavior for generations. The Beatles landed in the States in 1964, and Lyndon Johnson established the "Great Society," a set of domestic programs intended to eliminate poverty and racial injustice. The Civil Rights Movement gained momentum. Baby Boomers were discovering what seemed, at first, like an idyllic lifestyle at Woodstock and in the Haight-Ashbury section of San Francisco. Sexual freedom and experimentation, wife swapping, drugs, and rock and roll taunted the young married set. Husbands felt they were missing out on extramarital sex, while financially dependent wives discovered that there was either no joint property or that most of their husbands' assets had been cleverly hidden.

When it came to religion, Rome shifted powerfully in opposing directions over the course of a few years. The Second Vatican Council, announced in 1962 by Pope John XXIII, opened the windows of the Church to a spring of inclusiveness; under its influence, I participated in an ecumenical retreat movement in which men, women and, children from many denominations celebrated the Mass together. In the 1970s, however, due to the heavy rule of a rigid new conservatism, the Church of Rome outlawed these services, suppressing the shift toward ecumenism to which my friends and I had attached great hope. Eventually, numerous beloved saints and angels were marginalized as well, as Pope John Paul II, under the powerful influence of the future Pope Benedict XVI, instructed Catholics to reserve worship for Jesus. For many centuries, Catholic families had passed down the traditions of the angels and saints through rituals like celebrating feast days, praying novenas, wearing certain medals, honoring a different saint every day of the year, and the naming of children. Now, to the profound dismay of many Catholics, Rome forbade worship of all spiritual beings except Jesus.

I paid little attention to this decree. How could I push aside the protectors who were such an integral part of my inner landscape? I knew Mary, the angels, and the saints more intimately then I knew Jesus, who lived only in church. Jesus was the round wafer of bread I consumed every week, but he stayed within the four walls I visited on Sundays. Mary, however, along with the angels and saints, was always with me.

During this turbulent time in the Catholic Church, my children learned to walk and talk, and then entered school. I felt increasingly locked out of the Catholic Church as it continued to preach that my life's purpose was to obey my husband and Catholic doctrine without dissent. I was also increasingly aware of religious hypocrisies, both large and small. At our church in the vineyard, I didn't know how to explain to the children the priest's struggle with alcoholism, the tremors he suffered while celebrating the Eucharist. I didn't know how to explain why my sons could serve as altar boys, getting to eat the donuts and hot chocolate that were served outside after the Mass, while there was no role in which my daughter could serve at the altar. A fierce new sense of determination for justice rose within me. *Women had rights! I had rights!* I became increasingly angry and increasingly determined to find stable ground I could stand on as a woman and a mother.

I co-founded a religious school as a kind of rebellion against the priest, who in response to my concerns assured me that it was normal for children to hate Catholic religious education. A friend of mine, a mother of ten, shared my frustration, and we decided to help our children grow up with fond memories of religion, to give them opportunities to learn about miracles, good works, and love and to engage with interesting Bible stories. A quaint rural preschool, close to our little church in the vineyard, gave us permission to use their facility for an ecumenical after-school program of religious education every Wednesday. Mothers taught children to play musical instruments, and we baked bread. I taught inspiring material from a variety of churches and religions. We picked and stomped grapes, and made juice for our newly conceived Children's Mass. Everyone had fun, and I was happy to disprove the priest's theory.

At the same time, however, my marriage slipped into a vacuum of abandonment. Working to hold the disparate pieces of my life together took its toll. Like my mother, I was adept at maintaining facades and still labored to keep up appearances. I felt paramount that my children, our acquaintances, and my own ego should believe my husband and I had a happy marriage. Up to this point, I had found joy in my children, in the land, and in church, but the inner Light that I had always cherished dimmed as the life George and I had built disintegrated. It felt like I was falling apart, too. It got to the point where, one night, noticing a bottle of pills on the bedside table, I wondered how many I would have to take to kill myself. I thought: *If there is a God, then he must hate me.* For a few short minutes my world went dark. In the blackness, before I remembered the loving, trusting presence of my children, there was no loving God in my life, only a profound void. Terrified and unable to sustain such spiritual negation, I sat bolt upright in bed. And around the darkness appeared a narrow border of light, pure gold and effervescent. Tears stung my eyes. I was not alone.

Spiritual growth is sometimes likened to an onion or an artichoke, because we need to peel away layer after layer before we finally experience the luminosity at the center of our Being. My husband and I began marriage counseling as I undertook the slow, challenging, and necessary process of looking at my layers of denial, one by one. My therapist at the time guided me from the rigidity of my upbringing toward the dynamic and powerful liberation that was emerging all around me in the 1970s, until I finally came to embody it myself.

Words and writing were central to this process. It began with the doctor's suggestion that I compose a short autobiography, which seemed silly to me. Nevertheless, I began to write. To my surprise, my pen jumped into action. Words multiplied and chased each other as I attempted to capture thirty-one years on the page, cracking open the mighty dam of repression. After scribbling up to a hundred longhand pages a week, I purchased a small Corona typewriter. Penning poetry and short stories, and pleas for understanding to my parents, I stuttered blindly toward a new experience of womanhood. And, for the first time in my life, I shared my inner world with another human being, my therapist.

Scripture and the words uttered at Eucharist had always been holy for me, but now every word I wrote or read seemed a small, sacred key to hidden truths, an entry point into private lands of inner freedom. I transcribed conversations as accurately as a court stenographer because both my birth family and my husband constantly denied things that they had said. By recording these words, I began to capture a truth that no one could deny. But something else was happening as well. These rivers of words were slowly pooling into a recognizable entity: Me! I was discovering that I was not the inadequate person that my family made me out to be. I was neither weak nor stupid. In fact, I was strong, and I was smart.

Yet another aspect of my being was emerging as well. My therapist suggested various relaxation exercises, and I learned to meditate for twenty minutes twice a day. After each sitting, I wrote down whatever came to mind. Astonishing memories surfaced, as well as vivid dream scenes that my waking, day-to-day consciousness could never have imagined.

In one particularly notable dream, I walked out of my home toward the open field on the hill overlooking the valley. It was springtime. As I walked, a wind began to blow and quickly reached hurricane velocity. There was no visible life in the valley below. All living creatures, including humans, had burrowed into the ground to escape the violent gale. I was the only being who remained in the open, exposed to the ferocious wind. To stay upright with my feet anchored to the ground, I leaned into the blowing, howling fury at an extreme angle. I battled the deafening, destructive wind, beating at it with my hands and fists. In a voice filled with pain and rebellion, I cried for it to stop, but the terrible struggle persisted.

Then the wind suddenly ceased, and I stood on the beautiful knoll, surrounded by spring beauty. A perfumed breeze graced the environment. Green grass replaced the parched devastation that had been caused by the windstorm. Wildflowers—blue and yellow lupine, Queen Anne's lace, golden poppies, yellow buttercups, pink and white wild radish—decorated the landscape as far as I could see. In the valley below, people and animals emerged from hiding and resumed their daily tasks.

Why had I been the only one to stay outside? Why hadn't I sought shelter and protected myself like every other thinking being? Why had I been such a fool?

I turned and saw that the storm had reduced my home to a pile of rubble. Oddly, I felt little sorrow. All my pain and grief had been spent during the storm. I walked toward the wreckage, picking my way through the debris of wood shards, exposed nails, broken glass, and twisted metal until I came across my backpack. I found my toothbrush, a comb, and several other items, placed them inside the backpack, and calmly turned away from what had long been my home.

I walked down the hill to the long driveway beside the river. Lengthening shadows of dusk were cooling the air after the stormy day. I stopped on the driveway, took a Bunsen burner and cook pot from my backpack, sat down, and began to heat my evening meal. As I quietly stirred soup over the flame, several animals approached: a fox, an eagle, a rabbit, a mountain lion. We sat together in quiet peace.

After a while, my attention was drawn to my clothes, which looked like the attire worn in summertime by gentlemen of my grandfathers' generation: khaki pants, khaki shirt, and hiking boots. Contemplating my outfit, I felt neither male nor female—I was both. This was a pleasing observation. I welcomed the peaceful evening that followed the horrendous storm. My destroyed home was now only a vague memory. The next morning I would continue my walking journey, a journey that I knew would last for the rest of my life.

My therapist also helped me explore my intuitive capabilities. Putting a pad of paper on his lap as he sat behind the desk, he would draw images and ask me to tell him what they were, though I could not see them. I was often accurate. If he drew a necktie, for example, I would describe "a thick, downward-pointing arrow." He was impressed by this, and marveled when I wrote about events that later came to pass, but I brushed off his affirmations. I was struggling to survive in the "real world" and hardly had the energy to think about what he saw as my spiritual attributes. I confined my meditations to practices that would help me alleviate stress and guide me through my day-to-day challenges. While I appreciated his efforts to encourage me to embrace my inner power, I simply had no self-confidence as a spiritual being. Moreover, though I had always used my "psychic" gifts, both consciously and unconsciously, I also knew that the world I lived in was harsh toward psychics and fortunetellers and the like—terms that were basically interchangeable with "lunatic." I had no desire to be identified as one of them.

This was especially true at that moment in time, as my long and difficult marriage was no longer able to withstand the pressures of my newly emerging self, and my husband and I began a two-and-half-year divorce process. Because he came from a wealthy, high-profile family, I faced the possibility of public ruin, disgrace, and even the loss of my children—not to mention that divorcées were still treated as social outcasts. I refused to think of myself as such. I knew the world saw me as a good person, as a community leader and church member. I also knew that I was a loving mother. I could not afford to be labeled mentally ill while fighting to keep my children and negotiating with linear-minded lawyers. So I kept my psychic and spiritual tendencies to myself, as I had been doing my entire life.

At the time of my divorce, California had no community property statute. After twenty years of marriage, I effectively had nothing, and it was possible that I could leave the marriage that way, too. But I wanted both freedom and justice, and I knew I had to fight for them. I turned to lawyers and other professionals, who taught me how to defend myself. They explained my legal rights and made me memorize the names and numbers of newly passed legislative bills that protected women who had been married for many years, raised a children, then found themselves penniless. The term "no-fault divorce" entered the lexicon as the first impacts of the Women's Rights Movement were taking effect.

My mother and my mother-in-law were always ready with shaming diatribes concerning the divorce, but I learned to let their accusations drift by. When necessary, I would quote my lawyers, using specific pieces of legislation as reference points to defend myself. I observed with some surprise how weak and insecure a bully can be when confronted with either truth or legal facts. Once, for example, I informed my mother-in-law that a warrant for her arrest could be issued if she continued to use the phone to harass me, and she quickly backed off. As my rock-firm voice took control of the situation, my children stood in the kitchen listening, their eyes huge, their mouths open. How stunned I was as well, to realize that this confrontation could actually put a stop to my mother-in-law's ongoing campaign of verbal harassment. This was new territory indeed.

The local college offered "reentry" courses for newly divorced women, and I found them helpful, but I also knew I wasn't reentering anything—I was initiating a whole new world of single parenting and emboldened womanhood. I participated in assertiveness trainings, where I learned the "broken record" technique, which was to state my needs, repeat them, and then repeat them again and again, the goal being to break the habit of disregarding the validity of my own requests. I learned to give honest feedback and to perform "reality checks" during conversations. This entailed holding a hand up and saying, "I don't hear very well. I want to be sure I heard you correctly. What I heard you say is . . . ." This gave me and other silenced women a tool for navigating conversations that would otherwise have been predominantly controlled by men. And when my male divorce lawyers sat me down in their offices and stood towering over me, I learned to stand up, too, all 5' 10" of me (closer to 6' when I wore heels). Men were not used to this sort of behavior coming from a formerly compliant wife like me.

Through it all, I prayed and fumed against the stupidity, ignorance, and fear that had marked my life prior to the divorce proceedings. I berated myself for wasting so many years trying to be good, nice, loving, and patient, and to play stupid. I also wrote, meditated, begged for God's help, read scripture, and prayed. The divorce was final in June 1979, and I received a hard-won settlement that sufficed to keep a home and take care of the children.

If my twice-daily meditation had been important before, it was absolutely critical now that I was a single, bread-winning mother. I was deluged with intense demands, major decisions, numerous responsibilities, and ongoing identity crises. My periods of silent relaxation generated gradual but noticeable emotional progress, which my children helped protect. When I became agitated, short-tempered, and exhausted, the children would say, "Don't you think it's time to meditate, Mom?" Twenty minutes later, I would open the bedroom door and emerge peaceful and gentled.

I was forming a new faith system built on spiritual and material experiences operating hand in hand. I worked from my home office as a neophyte stock investor, conducting business between 8 A.M. and 3 P.M. The children and their activities consumed my remaining hours. When faced with a decision of any kind, I would retreat to my bedroom, lie down, quiet my mind, and ask for direction. *Should I buy this stock? Which broker should I listen to? Who should I hire? Who should I fire? Is my son safe going to this camp? Is my daughter safe going on this overnight? How can I meet the expenses of our home?*

Answers came in different ways. I was learning to rely on the inner voice that had always guided me, which I now took to calling my Inner Teacher. Sometimes I intuited answers in the same way you might know who was calling when the phone rang. Other times I received forceful answers of *Yes!* or *No!* I meditated, wrote, and learned to use a combination of tools like astrology and tarot. The answers that came often had nothing to do with being right or wrong, and more to do with exposing the true nature of my motivation, which was humbling. And I noticed that the answers always arrived when they were supposed to. If the timing of my answers did not meet with other people's expectations, then I strove to exercise patience and love in the face of their demands or frustration, while at the same time learning to love and be patient with myself.

I didn't let others know about my secret decision-making process, but I did fill the house with religious statues and posters with affirmative statements like "I don't believe in miracles. I expect them." I played sacred music to remind me and the children of the sacred beings—those same saints and angels that the Pope had pushed aside—that surrounded us at every moment. I was consciously reuniting with all of the unseen forces, which I had felt in childhood, that spoke to me through the rivers, wind, ocean, books, colors—the entire world around me. When the stress of daily life became too great, I walked to the river, perched on a rock, and listened to the soothing musical sounds of moving water, which washed away my inner chaos. Filled with gratitude and humility, I gave thanks to whatever or whoever serenaded me. I made my intention clear: I wanted to be one with a newly arising notion of God.

One of the first orders of business was to find a new church. Prior to my divorce, I was painfully aware that the Catholic Church's canon law forbade divorced people who remarry the privilege of receiving the Eucharist. This troubled me deeply. The Eucharist was an especially profound ritual for me, and at the time it felt like the one tangible connection to my God of church and religion. I hoped someday to remarry, yet could not imagine forsaking this sacred ritual.

There was also the fact that divorce was considered a sin. While the concept of no-fault divorce was entering the courts at the time, in my world divorce was still blamed on the woman, who was then marginalized at church. Sometimes people even crossed the street so they wouldn't have to speak with a divorced woman. I did not want to be victimized, ignored, or whispered about, especially in church. However, once my divorce was complete, I began to consider that the Catholic Church was unfairly discriminating against women and against *me*. In a support group I attended, someone suggested an idea that had never before occurred to me. "Mary Ann," she said, "you did not leave the Catholic Church. The Church left you!" This broke my heart, yet felt impossibly true. I had no choice but to move away from the church I had worshipped in since birth. And so I left the little chapel in the vineyard, taking my chances on salvation or damnation.

When I told Mother about my decision, she was furious. She and I were sitting in the family room, the children fast asleep in their rooms. She leaned forward, fueled by an alcohol adrenaline rush, and attempted to negate me with words like "failure," "ruin," and "guilt." I listened to her self-interested pressure tactics and her attempts to dissuade me, observing her as though I were a theatergoer.

"Your father and I have powerful connections in Rome," she said. "We have spoken with the Archbishop, who told us that if you insist on destroying your beautiful family, you can get your marriage annulled. You don't have to get divorced. Rome will recognize an annulment."

Enraged, I demanded her definition of an annulment through clenched teeth. "Are you telling me to go before some all-male ecclesiastical Catholic court and claim my marriage was a fraud?"

No one ever confronted Mother; she sat silent, stunned by my outburst.

"What would that make my children? Illegitimate? Bastards? And what does that make me? A whore? A prostitute?" The dam was breaking, the frustration of thousands of years of women's repression pushing through me. "Mother," I continued in an ice-cold voice, "don't you ever deny the validity of either my marriage or my divorce, nor what I have gone through these past sixteen years. I have left the Catholic Church, Mother. Understand me. I have left the Catholic Church, and I will never return."

She put her hand to her throat and wept. "How can you do this to me? How could you?" she wailed, then ended with another well-rehearsed threat: "I am going to call your father!" While she reached for the telephone, I went to bed with a new sense of lightness.

And so it was that the children and I searched for a new church. To my delight, it didn't take long. The beautiful Grace Episcopal Church at the corner of Oak and Spring Streets in St. Helena felt like home, its service and Eucharistic liturgies almost identical to those of the Catholic Church. Grace Episcopal became much more to me than a spiritual, religious, and social refuge—it was a revelation. Although I had been taught as a child that God was omnipresent, I was also taught with great conviction that God lived only in Catholic churches, and that it was a sin to cross the threshold of a non-Catholic church. Within weeks of joining the Episcopal Church I understood that what I had been taught was wrong. In my new church home, God's presence was overwhelmingly obvious.

Chapter 5

GOOD FRIDAY CALLING

The brain can change as a result of the thoughts we think.... Something as seemingly insubstantial as a thought can affect the very stuff of the brain, altering neuronal connections in a way that can treat mental illness or, perhaps, lead to a greater capacity for empathy and compassion.

—SHARON BEGLEY, *How the Brain Rewires Itself*

SPRING IN NAPA VALLEY can be heartbreakingly beautiful. Small-town streets become handsome arboretums as the trees awaken. Branches push spears of chartreuse foliage from dormant knobs along the winter lacework of bare limbs. These tiny, decorative green leaves and mostly bare branches create mosaics of light over sidewalk cracks and town gardens. A symphonic cadence of yellow mustard and white iceberg roses creates an explosion of color, and flowering fruit trees blossom deliciously throughout the valley's landscape.

On April 9, 1982, I was getting around on crutches, compliments of a winter ski accident. I swung my body in long arcs between the metal poles, moving along Spring Street through the dancing shadows of overhead branches and pointy new leaves. I was on my way to the serene and picturesque Grace Episcopal Church. It sat back from the street, surrounded by a rose-lined stone wall, that enclosed a well-manicured lawn. A path led to the small chapel, which stood in the shade of a magnificent redwood. Hundred-year-old hand-carved stones and hauntingly lovely stained-glass windows of sapphire, crimson, and gold gave the chapel's redwood interior an aura of mystery and miracle.

It was noon on Good Friday. Long gone were the days of large Good Friday church crowds, but I didn't mind the quiet simplicity or the near-empty chapel. I was there out of personal habit and to partake in the solemn rituals of this religious holiday. As there were only four of us in attendance, each congregant was sequestered in his or her private pew of choice. I navigated the blood-red carpet toward the altar and sat in the second pew from the sanctuary. I lifted my still-bandaged leg so it occupied almost the entire length of the small wooden pew and laid my crutches beneath the pew in front of me. I exhaled a deep breath of gratitude, feeling safe and blessed in the redwood serenity and lingering aroma of incense.

On Good Friday, we sit in remembrance of the ghastly torture and crucifixion of an innocent saint many devotees consider the sole Son of God. We contemplate the hours of darkness that accompanied Jesus' death and his subsequent visit to Hell. As the priest attended to the words of the liturgy, however, I wasn't concentrating on anything in particular. Relaxed and at peace, surrounded by beauty, I was unable to feel the sorrow and pain of the Crucified Christ. The service moved quickly, flowing by me. When the priest began the Eucharistic portion of the Mass, where bread and wine are transformed into the body and blood of Christ, he raised a large white wafer—representing the body of Christ—and broke it.

At that instant, a voice commanded, *This is what you will do.*

Startled, I looked around the chapel. My fellow worshippers sat quietly, with heads bowed in what appeared to be deep contemplation. They certainly wouldn't be sitting there motionless if they'd heard what I heard. The priest, too, continued to speak as though nothing had happened. Yet this voice of resounding clarity had penetrated every cell in my body.

When I heard that majestic voice of truth and power, I was both exhilarated and stunned, and in that moment seemed to lose the freedom of my individual will. Although unable to describe the experience to anyone—afraid of inviting ridicule or being branded mentally ill—I committed myself to what I considered to be my calling to the priesthood. However, I was unsure if women were eligible for the priesthood in the Episcopal Church, and felt too intimidated to ask the priest.

Unsure if women were eligible for priesthood in the Episcopal Church, and too intimidated to ask the priest, I wound up asking my prayer group the question burning in my mind: "Does anyone know if the Church ordains women?" Two were members of the vestry committee and assured me the Church was indeed admitting women to seminary and into Holy Orders. I knew all three of my children would be away at school the following September, which would leave me free to enroll in seminary. Blushing, I shared with the group my desire to become a priest. They were warmly supportive. I then met with the priest and told him I wanted to enter seminary. He said he would sign the necessary papers, which he did.

When I broached the idea with the children and shared my concerns about my age—earning the degree could take up to four years—my son Jim laughed and said, "It's best you begin now, while you're still young." He was right. It was time. I smiled at him and knew I would do it. From that moment on I never looked back.

Women had been denied seminary, monastic, and higher religious education for ordained positions of leadership for almost two thousand years, so I expected obstacles, but in fact the preparation and application process moved ahead smoothly. Within a few weeks I was interviewing at the seminary itself, and by midsummer I had been accepted into the masters of divinity dual degree program at the Church Divinity School of the Pacific (CDSP), an Episcopal seminary adjacent to the University of California's Berkeley campus.

As the school year approached, I helped the kids pack and sent them off with farewell dinners and bags of treats, then drove myself to Berkeley, my car filled with bedding, pillows, sheets, and other student paraphernalia. On a warm September morning, after twenty-one years of parenting, political and community activism, volunteering, driving, attending my children's activities, and learning to support myself, I pushed open the doors to the refectory, officially became a student again, and left my known world behind.

Nothing at CDSP was familiar. The handsome, two-story, red-brick buildings of the school were both thrilling and intimidating. As I walked into the crowded refectory that first day, the entire student body milled about, and I felt like a stranger in a strange land. CDSP was part of the Berkeley Theological Union, an ecumenical consortium of thirteen seminaries which shared both faculty and core classes in an area informally called Holy Hill. The schools were grouped together on tree-lined streets in an area, to the north of the Berkeley campus, known as Northside. Although I had been a student at the University of California twenty-five years before, I had lived in a Southside sorority with little sense of Northside culture. Now Northside students wore Birkenstocks, carried bibles, and walked under the leafy old elms toward quiet Euclid Street coffeehouses. There were neither bars nor boomboxes in Northside, and its small theater advertised foreign films.

Intellectual vibrations swirled about the seminaries of Holy Hill, and the large, silent libraries held stacks of knowledge I thirsted for. I loved my little dorm room with its simple bed, chair, and desk. During my first year, the clacking of typewriters echoed through the dorm halls. By graduation, personal computers had silenced the corridors. I crunched through dry elm leaves in autumn, listened to soft rains in winter, and visited the botanical gardens in spring.

Those years, filled with seemingly impossible academic demands, pushed my intellect to the maximum, as I learned how to navigate between library stacks and to manage my weekly commute between Berkeley and Napa. When the faculty demands seemed beyond my reach, my Good Friday calling would blaze through my mind like a comet. I was unable to go any direction but ahead, toward a master's cape in divinity and a life of ministry. Quitting was not an option.

Seminary was a slice of heaven, where I was housed and fed, both physically and spiritually. I treasured the opportunity to receive, to learn scripture, and to have knowledge transmitted to me by learned men and women who had contemplated the historical secrets of the sacred texts for many years. Living in an environment that emphasized the direct presence of what I experienced as sacred, I felt enwombed in a spiritual energy that continued to expand within me and free to discover myself in unprecedented ways.

The 1980s were a time of great social, economic, and cultural change. The eruption of Mount Saint Helens spewed ash that turned to cement as far east as my family's summer cabin in Idaho. There was an assassination attempt on President Ronald Reagan, and the first woman was appointed to the U.S. Supreme Court. Millions of viewers watched Lady Diana and Prince Charles's extravagant, wondrous wedding. The Falkland Islands, Reagan's Star Wars, and Sally Ride, the first woman in space, made headlines I barely had time to read.

Yet our professors pressed us to consider the urgent issues of the time in the context of various religious tenets. Our sexual-ethics professor, for example, who traveled between Washington, D.C., and Berkeley, was a well-respected moral theologian working in areas of medical ethics and human sexuality. Questions of homosexuality, monogamy, AIDS, extramarital sex, animal-to-human organ transplants, and euthanasia led to exploration of truths and higher truths, but which were which? How were rules and regulations meant to marry with human needs and higher consciousness in the areas of abortion, birth control, and contraception? How had views on abortion changed throughout the history of Christianity? Why? What were the various church teachings on the subject?

I learned to read scripture on a deeper level and basked in academic research correlating varying biblical interpretations with changing historical periods and cultures. There were hundreds more versions of the bible than I'd been aware of, and just as many interpretations. The first major feminist theologians in history were writing and publishing at Harvard and Yale. How would the telling of history differ when written from a woman's perspective? What sacred books written by Jesus' disciples had been hidden and were now being revealed? What were the Dead Sea Scrolls? What were the ancient texts discovered at Nag Hammadi? Why had I never heard the gospels of Mary, Thomas, or Philip? How many gospels were out there? Was Mary Magdalene a whore or Jesus' favorite disciple, the possible mother of his child, and carrier of all his spiritual teachings? How did religious teachings differ from spiritual teachings. We read and examined scripture word by word and compared them to texts on ancient papyrus whenever possible.

A nascent spirituality—inclusive of male and female perspectives—was beginning to take shape. Great female mystics of the Middle Ages, like Julian of Norwich and Hildegard of Bingen, were the subject of discussion at meals. It had never dawned on me to explore the lives and stories of women whose spiritual quest might so closely match my own—an experience that is now so openly and easily referred to as the Divine Feminine. Even though women of my generation were beginning to find their own voices, the voices of our female predecessors were still silenced in the patriarchal version of history. In truth, I wasn't sure what a mystic or a visionary even was. I had grown up hearing about the three children who saw Our Lady at Lourdes and at Fatima, but in those stories I was more focused on the appearance of the Virgin Mary than on the experiences of the children.

In chapel, which the entire student body and faculty attended twice a day, vested women officiated on the altar, which I had never seen before. My first paper was returned with red circles drawn around every instance in which I referred to God as "He" or to all people as "men," the professor pointing out that such sexist language was unacceptable. I was stunned and embarrassed. I'd been fighting for women's rights wherever I could, but had unwittingly continued to use sexist language. From then on, I focused intently on listening to my words and modifying my use of language to keep up with the gender revolution that was happening all around me.

My fellow female seminarians had a fantastic sense of humor in the midst of these seismic shifts. An altar to the Virgin Mary was set up anonymously in a school elevator, and the women seminarians, half-smiling, took bets as to how long this shrine to the Divine Feminine would last. The altar remained intact at least until my graduation, and additional pictures of Mary appeared, along with a lovely picture of Jesus laughing uproariously.

Luckily, I had managed to create enough financial independence to immerse myself in my spiritual and religious passions. When I was still married, I had asked a male stockbroker friend to invest some cash I'd saved over many years. He was pleased to do that, he said, but first he'd need my husband's written permission. I'd known this man since childhood and, furious, asked if he was joking, then informed him that he was never to ask me to sign such a paper again. Soon his well-known, nationwide brokerage deleted that requirement from their mission statement.

My newfound financial freedom meant that my academic explorations were relatively unburdened, optimistic, and spontaneous. I reveled in being free to live at the seminary, in what I perceived to be God's home. For me, it truly was a holy sanctuary. Fifty percent of the student body was women, some of whom were balancing the demands of study, marriage, and parenting. The average age was around forty. We were a mature group, unlike in prior years, when classes were limited to young men entering seminary fresh out of college. Our presence on campus seemed so natural and powerful that it was a stretch to remember that only a few years before women had been excluded for no other reason than gender. Whatever self-doubts I may have harbored about my gender quickly vanished. I would be ordained to celebrate my most cherished ritual, the Eucharist, and I would finally have the opportunity to be of public service.

Chapter 6

INTO THE
WILDERNESS

There's a common misunderstanding among all the human beings who
have ever been born on the earth that the best way to live is to try to
avoid pain and just try to get comfortable. You can see this even in
insects and animals and birds. All of us are the same.

A much more interesting, kind, adventurous, and joyful approach
to life is to begin to develop our curiosity, not caring whether the object
of our inquisitiveness is bitter or sweet. . . . To lead a more passionate,
full, and delightful life than that, we must realize we can endure a lot
of pain and pleasure for the sake of finding out who we are and what
this world is, how we tick and how our world ticks, how the whole
thing just "is."

—PEMA CHÖDRÖN, *The Wisdom of No Escape*

F irst-year seminary students were encouraged to find a priest and
parish to sponsor them as interns. The priest of my home church
was a friend, and we met to discuss the possibility, sitting across from
each other at the parsonage desk. After I had expressed the joy that I'd
felt at seminary and my hope to intern with him at Grace Episcopal,
he leaned forward in his chair and spoke sternly.

"I said nothing when you decided to go to seminary, but had I known you wanted to become a priest, I would have told you what I am going to tell you now." Gone was the façade of the Good Shepherd protecting his flock. His face was now flushed with anger. "I will do everything I can to thwart your attempts to enter the priesthood. It is a sin to ordain women to the priesthood." He walked over to his built-in bookcase, which stretched floor to ceiling. "You see these books? Every acclaimed author here teaches that the ordination of women violates Christianity's most sacred teachings."

Whatever intellectual argument the Church may offer to explain its history of opposition to the ordination of women, I knew that within those books was evidence of a tradition that considers women fundamentally unclean and evil. From that perspective, women must be subjugated and regulated in order to preserve Divine Order. The liberation and enlightenment of women thus stands as a mortal sin. While the Episcopal Church had recently anointed its first female priest, the culture of the Church had been so profoundly influenced by this ancient prejudice that these ideas had yet to be fully uprooted. The modern emergence of feminine power in places like Berkeley had only intensified resistance to the ordination of women in others. And whatever my personal insecurities might have been, I could certainly have been perceived as a figure of female empowerment: I was determined. I was wealthy. I was tall. I was intelligent. I was a mother and a businesswoman. I was active and well received in the community at large and in our church community.

"The ordination of women is a sin against God and Jesus," my priest stated emphatically, firmly ensconced in the religious orthodoxy that spiritually demonizes women. "I will never allow you to set foot on my altar!"

59

Stunned, repulsed, even nauseated, by his self-righteous fury, I could not think how to respond and quickly left his office without a word. I stumbled outside where I stood on the corner, shaking, trying to comprehend what had transpired. Across Spring Street, a hand-painted banner hung from the roof of the Native Sons Hall: "Come! Crab Feed, Dancing, Live Music, Saturday Night." Next to the hall, the tiny Baptist church was quiet, as was the Presbyterian church to my right, where I had taken yoga and my children had attended preschool. This was my home. This was where I worshipped. This was the church I'd discovered after my divorce. And now my priest—a man who had received a sacred ordination by powers that I believed came directly from the Son of God—had threatened me. In that moment, I didn't consider that the threat had been issued by an insecure man who hid behind priestly robes. I had always believed that the priest represented God—and I felt like God Himself had rejected me.

Something inside me was shattering. Seminary had awakened me to gender equality, and I'd been induced to face my own sexual bias. I had become careful to use inclusive language and winced when others outside seminary used sexist language. In that explosive instant outside the chapel, however, I saw how my own unquestioning belief in and dedicated reverence for an all-male God had created so much pain in my life. If I believed God was all male, did I believe men were gods? Was God delivering a message to me through the male priest who had just declared me unfit for ordination? Now who did I believe God was? Had I on some level believed that I was receiving God's presence into my body when I had sex with a man? I certainly believed it regarding the Eucharist. Until I entered seminary, I operated on the belief that only a male, through the Eucharist, could enter my body, make me holy, and save me from eternal damnation.

One thing was clear: if I wanted to be ordained, my only choice was to change churches. Again. This time I felt excommunicated from Grace Episcopal Church, which left a part of my heart so vulnerable that for several years I was unable even to drive past the little church on the corner of Spring and Oak. The pain was too great. When I later spoke with the dean of the seminary, an extraordinary biblical scholar who was always kind and gentle, he explained that the priest at Grace Episcopal was one of only three in the diocese who adamantly opposed the ordination of women. Apparently, many priests from Northern California had tried to reason with the priest on behalf of women, but he had refused to budge. The dean recommended that I find another parish, one that would accept a female intern, since internship was a requirement for ordination.

So I swallowed my pride, left my beloved parish community, and joined St. Martin's Episcopal Church as their seminarian. The priest there seemed thrilled to have me as an intern and even turned to me as a confidante as he was coming to terms with his own homosexuality. For three years, I worked hard to fulfill my duties at St. Martin's, at one point managing the church while the priest participated in a program designed to help gay priests embrace their sexual identity. I invited speakers from Berkeley and hosted seminars on subjects we were discussing at seminary. The church was full during this time.

My role within the church community grew strong, as did my confidence and my bonds with the congregants, who offered praise for my preaching and teaching skills. (Those who were less impressed kindly kept their silence.) I was fortunate in this; my fellow female seminarians were seldom given an opportunity to preach. Women seminarians and newly ordained female priests who visited the

Church Divinity School advised us to be prepared to preach only on Valentine's Day, Mother's Day, and Low Sunday (the Sunday following Christmas), when churches were traditionally empty. I appreciated my good fortune at St. Martin's, officiating at weddings, funerals, and retreats in my role as chaplain, offering spiritual guidance and counseling to the parishioners, who often turned to me. All of this unfolded naturally, and I was thrilled to be finding my way along the path of service and ministry.

In 1986, I graduated from seminary and completed a challenging but rewarding residency as a hospital chaplain, all while preparing for my exams, which I passed in early 1987. At long last, the regional bishop summoned me to his office to discuss my ordination. On the drive to Sacramento's Cathedral of the Blessed Sacrament, near the state capitol, the events of the recent years passed through my mind—all the very hard work, my "incident" with Grace Church, the excitement and satisfaction of an active ministry. I looked forward to my visit with the bishop, who had always complimented me on a job well done. We were friends, and I was deeply grateful for his steadfast support.

Late spring temperatures were beginning to rise, but his large, carpeted office, which doubled as a meeting room, was comfortable and cool. We sat across from each other at his cluttered desk and reminisced about the years which had so quickly passed. Eventually, he settled into the business at hand.

"It has just been called to my attention that in the three years that you have been at St. Martin's, your priest has not filled out a single form that you need for ordination," he said. "He refuses to do so."

This came as a complete surprise. I had devoted years to becoming a priest worthy of my calling and thought I'd helped to grow the church along the way. What had gone wrong? How had I failed?

The bishop explained that St. Martin's, as with many other churches, was faltering because more parishioners caused more work for the priest. "The priest doesn't want the church to grow, and he doesn't want more church members." I sat in silence, trying to absorb the meaning of his words. But he wasn't finished. "I feel that it would be a disservice to you to ordain you, and I'll tell you why. I think that on some level my clergy don't believe the wealthy are capable of empathy, that they can relate to the struggles of those less fortunate. And they may also harbor personal envy that would begrudge you, a woman— and a wealthy woman, at that—success in the ministry. If I ordain you, they are likely, whether consciously or unconsciously, to sabotage your efforts, even if it's just a matter of hampering you with bureaucratic trivia or simple unhelpfulness, as with the priest from St. Martin's."

The bishop, my most staunch supporter, now looked defeated and tired. To administer the many duties involved in running the diocese, he was dependent upon his clergy advisory board—the same people who were opposed to my ordination.

"If I ordain you, I suspect that you will end up with no time or energy to minister to anyone. Go home, Mary Ann," he concluded, "and establish your own church. I think you would do better to become a freelance minister."

I was dumbfounded. I considered his words, recalling earlier visits when he had mentioned how eager he was to retire, explaining that he had never wanted to be a bishop but had been called to service nevertheless. Accepting this call to the bishop's office was his way of expressing gratitude to the Church, and he described the many wonderful years he had known serving a parish church. He was a wonderful pastor, loving, kind, and knowledgeable, and I trusted him. The matter, however, was closed.

I couldn't think what to do, for at that moment the male God of the church died at the institutional altar of dogma and creed. It was the God I'd always known, the only God that I'd considered "real," the God I wanted nothing more than to serve. But that God appeared to exist outside of and separate from me, only in church, where male priests administered that God through the Eucharist. I had not only depended upon those religious rituals for my sense of connection, but had devoted my heart and soul to them since childhood. And now that my service had been denied, this God was no longer alive to me.

I thanked the bishop for his time and tried to keep my balance as I walked out of his office in the Cathedral of the Blessed Sacrament. In the parking lot my body seized up, nausea and pain in my womb. I still had a long drive. "Please help me," I called to the presence that was always with me. "Help me drive. Keep me safe. Help me get home." When I finally arrived, I fell into bed and remained there, fully dressed, until the next morning.

With time I healed, but never again did I associate the male god I knew in church with the inner spiritual visions of certainty I experienced no matter where I happened to be. While I still held deep faith in the principles of Christianity and the great commandment to love, I could no longer overlook the patriarchal roots that were a systemic force of conflict within the Church. I was also beginning to see that, despite my devotion, my very success in ministering and my economic status might be serious impediments to achieving my vision of ministry.

At St. Martin's services the following Sunday, my heart pounded with wrath. The priest nervously delivered a sermon on envy, of all things, confessing to the congregation his resentments around money and status, though he did not refer to me directly. He kept wiping his face, clenching and unclenching his long fingers. He did not apologize. From my volunteer work with sexually abused children I'd learned that perpetrators never mention their victims and never ask for forgiveness, because they don't perceive themselves as guilty. Rather, unable to recognize the pain and suffering they have inflicted, they tend to feel persecuted themselves. The degree to which abusers focus on their own pain to the exclusion of their victims' suffering often correlates directly with their own actual guilt. Accordingly, the priest of St. Martin's was asking the congregation to understand him as a victim, even if only of his own psychology. I had been treated unfairly, profoundly so, and the priest's silence on the issue corresponded with the psychology of a perpetrator. There would be no recourse.

As I listened to the priest sermonize, I prayed a too-familiar prayer: *Don't let me act like a victim. Give me the grace to leave this church today standing tall, firm, and wise. Stay with me. Please don't leave me. Don't let me hate or be angry, help me love, help me love.* After Mass, I walked across the altar, through the sacristy door, and directly to the vestment closet. I removed my robes from their hangers, draped them over my arm, and walked out of St. Martin's and the Episcopal Church for good. The priest stood outside the church door with a group of congregants. When I came up to him, I simply said, "Goodbye."

Some of the lingering parishioners, seeing me with my vestments and probably registering the finality of my tone, became distressed. They sensed that my exit was in fact a departure, which only added to the financial and congregational crises that the church was already facing. When they asked me not to leave, I didn't reveal what the priest had done. I knew that I could not blame him entirely, that somehow I, too, was responsible, even if at that moment I couldn't understand how. Eventually I saw that the priest and I had not been forthright with each other. If he was deeply conflicted over issues of status and power, for my part I refused to claim ownership of my true power, out of fear that I would bruise men's egos and thus be subjected to more rejection, as with my birth family, in my marriage, in the Catholic Church, and with the Episcopal priest who refused me internship.

I chose to tell no one about my difficulties with the male clergy or about their abusive behaviors. While it is true that victims often remain silent, something else held me back. Not only did these men face enough opposition as it was—many congregants were dissatisfied and felt helpless to change the direction in which their churches were headed—but I felt that it would be wrong to speak ill of a fellow clergyperson; in any case, I could do no more harm to these men than they were doing to themselves. Moreover, I suspected that any criticism I leveled at them would come back to haunt me. The Church had clearly revealed that it was not a democratic institution sympathetic to the complaints of a woman. In the end, I knew I could further damage the reputation of these churches, but I had no interest in doing so. I called to mind what Jesus answered when asked how many times we must forgive: again and again and again.

I now had to focus my energies on establishing my own freelance ministry—a ministry of justice, love, and forgiveness.

Chapter 7

THE DEATH
OF MAGDALENA

The world breaks everyone and afterward many are
strong at the broken places.

—ERNEST HEMINGWAY, *A Farewell to Arms*

AFTER MY EXODUS from St. Martin's, life overflowed with activity. My sons graduated from college, and the house filled up with my children and their friends as they returned home before moving on to graduate school or jobs elsewhere. My daughter visited during her summer breaks, and I hosted large family reunions for the various holidays.

I had interned as a chaplain at a large hospital in Washington state to complete my graduate training and now became the chaplain at Napa Valley Hospice. I participated in meetings of the local clergy, and at one such meeting I met a Presbyterian seminarian, Jeff, who shared my interest and passion for inclusive ministry. He and I joined forces and organized the first Taizé services to be held in the Napa Valley.

Taizé is an ecumenical Christian movement, founded in war-torn France after World War II by a man known as Brother Roger. The monastic order in the town of Taizé comprises both Protestant and Catholic brothers from all over the world. Brother Roger envisioned a place where people of different Christian denominations could come together to heal, work, and worship in silence. Young people rejecting fire-and-brimstone messages of sin and eternal damnation in favor of a ministry of love, simplicity, and kindness were especially drawn to Taizé. By 1960, 100,000 young people were making pilgrimages to the Taizé community, and the movement grew in size and popularity throughout the 1970s and 1980s. A French composer of liturgical music, Jacques Berthier, composed a hauntingly beautiful liturgy around biblical scripture for both musicians and cantors, which Jeff and I were eager to introduce to the Napa Valley.

The inspired candlelight Taizé service drew increasing numbers of people and kept me busy. I received calls to help those who were dying or to preach at memorial services. Young couples heard about me and asked me to officiate at their weddings. One day, I received a call from a woman named Angela, who asked to meet with me to discuss some personal issues.

Angela was a quick-witted, cynical, entertaining woman. She arrived at my office with her baby daughter, Magdalena, who was clad only in wet diapers. Magdalena was a beautiful child, like a lovely Botticelli angel, and profoundly asleep. I was deeply moved by this child. I held her in my lap and sang a little song as I rocked her. She remained still as I stroked the flawless, rose-white skin of her arms and legs. I cooed motherly sounds and was sad when the short visit ended.

"I want to keep her," I laughed when they left.

The next morning at 3 A.M., I received a hysterical telephone call from Angela. "She is dying. Magdalena is dying. You have to help me. Please come right away."

Magdalena was at the local hospital. When I arrived, I asked a nurse if I might be allowed to visit Magdalena, given my time as a hospital chaplain. I was admitted to the intensive-care ward, where Magdalena lay naked on a raised crib, more beautiful even than she had been the day before. Her lovely skin glowed under red heat lights as I whispered silent prayers to her. This child somehow reminded me of myself, and feeling a strong bond with her, I stayed with her for a while before joining Angela's family in the waiting room. In the late afternoon, the hospital chaplain came to tell us that Magdalena had died.

Dead? I thought numbly. *Magdalena is dead?* Surely the chaplain was mistaken, for that radiant child could not possibly have died. A wave of faintness rose in my head, but I took hold of myself quickly. *The family needs me. I am a minister. I must stay strong. This is my calling.* It took great effort, but I managed to remain steady in the presence of those gathered, as they, too, struggled to comprehend what had happened.

As I was leaving the hospital, the chaplain approached me with a grave expression. "You could be in serious trouble, Mary Ann," he said, sweating slightly. "Angela has just been arrested for suspicion of first-degree murder and is insisting that the police speak to you, as you are her priest. She has said over and over that you know everything. You were the last person outside the family to see Magdalena alive, and the police are saying that you should have reported child abuse to the authorities."

My blood ran cold. "Child abuse? Murder? Priest?" I exclaimed. "I've only met Magdalena once." I heard my voice as though it came from a great distance.

"Magdalena had extensive brain damage and multiple broken bones in various stages of healing," the chaplain said.

I began to shake and reached behind me for the wall, a railing, anything to lean against to keep myself upright.

He continued: "You will need all the legal help you can get, so you should contact a lawyer as soon as possible."

During my first police interrogation, a heavyset detective sat at a desk in front of me. Behind me, where I couldn't see him, stood a sharp-tongued deputy who jumped in periodically to question certain statements I made. When I informed them I was not, in fact, a priest, the deputy broke in: "We know you were running St. Martin's, and you are well known as a practicing minister. You went to seminary, didn't you?" I had a hard time making them understand that I had been only a voluntary intern at St. Martin's. At stake was the question of whether or not I was ordained. If I had been, I would have been categorized as a professional and therefore required by law to report child abuse.

As the investigation proceeded, horror stalked me at every hour. I withdrew into myself, refusing all phone calls except those related to the trial, wracked by fear and guilt that I could share with no one. In particular, a memory of the inner voice I had heard during my first brief meeting with Angela haunted me. The voice said one word: *Danger!* When I heard that inner warning, I instinctively pulled back in my chair, but only for a moment—then I ignored it, utterly. Although I could not have known about the heinous torture that beautiful child was suffering, my sense of responsibility, failure, and guilt was monumental. This event, coupled with my recent betrayal by the priest at St. Martin's and my earlier rejection for ordination, overwhelmed my body, mind, and spirit. I never wanted to minister again, yet it was imperative that I follow my calling. Knowing I had to make a radical shift, I vowed never to make a decision without listening to my

Inner Teacher. As I made this commitment, all my discomfort around accepting the esoteric validity of my intuition vanished.

For the next few months, I prepared for the trial by meditating on every minute I had spent with Magdalena and her mother the day before she died, the timeframe about which I would be questioned during the trial. I retreated into my home, shut the doors, and listened inwardly day and night, searching to understand the ways in which I had been complicit in the heartbreaking tragedy of Magdalena. *The truth, I prayed, please help me, please let me see the truth, don't leave me.* I wrote down my dreams, cried for Magdalena, and wept for my stupidity and ignorance. I examined as honestly as possible how, despite good intentions and worldly advantages, I had gotten myself embroiled in so many high-stakes predicaments over the years. I surrendered myself to the process.

During this period of self-examination, I was forced to confront both my highest and my lowest instincts, and allow that which was the highest to dissolve the lowest. I came to see with excruciating clarity the ways that I had contributed to these complicated *entanglements*. My whole life, I had feared my own intuition and had not trusted the validity of what I sensed; instead, I often told people what they wanted to hear in efforts to comfort them, a habit I had learned with my mother. I feared being honest because of what the consequences might be. I feared rejection. These were simple enough truths, but my understanding of them was hard won. What I now could see was that my Inner Teacher represented the highest and most sacred religion for me, and that my ignorance and insecurity regarding this truth had contributed to every difficult situation I had ever faced. From that moment on, I vowed, I would honor and revere the truth according to my Inner Teacher's revelations.

Having spent months in contemplation, I found the resolve I needed to enter the courtroom and speak clearly to the events about which I was to be questioned. As I sat in the hallway waiting for the bailiff to call me, my lawyer friend Bob, who happened to be at the courthouse that day, saw me and stopped to chat. He wasn't interested in the trial, but wanted, as he always did, to hear about my time in seminary and my ministry.

Thankful for the diversion, I smiled weakly. "Bob, for four years you have been grilling me about seminary. Maybe you should put your law practice on hold and enroll in seminary yourself."

His face lit up. "But, Mary Ann, I've met the most remarkable teacher. He is a Buddhist. I'd go anywhere in the world to hear his teachings. Wait a minute—aren't you the hospice chaplain now?"

I nodded, but my heart turned icy with shame and guilt.

Bob leaned toward me, his eyes boring into mine. "This man is known worldwide for his teachings on the transference of consciousness that occurs at death."

Nothing else could have affected me as profoundly in that moment as those few words. At the hospital in Washington where I completed my graduate training, I had been assigned to the intensive-care unit. On my first day working the floors, there were seven deaths. To my great surprise, I discovered that in critical situations of life, death, and dying, I was able to minister to patient, family, and medical staff in meaningful ways. Somehow, in stressful situations of intense grief, I entered a state of gentle ease, confidence, and knowledge. The work itself, although it left me drained, was effortless in the moment. I soon found myself in demand.

Although I received accolades for "caring" and "professionalism," however, I remained profoundly uncertain about my aptitude. I'd had no training in death and dying. In seminary, the subject of death had been mentioned only once, in the week before graduation, when we learned what sort of music should be played at a funeral, and that it was best to visit the family of the deceased at least once afterward. Therefore, while it seemed that I was able to help those I ministered to, I questioned whether I was really saying and doing the "right" things. I was haunted by doubt, which Magdalena's death had only strengthened.

Bob continued, vibrant in his enthusiasm about the teaching he'd recently received. "This teacher is an acclaimed master of *p'howa*."

I had no idea what Bob was talking about. I'd never heard such words or concepts before, yet they magnetized me. I suddenly felt that I had to know where I could find this Buddhist sage. A trek to the Himalayas for the next year was already booked on my calendar, and I sat there calculating how to arrange one more stop on my airline ticket. That wouldn't be necessary, however, for as Bob explained, the Buddhist master was teaching in Napa, behind the Carmelite monastery about a mile from my home, where he'd be for two more weeks.

The bailiff appeared and ushered me down the wide, beautifully handcrafted hallway of justice to the witness stand, and I managed to deliver my testimony with clarity. After the judge excused me, I went home, changed clothes, and drove into the hills.

In the end, due to lack of evidence, Angela was acquitted.

Chapter 8

HIS EMINENCE CHAGDUD TULKU RINPOCHE

Rest in great natural peace
This exhausted mind,
Beaten helpless by karma and neurotic thoughts
Like the relentless fury of the pounding waves
In the infinite ocean of Samsara.
Rest in great natural peace.

—NYOSHUL KHENPO JAMYANG DORJÉ,
A Marvelous Garland of Rare Gems

I MEANDERED ALONG mountain roads and passed a crooked, hand-painted sign that read "Llama Ranch." *Isn't 'Llama' a Buddhist word?* I mused. *Weird way of advertising a place where such a holy man might be.* An arrow pointed left, and I drove in that direction, up a dirt road, until I came upon a small herd of four-legged llamas grazing on the hillside above a small, unkempt dwelling. The owner of Llama Ranch wasn't sure exactly what I was seeking, but he suggested another road, which I eventually found and followed deeper into the hills. This may have been in my backyard, but it was wholly new terrain to me.

The roughly graded fire road led me to a cluster of dust-covered manzanita trees under which a number of cars were randomly parked. I parked there, too, and followed the sound of voices uphill through the leafy, gnarled branches of the old oak forest until I happened upon His Eminence Chagdud Tulku Rinpoche, who, though I didn't know it at the time, was widely considered to be among the most gifted masters of Tibetan Buddhism teaching in America.

HE Chagdud Tulku Rinpoche sat serenely in the lotus position on a makeshift platform in the middle of the grove, wearing a loose yellow shirt and a long maroon wraparound skirt, in observance of the traditional monastic colors, which date back 2,500 years. He was barefoot and had a wispy, drooping mustache, and his long, thin gray hair was gathered into a topknot skewered at the crown of his head. His round, weathered, smiling face and relaxed manner belied the observant depth of his eyes and the air of wisdom that emanated from him. He spoke gently but with undeniable authority to his students as leaf-shaped shadows swayed across the assembly. Several empty, rusted folding chairs were set up at the back of the group. I sat in one closest to the rear.

The strangeness of finding my way to this place via back roads and the residual tension from testifying in the courthouse earlier that day started to ease, and I was able to think and see a bit more clearly. Chaplaincy training in the emergency room and intensive care unit of a large hospital had taught me how to shift my mind quickly from one extreme experience to another, and I could feel such a shift happening now. I knew that there was something here I needed, something indefinable perhaps, but necessary. I did not question this, but let the feeling pull me forward. Entranced by the woodland ambience and this soft-spoken holy man, I was no longer aware of my emotions. I knew only that I wanted to remain to listen to him. In some uncanny way, I felt that I had come home, and for the first time in many months, I began to breathe more easily.

When Rinpoche's talk concluded, the students chatted among themselves, and several approached me to offer tea. As this was my first Buddhist meeting, I didn't know the protocol, but they put me at ease and invited me to meet Rinpoche. Bells from the Carmelite monastery, located several hills from our private forest hideaway, rang out the Angelus, and I introduced myself to Rinpoche as a Christian minister and hospice chaplain. I paused between sentences, listening to Rinpoche's translator, trying to absorb what my words sounded like in the Tibetan language.

Rinpoche's face opened into a wide smile as he took my hand and motioned for me to sit next to him. He asked many questions about my ministry, then taught me the Sanskrit word *dharma*, explaining that it meant "Truth." As I listened to him, something deep within me, like a distant but harmonious memory, resonated with his unusual presence, and I suddenly knew that Rinpoche's *dharma* and the Truth I'd experienced through my Inner Teacher were identical. It was the same sacred, expansive essence of unbridled love and joy that I had secretly held dear since childhood. And, thinking of Magdalena, I knew that I would never again ignore it.

Rinpoche offered to teach me about Truth—a rare honor, although I didn't know it at the time, conferred because he had already recognized the possibility that I was a reincarnation of his mother, Dama Drolma. As a *delog*, she had traveled the afterlife and returned with spiritual wisdom teachings, so Rinpoche had been struck by my work with the dying, which had come so naturally to me as a hospice chaplain. Rinpoche made sure the translator told me about the Red Tara and *p'howa* empowerments he would begin the next day. An empowerment, as I later learned, is a ceremony, unique to Tibetan Buddhism, that initiates students into a specific spiritual practice by helping them to realize themselves as divine through readings, rituals, meditation, or identification with particular deities; crucially, a qualified master must transmit the corresponding power of a practice directly to the student. At the time, I had no questions, felt neither doubt nor hesitation, and assured him that I would return early the next morning and stay for his week of teachings. I was welcomed into the group and given the weekly schedule.

Tara is a great feminine deity of Buddhism, of whom Yeshe Tsogyal was one incarnation. She is said to be the mother of all sentient beings and appears in twenty-one manifestations, in different colors of love, beauty, strength, wisdom, and compassion. In her form as the Red Tara, she is considered beneficial for removing fears and for increasing wealth, longevity, and spiritual power. Padmasambhava had given the Red Tara empowerment to Yeshe Tsogyal, asking that she hide it as a *terma*. The teaching remained hidden until the twentieth century, when it was rediscovered by the renowned lama Apong Tertön and was passed on through the lineage to Rinpoche. When the Red Tara first appeared to Rinpoche, she instructed him to spread her teachings on love and compassion the world over. He did so, offering the Red Tara empowerment only to students whose minds had been purified through their spiritual practices.

When Rinpoche offered it to me as my first empowerment, I did not comprehend the privilege it represented. What I did know was that the Red Tara was familiar to me as a form of the Blessed Mother whom I knew so well. For the first time in my life, I was fully estranged from the Church, without a Christian practice, and with the Red Tara empowerment, Rinpoche gave me a new practice, with a *mala* (string of prayer beads), a book, and a ritual. I experienced profound peace and a sense of homecoming. In this way, the Red Tara met me at the gate and helped me effortlessly cross the threshold between cultures.

For the next three days, Rinpoche also offered *p'howa* teachings, for up to ten hours a day. *P'howa* is an ancient death ritual with specific ceremonies for transferring one's soul or inner consciousness at the moment of death to what Buddhists call the Pure Land, the celestial abode of the Buddhas. In other words, it is a practice of conscious dying and conscious rebirth. Rinpoche said he did not believe in reincarnation, because that word implied the validity of death.

"We don't die," he said. "We change bodies."

I sat with thirty-some students in a canvas yurt, all of us on cushions atop a rough wooden floor. Rinpoche's personal incense mixed with the woodsy aromas typical of Napa Valley's western hills, scents of pungent, sunbaked, dusty bay, redwood, and oak forest. We performed specific meditations, hours of chants, and mystical visualizations. Primary among the practices was that of moving the energy of our life force upward through the *Sushumna nadi* (in Buddhist theory, the body's central energetic channel), then out through the *Sahasrara chakra* (the energetic center at the crown of the head).

These experiences were intriguingly esoteric, and I tried them out with the openness of a child, gratefully forgetting all that I'd left behind in the valley below and, above all, trusting my intuitive draw to this great master teacher and practitioner. Rinpoche proceeded with profound seriousness and caution, reassuring our group that we were too novice to worry about actually transferring our life force or consciousness during these practices.

"You will not die learning how to perform *p'howa*," he said, "but you will master the skills you will need when your actual death approaches. You will also be able to help others navigate the process of dying." Such assertions both mystified and fascinated me.

Discussions among students were equally confounding.

"You get signs after receiving Rinpoche's empowerments," someone said while we were standing in line during lunch break one day. At that point, I had no idea what an empowerment was, but given the direction my life was going, I was drawn to the idea of gaining power in those areas of my life where I believed I had too little.

"Signs?" I asked. "What do you mean by signs?"

"You know, physical signs, on your body."

I neither disbelieved nor doubted, but I had never heard of Protestant Christian ministers receiving signs on their bodies. This odd exchange reminded me of a remarkable statue I had once seen during a visit to Thailand: a huge, golden sleeping Buddha, whose feet were covered with beautifully intricate symbols and lettering. Now I thought, *Surely these students don't think hieroglyphics are going to show up on the soles of their feet...do they?*

It didn't take long to find out. Rinpoche stated in the next teaching session that we might experience an itching on our heads at some point during the retreat and find a sticky fluid there. Such a sign would simply indicate that the practice had been successful. I looked around at the others, wishing I were Buddhist so that I, too, could have signs. But on the last day, having allowed my consciousness to flow into the magic river of the mantras, I reached up to scratch my head and discovered a sticky substance on my fingers, which I gazed at with wonder—Rinpoche's odd prediction had borne out!

That night we went to Rinpoche's tent, and he told us to kneel in front of him. He felt our heads one by one, then with each of us took a piece of straw and stuck it into... what? A hole? The fontanel, that soft membrane between the cranial bones of the skull? I didn't know, but we all joined in his laughter, looking at each other standing there with straw antennas sticking out of our heads. At the time, I was so overwhelmed with all the new and strange experiences I was having that I couldn't attend to making sense of them.

With time and study, I eventually learned that consciously directing energy through specific meditative practices can have powerful transforming effects not only on the heart and mind, but upon the physical body as well. During our *p'howa* practice, we had channeled our inner energy upward to open the *Sahasrara* energetic center at the crown of the head, which corresponds to the fontanel. Having chanted for three days and three nights with Rinpoche, I had entered a zone where such phenomena somehow seemed natural and unremarkable. I was simply pleased that the practice had been successful, at least according to the signs we were getting. And, above all, for the first time in years I experienced happiness and a phenomenal sense of ease, a feeling of being at home in the compelling presence of mystery.

Within weeks, I was immersed in a strange and expansive new life. Rinpoche began to visit my home in Napa, a ten-acre estate I had received through my divorce settlement. Due to my years of stock-market trading, I had been able to transform the Family Home, as I called it, into a wonderful retreat space, which I loved to share. I invited Rinpoche to give teachings there to the hundreds of students who flocked to him.

One warm July afternoon in 1988, he sat in lotus position under the Family Home's tulip tree, eating homemade apple pie and sipping iced tea with a small group of senior students.

"The oldest part of your brain is at the base of your head. It is called the medulla oblongata. My English correct, yes?" At first Rinpoche's English had been difficult to understand, but with time I had become familiar with his unusual syntax and was able to follow without a translator. Rinpoche pointed to the back of a student's head. "All ancient wisdom reside here. Your mind like a television receiver," he said and laughed merrily. "You are all television receivers and transmitters!"

The others watched him with the same smiling curiosity I was feeling.

Rinpoche told us how truly stunned Tibetans were when they first heard about boxes with small talking people inside. "We couldn't believe such a thing. 'Impossible!' we said. Then we hear about a handle with long wire attached. Hold up to your ear and hear people's voices talking even when people talking are far, far away. We laughed and said, 'Ridiculous!' Soon in Tibet we see West a place of mystery and magic. More and more we hear of your science and technology, more we are in awe of you. Now you in West meeting people from Tibet, you hear stories about Eastern spiritual accomplishments, our spiritual science, and you say, 'Impossible, ridiculous!' You hear stories about our visionaries, mystics, and healers, and you say, 'Miracles!' Just like we say television and telephones are miracles." Rinpoche loved Western science and he loved the television, often using them as metaphors to teach us about meditation.

"Meditation quiets the mind, slows it down," he continued. "You see pictures, like movies in the mind. Some of you learn meditation in past lives, so you learn very fast. Others learn now for the first time, for you meditation skills come more slowly. Human mind is like a giant television set—human mind powerful broadcasting station. Be careful! Don't attach your mind to these mind movies. Have clear minds, discriminate between visions from very high sources and destructive, potentially dangerous chatter from *samsara*."

I knew by then that *samsara* referred to attachments to the constantly shifting realm of mental suffering and ignorance, the realm of impermanency, of everyday reality. *Samsara* describes the world I experienced at my childhood dinner table with my family. *Samsara* is the ongoing, frustrating effort to save a failed and destructive marriage; it is envy and jealousy; it is the world of poverty, of constant worries about money; it is the fear of violence we feel walking around most of our large cities and the constant headlines of murder and war. *Samsara* refers to the ongoing difficulties of the world, where nothing lasts, not even the good things. Often we hear about getting off the hamster wheel—or, as Rinpoche described it, cyclic existence where we spin around and around, never finding true happiness or lasting inner peace—but we question whether it is indeed actually possible to get off that wheel.

Rinpoche then urged, "Look around you. What can you see that is permanent? Even when meditating, look into your mind, test your thoughts against sky. Are your ideas like footprints in sky? Can you see them? Are they permanent?"

I looked across the lawn to the giant oak, to the vineyards below, the blue agapanthus, the colorful roses bordering the lawn, my fellow students, my golden retriever, my white cat.

"What can you see that is permanent? What will be here two hundred years from now? Even sky has boundaries. It is limited. Even sky no more when our planet ceases to be."

He picked up his glass, which was filled with pure, clear water, then scooped up a handful of dirt from the flowerbed beside him. He tipped the dirt into his glass, stirring water and dirt together with my grandmother's silver teaspoon.

"Agitated mind filled with ignorance or negative emotions, it like this," he said, tapping the glass with the spoon. "Difficult, negative thoughts like dirty, cloudy water. Cloudy mind see no truth. Thinking mind never discern its own true nature." He pointed at the glass in his hands. "See? No clarity, muddy."

He put the glass down. In the stillness, the dirt settled to the bottom of the glass, leaving the upper portion of the water clear again.

"Knowledge, wisdom, permanent. Compassion, truth, permanent. Don't confuse permanent with impermanent."

I had never heard such ideas articulated so clearly before. As I sat with Rinpoche in the shade of the tulip tree, I wondered why, after a lifetime of faithful church attendance and four years in one of the West's finest seminaries, I had never encountered discussions relevant to the nature of the mind, the world we live in, the nature of the elements and how they interact. Why had I never been introduced to the esoteric planes of reality surrounding us, our planet, permeating the universe?

On numerous visits to the Family Home, Rinpoche and other visiting lamas introduced me and many others to these essential teachings and to what Western students might call the "spiritual sciences" of the Nyingmas—for example, what it means to be a Light Being, the concept of the Billion-fold Universe, and terms like *heart-mind*. They described how an eternal *heart-mind* consciousness resides in every atom of the universe and is irrevocably connected to every other aspect of the universe. Joined with but different from the intellectual capacity of the brain, the *heart-mind* is an intuitive, emotive state that provides an additional *quality of knowing* to our experiences. It also serves as a conduit for connecting to others and the Billion-fold Universe.

During this period, I saw my first Tibetan *thangka*. *Thangkas* are sacred paintings that serve as maps of the multilayered and multidimensional spiritual world of the pure mind. A single *thangka* will often depict one of the many Buddhist deities, each of whom is represented in a specific color, in a specific and spiritually resonant posture, holding significant artifacts. The deity will be surrounded by tens or even hundreds of associated awakened beings, which represent the countless aspects of the deity's supreme nature. These gorgeous and elaborate paintings reminded me of the protectors of my childhood faith—Mary and the myriad prophets, saints, angels, archangels, cherubim, and seraphim.

I learned that we are "electrical beings" because electrical currents continuously transmit messages to the brain, *heart-mind*, and body. I learned how to hold a golden *dorje*—a ritual tool that symbolizes spiritual power—next to my heart during certain prayers. While holding the *dorje* in this way, one concentrates on receiving rays of loving-kindness from a chosen deity, harnessing that Light energy in the body and sending it from the *heart-mind* back out to the universe.

For a lifetime, I had saved Roman Catholic holy cards depicting both Our Lady the Virgin Mary and Jesus surrounded by golden rays. In many of these images, Jesus' heart emanated brilliant shafts of light. The convent I'd gone to as a girl was named Sacred Heart, but it wasn't until I met Rinpoche that I was confronted with how vital our own heart chakra truly is. I understood that I, too, was surrounded by a field of Light that was just like the beautiful auras pictured in my holy cards of Mary and Jesus. I was taught how to transmit that healing, compassionate energy outward from my *heart-mind* and how to partner with beneficent divine forces that I'd previously assumed resided only "outside" myself. My inner world was bursting open as I learned about the extraordinary power of prayer, mantras, compassion, and meditation.

Nothing from my life before meeting Rinpoche could explain how passionately I responded to his teachings. The fifty years that preceded my first encounter with this great master, as he sat in the lotus position in that oak grove in the hills of Napa Valley, seemed to be merely an accumulation of random actions and reactions. But in the midst of the strange familiarity and overwhelming resonance I felt in Rinpoche's presence, I began to contemplate the possibility of past lives. I experienced an inexplicably profound sense of refuge in the haunting vibrations of the mantras we recited and in the very sound of Rinpoche's voice as he imparted the ancient teachings. It was like remembering a long-forgotten song from childhood. No one had to tell me I had known Rinpoche from past lives. *I knew it.* The doors of an eon were rumbling open on their hinges.

In the midst of my Tibetan Buddhist initiation, my work as chaplain at the Napa Valley Hospice continued to be profoundly rewarding, as did the Taizé services in Napa Valley. I became a card-carrying minister of the Universal Life Church, which served as my legal certification for ministering at weddings and the like. And, at the urging and invitation of friends, I joined the United Methodist Church in St. Helena. Wary of joining another institutional church, I had meditated on this possibility for quite some time, but wistful memories of church community, preaching, teaching, the study of scripture, and congregational worship won out. I would simply be careful, walk softly. To my surprise and delight, I was welcomed with open arms.

Meanwhile, Rinpoche continued to guide me through what at times felt like a maze of opposing forces. My partnership with him and my role as his student felt like a natural extension of my ongoing ministry. Rinpoche appreciated having access to my Christian education and enjoyed meeting the clergy I introduced him to. Given how at home I felt in my Buddhist studies, however, we discussed whether I should stay with the Christian Church or pursue formal Buddhist training instead. Rinpoche dissuaded me from the latter, explaining that I'd spent this lifetime as a Christian, was a highly a trained theologian, and could speak with dissatisfied former Christian students in ways he couldn't.

"Take you too many years to learn new formal Buddhist system. New language not necessary for you. In many past lives you do much work. You learn already," he said. As it pertained to my hospice work, he suggested, "Old age, dying, most important time in people's lives. Future life depend upon good peaceful death. Good you help them. Hospitals, churches don't want Buddhist lamas from Asia. They want Western minister."

Whether I was a Western minister or Buddhist lama, I was now also exploring many soul-nourishing aspects of truth in Tarot, Ancient Christianity, Buddhism, Western mysticism, astrology, psychology, philosophy, and multiple healing modalities. And I was driven to embody and to serve this expanded experience of Truth as much as I possibly could.

Chapter 9

IN SEARCH OF MY YOGI:
THE HIMALAYAS

The Himals may be the birthplace of Asian imagination and the fountainhead of the two oldest religions, and the natal home to gods, demi-gods, spirits, and emanations in abundance. It is not surprising the Lord Buddha took birth in the foothills of the Himals. No other area in the world is so populated with power spots or places imbued with spiritual energy, where travelers are touched by purifying winds, by caves or rivers, and by the images of deities that have spontaneously and intentionally emerged from the earth. Here is the home of serpent deities called "nagas" which control the fertility of fields and forest.

—MICHAEL PALIN, *Himalaya*

LIKE MANY MAJOR DECISIONS I've made in my life, my decision to join a trek in the Himalayas was a spontaneous response to a friend's invitation. If the phone rings, you answer it. I was nearing my fiftieth birthday and knew that if I wanted to make such a journey, it was as good a time as any. To address my shaky hiking, athletic, and endurance abilities, I undertook a diligent training program, climbing the hills around Napa Valley with backpack and trekking poles.

One late afternoon, while trudging up the Oakville Grade Road, I was stopped in my tracks by the apparition of an ancient man. He did not have the fleshy appearance of a physical being, but he seemed quite real. In the vision, he sat on a stone ledge that seemed to be high up in a place I sensed must be the Himalayas. A beautiful, cerulean-blue sky surrounded him. His thin white beard hung down, as did his long white hair. He wore a tunic so threadbare that light shone through it. In fact, light seemed to radiate through his entire body. He spoke no words, but his gaze and his being radiated indescribably profound love and stillness. Though this seminal "meeting" lasted but a few moments, the feeling of love lingered long afterward. In my mind, I called the ancient man My Yogi, though in truth I had no idea what a yogi was.

I became convinced I would meet him in the flesh on my trek, which only deepened my thrill about and commitment to going to the Himalayas. I now felt as called to make this journey as I had felt called to the ministry on that long ago Good Friday. I trained with renewed vigor and excitement, and contemplated what to do when I met My Yogi. What would I say? That I had met him in a vision while hiking in mountains clear across the world? Would I be too intimidated to speak? Would words be necessary? Would I be comfortable being silent?

My dedication to making this trip was so strong that when the trek was suddenly canceled for unexplained reasons a few weeks before my scheduled departure, I didn't interpret it as a sign that I shouldn't go. I found another trek that was planned for the same time and needed two more people to complete the team. The new trek would take us deep into the Himalayas, separating us from the outer world—friends, family, and medical help—by hundreds of wilderness miles. It would take us to many revered sites in ancient Tibet. I meditated on the possibility and even visited the trek leader, Hari, in Wyoming, so that he could determine whether my hiking abilities were up to snuff. In truth, he seemed more interested in signing me up to meet the trek quota, but he did assure me that my pace was fine and that the trek would be well within my capabilities. I passed the endurance test, signed the papers, and prepared to honor the bond between me and what felt like my destiny.

When Rinpoche heard about the trek, he tried to talk me out of it. There was a crisis in Kathmandu, and his own monastery was in lockdown. He suggested that a trip to the region could be unsafe. Had I shared the visions of My Yogi and the urgency of my call, perhaps Rinpoche might have changed his point of view, but I did not. Instead, I listened to his concerns, then checked in with Hari, who told me that the political situation in Kathmandu was under control. But Rinpoche called again, stressing the dangerous nature of travel at that time.

I decided to consult my Inner Teacher on the matter. One late September afternoon, I meditated outside, under the tulip tree. Warm, dappled light filtered down through the overhead world of green, and swaying leaf shadows danced over my body. Gold honeybees, thick-legged with pollen, buzzed around the tree. I closed my eyes and felt Ezekiel's wheels—those biblical wheels within wheels that signify the presence of God's will to action cycle after cycle—spin a warm, assuring iridescent blur around and through me. Outer and inner benevolent forces seemed to be calling me into motion. My Yogi sat with me at the center of these forces, giving me the confidence I needed.

I departed from the San Francisco airport for Kathmandu on a clear October morning. Several days later, when the pilot announced that the Himalayan mountain range was now visible, many of us leapt from our seats and leaned over passengers with view windows. Transfixed, we gazed with wonder at the snow-capped peaks, ice-blue glaciers, and forests that lay under Nepalese morning skies.

We deplaned under a hovering gray haze and crossed the tarmac toward Kathmandu's attractive modern terminal. At the baggage claim was our expedition leader, Hari, who was just as handsome, virile, and muscular as he had been when I met him in Wyoming: six feet tall, built of solid muscle, with thick, dark, wavy hair, blue eyes, and finely chiseled facial features. His vibrant physical health radiated competence, energizing everyone around him. He organized the unfamiliar faces with an air of efficiency and organized haste. The man who helped me with my bags seemed to be Hari's assistant, and the two of them handed out long red-and-white checked scarves to our group of nine as we took seats on a long bench. Hari launched into his welcome speech.

"The air in Kathmandu is highly polluted with fecal dust, so tie these scarves around your nose and mouth now." We all opened the long scarves and began winding them around our heads as we listened. "Do not touch your face or mouth for the next month. If you see someone from our group doing this, stop them. Don't let anyone touch their face. If we can get you into the high country healthy, we can keep you that way. Be responsible for yourself and remember, don't touch your face."

Something in this exchange reminded me of my days at the convent. Each Monday morning, the entire student body of girls sat at attention while the Reverend Mother and the Mistress of Studies gave recognition to those who had excelled during the past week and reproached those whose behavior needed improvement. I was called for correction once, because I had touched my face during the previous assembly. I learned that a proper lady did not touch her face in public. I grinned at the memory. And I felt relieved; I didn't have to make decisions. Hari was in charge, and I felt safe. I assumed that he would now guide us to a chartered bus and deliver us to our hotel to unpack and freshen up, after which we'd socialize over a refreshing cup of tea.

But our "Welcome to Nepal" lecture continued. "You all have jet lag, which you must get over by tonight. The best way to do that is to exercise. This will oxygenate your system immediately. There are bicycles outside. We will begin riding right now. This is your first exercise operating as a unit. Remember, you must keep your trekking partner ahead of you in sight. You must be constantly aware of your surroundings. This is a matter of life or death."

I was totally unprepared for this pronouncement. We were hurried past the empty space where our luggage had been, then out the airport's front entrance, where ten clean but dented black bicycles leaned against sturdy kickstands. I took pains to look nonchalant, as though I regularly mounted a 1950s-style Chinese bicycle to ride single file, with a bright scarf tied around my face, through the streets of exotic cities.

In Kathmandu, it turned out, there was no discernible right or left side of the road—cars, pedestrians, buffalo, wheelbarrows, donkeys, and buses wove their ways through openings wherever they appeared.

"Use your bells!" Hari yelled.

Bells were ringing on every moving object. Even the buffalo wore bells. Nevertheless, I channeled my anxieties through my thumb, continually pumping the bicycle's silvery bell as we pedaled through the city.

Trying to keep sight of the other group members, to whom I had yet to be introduced, was nightmarishly difficult. Fortunately, no one else in the entire city of Kathmandu wore red-and-white checked scarves wrapped around their heads. I followed these scarves until they vanished in the city's hazy chaos, then reappeared on the far side of an exhaust-spewing bus. We pushed on through the deafening, rapidly changing sights of Kathmandu. Camels lumbered in front of me, once again temporarily separating me from the group. We rode past aging, patched, but picturesque two-story wooden buildings whose balconies were partially covered with chipped paint. We pedaled around rice paddies and barley fields, through dried dung, smog, exhaust fumes, and cigarette smoke. Sidewalk vendors' barbeque-scented cook fires commingled with the pungent aromas of diesel. Tall blackboards with menus written in different shades of bright chalk stood outside small eating establishments. I pressed on in a blurred state of sensory shock. At one point, we passed a water hole or cistern dug into the tan earth. Rudimentary stairs carved out of its rounded sides led down to a pool of brown water in which women washed clothes and with which children filled cracked plastic jugs. I prayed this wasn't their drinking water.

Our morning ride ended for lunch at Kathmandu's best hotel, the Yak and Yeti. Hari sang its praises as we walked through a comfortable lobby to the dining room, where we sat around a single table. I relaxed into my chair and looked at the four men and four women with whom I would spend the next month. They all appeared to be gentle and nonthreatening, so I suggested we introduce ourselves. My enthusiastic proposal was met with sober reserve at first, but soon, one by one, we all exchanged introductions.

It seemed that the entire group were friends from Salt Lake City, and even Hari had roots with the group. I wondered how to present myself. How would Mormons feel about a Christian minister? Should I instead introduce myself as an investor, a writer, a mother? Though my life revolved around my ministry, I was at the time a confusing mixture of Christian and Buddhist. I decided to leave out the Buddhism and identified myself as a Christian minister and hospice chaplain.

Conversation ceased as lunch was served. After eating, Hari pushed his chair back, stood up, and told us to hurry as we had a long ride ahead. I began to fear that this grueling physical-fitness program would never end, but I remounted my bicycle and pedaled off after Hari. The afternoon passed in a daze, but eventually we stopped for a dinner break, during which we again remained silent. When that meal was over, we once again climbed on our bicycles, and rode through the outskirts of Kathmandu into dusk's deepening light. We reached the outskirts of the city as the moon, huge and golden, began her slow ascent above the dusty, smoggy horizon.

Still we continued. We pedaled up a slight incline. We steered around newly planted rice paddies glistening with the fairy dust of the now fully visible, silver harvest moon. Careful to stay dead center on the narrow paths, we rose out of darkness into magical moonlight and saw bright, welcoming lights inside a small hotel popular with European trekkers. Twelve hours after leaving the airport, our hellish bicycle ride ended.

The hotel had varnished, clean, wood-paneled walls, tall, narrow windows, and canvas-covered floors. The group's women were shown to a single spacious room. My duffle bag sat next to a neatly made bed. I spoke briefly to the other women but soon collapsed onto the mattress, wondering how I had survived Hari's surprise welcome to Nepal. As I fell asleep, quickly forgetting my roommates' names, flashes of fairy dust and glistening rice paddies mingled with scenes of incredible poverty and my first glimpse of the Himalayas.

In the cool darkness of the next day's dawn, a green bus met us outside our hotel. Lashed to the roof and filling the rear seats of the aging vehicle were large piles of gray canvas bags, which contained our tents, ropes, tables, chairs, cooking utensils, food, sleeping gear, and clothes. All the members of our expedition were present. Americans, Sherpas, and porters filled the bus with shivering waves of excitement. Our hot breath met cool glass windows, and we wiped the condensation away with our hands as we left on the Araniko Highway, driving through a gap at the eastern edge of the Kathmandu Valley. This road connects Kathmandu to both the Nepal-Tibet border and to Lukla, the starting point for many Mt. Everest expeditions. The Araniko is Nepal's only road to the Tibetan border and is among the most dangerous highways in Nepal. Speeding Chinese lorries, extremely steep slopes on each side of the road, and massive mudslides make the route notoriously treacherous. It is not uncommon to hear of buses plunging off the sides of the highway, especially after the rains.

As our altitude increased, the highway narrowed, and our top-heavy bus swayed, navigating sharp curves and dangerous holes in the poorly maintained pavement. Laughter helped dilute our terror, and an infectious camaraderie blossomed. I shared a seat with Tanya, a delicate woman in her early thirties who wore her dark brown hair in a neat bob. We shared anxieties and concerns about the upcoming trek; she confessed that she was also worried about her ability to survive this trek, but her brother had strong-armed her into coming. She eventually explained who was who from Salt Lake City: she herself was a nurse, and there were two doctors, an anesthesiologist, a classical-music disc jockey, a teacher, an accountant, and a dancer. After we consumed boxed lunches, the DJ, James, stood at the front of the bus entertaining us with taped music no one could hear above the mechanical din of the engine.

At one point, Hari steadied himself at the front of the bus and yelled over the engine: "Every day you will ask yourself, many times over, what deluded idea was behind your decision to join this trek. You will be convinced it was the most imbecilic decision you ever made." He clung to the seat back next to him as the bus swerved side to side. "When you are on the trail, however, don't let your mind wander. Stay aware of your surroundings and keep the person in front of you in sight. This is a matter of life and death."

Inwardly, I fumed. I knew after the bicycle ride around Kathmandu that I couldn't physically keep up with this group, but what good would it do now to raise my hand and argue? I decided not to worry and thought back to Hari's advice in Wyoming: "Just find your pace and maintain it." I never questioned him or my motivation for being on the trek, so I settled into my discomfort and trusted that I would survive the trek and all would work out in the end.

Our first camp would be pitched on private property, Hari announced, and we were to show respect to the farmer who owned the land. Hari intoned in the strictest terms, "Never enter your tents while wearing your boots. Sit inside the tent's doorway, remove your boots, and leave them outside under a plastic covering. Leave no toilet paper, Kleenex, or garbage of any sort behind in our campsites or on the trail. Carry your soiled toilet paper with you until you can either burn or bury it."

Several porters and Sherpas had chosen to ride on top of the bus, scrunched between the lashed bags. When Hari was done with the orientation, some Americans shouted over the engine noise, "Can we ride on top of the bus with the porters?" I figured that if we plunged off this treacherous road, there would be no survivors anyway, so what difference would it make if we were inside or on top of this old rattletrap bus? Hari must have come to the same conclusion, for he nodded to the driver to pulled over. He and his friends laughingly climbed to the roof, where they rode for the rest of the drive.

At our destination, we ate boxed suppers in the bus while the porters unloaded and erected the tents in the dark. Recent rains had muddied the tilled field in which we were to camp. The bus lights, our headlamps, and the lanterns set around by the porters barely illuminated the soil, which looked black and rich, fertile. As I walked to my tent, however, a strong smell filled my nose, and I gagged. The field was covered with manure—human, as I was informed.

No one had to remind me about my boots when I entered my tent. They came off and were covered in a flash. I scooted backward into my pup tent, still gagging, trying not to breathe through my nose. I thought about the farmer and his family. Who brought the chamber pots out each morning to fertilize these fields? Was it a woman's job? After the extreme poverty I'd witnessed in past couple of days, I noted to myself that this family was fortunate in that they could probably feed themselves from produce grown on this land. I also reminded myself that the human sense of smell neutralizes odors in a matter of minutes. Covering my head and face with my scarf and sniffing a scented towelette, I fell asleep wishing I didn't have to personally test this theory for accuracy. But when morning arrived, the world was indeed free of stench.

Chapter 10

CROSSING OVER

May I take on this suffering for other beings.
May this suffering ripen within me instead of them.
May not even a single sentient being experience this kind of suffering.
May it be so.
May all sentient beings be parted from their suffering.
How fervently I wish it to be so.
May they never experience suffering.
How wonderful it would be if others no longer endured any torment.
I still work hard to eradicate all the suffering of beings.

—THE FOURTH DODRUPCHEN RINPOCHE'S
Compassion Meditation, in Sandra Scales's
Sacred Voices of the Nyingma Masters

O N THE FIRST OFFICIAL DAY of our trek, we walked like
European aristocrats through fragrant, grassy fields filled with
wildflowers and lichen-covered stones, inspired by the poetic majesty
of the vast, snow-covered mountains that surrounded us. Along the
route, conical rock piles were adorned with colorful prayer flags
fluttering in the soft breeze. Tribal porters trotted past our column,
later greeting us with hot tea and biscuits in a romantic meadow,
where we picnicked near a small fire that carried delicious aromas
skyward on white feathers of smoke. After lunch, Janelle, the dancer,

who was to perform the role of Clara in a London production of *The Nutcracker*, practiced elegant arabesques in front of near-vertical granite walls whose summits were lost in high countries of ice and snow. Her father looked on, eyes shining with pride, as she dazzled the rest of us with her youthful grace and beauty. Entranced, happily ignorant of the challenges ahead, I rested on a Tibetan rug and gazed up at lazy puffs of cloud drifting slowly above, then dozed in the heat reflected off the granite. When our guides called us back to the hike, I hoisted my backpack, eager to get under way.

That meadow was the last piece of flat ground I would see for weeks. The next stage of the trail was essentially vertical, with three-foot-high steps. There were no secret passages through these stony heights. I had to claw my way up. Then, after the trail crested at the first ridge, the path headed straight down, which required me to sit and scoot from step to step. Having climbed four thousand feet, we now had to descend three thousand. This was the challenging reality of the Himalayas.

We eventually arrived at a steep subtropical jungle. Musk deer, over five hundred species of birds, and forty species of rhododendron thrive in that valley, but I saw nothing more than the next root or branch to grasp as I descended through the increasingly moisture-laden undergrowth into a ravine. I was exhausted, and my heart pounded a furious staccato, yet over its cacophony I could hear and feel the vibrations of a distant roar. As it was all I could do to hang on, I paid little heed to the increasing roar, although it reverberated through my body. Through great effort, I managed to slide to the bottom of the ravine without actually falling.

My Lord, I thought, *there must be waterfalls the size of Niagara ahead.*

The possibility of seeing something so magnificent galvanized my shaking legs once I was on level ground, and I moved toward the sound, accompanied by Norbu, an extraordinary Sherpa guide with whom, from that day on, I brought up the rear. What we encountered, though, was not a waterfall, but a massive gorge.

Hearing thunder in its depths, I approached cautiously and peered over the rim. Carved into the mountain range by the Bhote Koshi River, the gorge pierced me with awe and terror. River torrents, swollen into angry tumult by monsoon rains, boomed over granite boulders, water pounding stone with overwhelming power. Although struck by the beauty of the spectacle, I was sapped by the journey that had brought me here and terrified by the extremity of the drop. I stepped back quickly and collapsed on the damp, green ground—all but ensuring that I would lag even farther behind my fellow trekkers.

Norbu quickly signaled that we had to push on, so I forced myself to stand. Back home I had studied *National Geographic* pictures of rickety bridges stretched across deep ravines and had wondered whether I could make myself walk across a two-rope bridge with missing slats and a handrail of thin wire. After having repeatedly practiced such a crossing in my imagination, I had finally concluded that I could do it. With this resolve in mind, I took a few steps upriver, looking for a bridge, but Norbu shook his head and gestured instead at a wet, slippery log that straddled the gorge.

I froze and considered my situation: I was alone with a man who spoke no English, and he thought I was going to walk over that log—which was patrolled, it seemed to my terrified mind, by *nagas*, the howling serpent gods that guard the abyss. I wanted to cry.

Pointing upstream, I said fiercely, "No, absolutely not. I need a bridge to cross."

Norbu gently took my gear and again gestured at the log. Holding my backpack in one hand and my trekking poles in the other, he walked across the log in a sprightly manner. Within inches of the other side, he returned, walking backward and grinning. Then he crossed the gorge again, depositing my gear on the far side. He danced a jig back to me, waving his arms and laughing.

Perhaps I became hypnotized because when Norbu returned the third time and offered his hands, palms up, I saw an opening. The demonic force of the *nagas* transformed into a field of glistening rainbow lights that illuminated every drop of moisture. I approached the edge of the gorge, laid my hands lightly atop Norbu's, stepped onto the log, and began to cross over, each step somehow landing squarely in the center of the log. The energy I felt flowing from Norbu's hands was at once stimulating and sedative, and my fear evaporated. I placed one foot in front of the other and soon was able to stop looking at my boots. In a dreamlike rapture, I gazed outward at the surrounding environment, straight down at the crashing waters, captivated by the beauty below me. It was as though I had crossed into a different dimension when we reached the far side of the gorge.

Norbu shouldered my backpack. After a short distance, as darkness descended, we reached our first overnight camp and joined the other trekkers for dinner, which was a minimal affair. Everyone in the group had crossed the gorge by way of that log, yet no one mentioned it. My fellow trekkers had evidently agreed not to dwell on hardships, but instead to transcend them. With heads bowed, we ate in silence. From that point on, we rarely expended energy on either talking or dancing.

Our goal was to reach the Sacred Rolwaling Valley high in the Himalayas. Although located in today's Nepal, the valley is one of

Tibet's oldest and most sacred landmarks, considered a destination for Tibetan Sherpas should they need to escape to Nepal in the case of a national crisis. My fellow trekkers and I would be among the first Westerners allowed to visit these lands. After the Communist takeover in the 1950s, the Chinese government had closed all borders into Tibet. Thereafter, the Chinese considered the United States and other Western democratic nations friendly to Tibet suspect, and thus instituted daunting bureaucratic obstacles that would make it difficult for citizens of those countries to enter Tibet. Fortunately, Hari had established strong local connections in Nepal and had been able to secure visas for us to enter the valley.

Though I slept well that first night, I awoke to the river's nearby roar and suddenly felt a choking wrath at Hari, who I felt had not prepared me sufficiently for the physical challenges I was up against. As I lay fuming in my sleeping bag, a porter unzipped the tent door and entered with a thermos of tea, a civilized British colonial custom that roused me from my reverie. Once dressed, I crawled out of the tent and started back toward the gorge—I wanted to see that log bridge one more time—but Norbu hurried me to breakfast instead.

Presiding at a vinyl-covered folding table, Hari gestured to a dishpan filled with an iodine solution and lectured us in the dire language that we had to come expect from him. "Do not eat anything unless it is prepared by the Sherpas, who are both our cooks and guides," he intoned. "The Sherpas have already cleaned your eating utensils and plates, but you still need to sterilize them in the iodine. We will follow this procedure before each meal. Take no chances. Dysentery is rampant in the Himalayas. If one of you gets sick or injured, we will have to leave you behind. The villagers are good people. They will feed and care for you until we return."

We had seen several village huts the day before: thatched roofs, dirt floors, animals in and out of the living spaces. Alarmed at the thought of being left behind, I vowed to do whatever I had to do to stay safe, even if that meant washing my hands ten times at each meal. Hari instructed us to use designated "wash" and "dry" towels, then to swish our hands in the iodine solution, air-drying them as we entered the mess tent. Once we were seated, the iodine basin was passed among us again.

Hari looked around the camp table, a portentous gleam in his eyes. "We will eat breakfast quickly this morning because we need an early start. You need to learn right now, a trekking group acts as a single unit. While climbing, you must be constantly aware of the person in front of you and always keep them in sight. Their movement could be a matter of life or death to the entire group."

On hearing this, I again flared with anger. Hari knew that I walked much more slowly than the other trekkers. I had decided to trust him, but it was something else entirely to learn that I could actually die, or cause others to die, if I was to lose sight of the person in front of me. I caught his attention.

"My pace, as we have discussed, Hari, is quite slow."

"Your pace will be fine," he assured me, peremptorily. "Just find a comfortable speed and maintain it."

I was in way over my head. I couldn't look him in the eye. As I stifled my anger, Rinpoche's attempts to dissuade me from the trek flashed through my mind. I forced myself to focus instead on fortifying myself with breakfast. Under no circumstance would I let the group see how insecure and terrified I felt.

Shortly after our meal, I dressed myself in multiple layers—long johns, fleece pants, shirts, jacket, an army-surplus hat, and a long cotton skirt (the women trekkers had been asked to wear overskirts to avoid insulting the locals). I stood with similarly garbed fellow trekkers in single file near the mess tent as camp was disassembled. Our co-guide, Cathy, in her mountain-chic wool wraparound skirt and with a lustrous blond ponytail, moved about with the confidence of a sleek racehorse anxious for the gates to open.

Hari and Cathy led us to the trail with yesterday's still-wet clothes tied to our backpacks, flapping in the still morning air like flags of surrender. Our positions in line had been established, and they would not vary. Down the line, each hiker stepped aside as heavily laden porters, each carrying a portion of our camp on his back, trotted past us toward our next destination. The porters were small, wiry, and tough. Most were dressed in ragged pants cut off at mid-calf, and some wore flip-flops, while others wore tennis shoes without laces or walked barefoot. Their loads were larger than they were.

Once the porters passed, I pushed on, trying to keep up, but the other trekkers nevertheless quickly pulled ahead. The narrow but well-traveled trail followed the now placid waters of the Bhote Koshi River, eventually leading us into a lush jungle whose beauty overcame my preoccupation with being last in line. Due to the winding topography, we again crossed the river, this time via a suspension bridge. The gorge widened as we traveled up a series of steep switchbacks adjacent to a huge granite wall, dark in misty shadows. Yet I could clearly see the surroundings, illuminated by descending rays of sun that, as they pierced the green layers of foliage, seemed to convey hidden and incomprehensible truths.

Chattering bands of monkeys clung to giant boulders as we ascended beyond the tree line, leaving behind the forests, the alpine fir and birch, the waterfalls, the colorful birds. By midmorning, the trail had dwindled in width until it could barely accommodate a single person, and it now sat right on the edge of a near-vertical cliff of copper-colored earth. Two thousand feet down was the river, a distant dark ribbon snaking its way toward the Indian subcontinent. Leery of vertigo, I did not look down, but my stomach knotted with nerves. *Focus!* my Inner Teacher directed suddenly, and I knew to keep my arms and poles close to my body to avoid hitting the mountain wall on my right, which could knock me off balance.

Keenly aware of my limbs, I focused intensely on the trail—until it vanished. Suddenly there was nowhere to place my leading foot. Ahead of me, a mudslide had eradicated the path and left behind a hard, smooth, coppery expanse. To my left was a sheer drop. In that moment I envisioned a shadow-body falling from the trail, down through the air, but with an eerily floating quality, as though suspended from an invisible parachute. I jerked my head, dizzy, for I knew it was my own body that I saw. It was me falling to my death. With that vision came an instant and utter comprehension of the fragility of my physical life force. I was a small creature on the cliff of life, unable to turn back or go forward.

From the far side of the sun-baked mudslide, a Sherpa named Pema inched back toward me, deftly traversing the hard-packed slope like a spider. As Pema approached, Norbu gingerly reached around to ease the poles from my wrists and the backpack from my shoulders. I had no choice but to surrender.

Again I envisioned the falling figure, but I heard the voice within me: *This is not your day to die.* At certain times, the momentum of my life plays out as though against a cloudless sky, and I can see past, present, and future free of obscurity—this was such a moment. When I looked again, I knew that the falling body was my fear-body being released from a past experience. Now when I looked into the abyss, I experienced no fear, no threat of vertigo. I had braced myself to encounter howling demons, their eyeballs bulging and teeth bared, but like the trail they had vanished into the quiet of the mountain. Instead I now saw, or rather felt, a panorama of countless lifetimes and knew that for the time being I was safe.

Pema reached out to me, seemingly glued to the polished earth. He took my left hand and placed it into a small, hard indentation. Then, like a contortionist, he leaned over, took my left foot in his hand and placed it into another small, hard indentation. Norbu placed my right hand on a small outcropping and my right foot into some sort of pocket, which I never saw. In this way, we inched across the mudslide. Suspended, body flat against the slope, head to one side, I saw nothing but Pema's faded blue cotton pants. My senses of touch and smell, however, were all-pervasive. There were the men's hands on my hands and feet, the smell of the dirt wall as it pressed against my cheek, my thighs, arms, and chest. Gravity anchors us to planet Earth, pulling us downward, but on that copper-hued slide, gravity pulled me sideways into the face of the cliff, much as a mother holds her child to her breast. The cliff wall held me in a nurturing embrace, and I clung to it with the tenacity of an abalone. I experienced trust.

How Pema, Norbu, and I were able to accomplish this cliff-crossing feat, I'll never quite understand. I do, however, understand why people return time and again for these dangerous mountain climbs. Michael Palin has written that we return to be with the Sherpas, and that is simply true. There may be other mountain ranges in the world as challenging and glorious as the Himalayas, but nowhere else can one encounter these beautiful, gentle people. Indeed, the Sherpas outshine even the majestic Himalayas. The more time I spent with them, the more my worldview changed, the more I grew to cherish the fundamental human values that they embodied—generosity, cheerfulness, peace.

I moved forward, almost floating, in a state of complete relaxation. Although every fiber of my body had been maximally stressed, I was neither sleepy nor drowsy. Instead I felt liberated, euphoric, and internally free from the dimensions of time and space. I basked in the light radiating off the coppery walls while we walked silently. When we reached the rim of the canyon, I paused to gaze at the Bhote Koshi River for the last time. My Inner Teacher said, *Child, this is holy ground, where veils between realities can part for the questing pilgrim. You have paid a high price to come here. Keep your mind clear, pay attention, and remember—you will not return to this spot again in this life.*

Our overnight camp was perched atop a slight plateau. Unseen by our trekking party above, Norbu, Pema, and I climbed the last steep portion of the hill. At the top, I jumped into view with my poles held high in a victory sign and shouted merrily, "Women on top!"

Rather than the laughing camaraderie I expected, silent stares greeted me. Everyone in the group looked discomfited. Then I noticed that five rifle-toting Maoist soldiers had aimed their guns at me without pausing in their heated debate with Hari. The Sherpas translated, matching the forceful tones of the soldiers.

Our trek had brought us near a highly restricted area close to a checkpoint at the village of Lamabagar. The Chinese vigilantly guard this political barrier, keeping it closed to all Tibetans. Our hours in Kathmandu's government offices had produced the visas and permits we needed, complete with photographs and official stamps—all except for Hari's, but he had assured us that the authorities would find us on the trail to deliver it. It was when the soldiers arrived, hot and sweaty, with Hari's visa that the crisis ensued: although nine trekking permits had been issued, only eight trekkers were present and accounted for, as I had not yet arrived.

I later learned that one soldier had waved a pink visa in Hari's face and shouted, "You have an extra visa? Who are you smuggling into the Rolwaling Valley? Maybe you are helping a Tibetan criminal escape?" The other four soldiers held their rifles at the ready, prepared for hostile action. This argument was in full swing when I popped up over the embankment and hollered at everyone in my excitement. Once they saw me, the soldiers indulged in a few more barbed exchanges with Hari, but finally slammed shut their folders and marched away disgruntled.

Nevertheless, the encounter had affected the mood of my fellow trekkers, who wheeled like a flock of birds and entered the mess tent for dinner. I followed them in, not knowing what had happened. One of the other female trekkers paused at the tent door to hiss in my ear, "Maybe you could walk just a little bit faster on the trail?" I stared at her, stunned and confused, but she walked over to sit with the group that surrounded Hari. Chastened, I sat on a folding campstool at the far end of the table.

As dinner was being served, I ventured to ask what had happened. There was silence. Politely, I tried again. "What was going on with the soldiers? It looked rather grim when I arrived." More silence. I asked a third time. "Can anyone tell me what's the matter?"

James, the DJ who seemed to have assumed the role of group spokesperson, said, "We are practicing the Buddhist way on this trek, Mary Ann."

"Yes? And what does that mean? Why won't anyone talk to me?"

"We are practicing nonattachment and silence," he replied. However this practice of silence had come about, I certainly didn't know about it. While everyone suddenly took intense interest in what was on their plate, James's direct, probing gaze made it clear that he was speaking for all.

An uncomfortable memory flashed through my mind, of the reluctance the group had displayed when I had suggested we introduce ourselves, of how they had looked at me as though I had breached an unspoken rule of etiquette. I had also since learned that they were not in fact Mormons, but members of a Buddhist community in Utah, so my gambit to present myself as a Christian minister had misfired. Now, paradoxically, I felt that precisely because I was a Christian ecclesiast—and a slow-walking one, to boot—I had become persona non grata with my fellow trekkers. Swallowing my pride, I bent my stiff neck to eat.

The magnificent golden hues of the sun's low orb greeted us as we exited the dining tent. The moon joined her mate and reflected the sun's majesty in the blue translucence of the evening sky. In my tent, I found myself restless, bored, trying to think of something to do before darkness fell. Then I heard the sound of playful, exuberant laughter rippling through the crystalline mountain air. Hari and Cathy were rollicking in their tent.

A force of longing seized me—how I disliked that merriment! Their delight was like a rusty sword piercing my heart. I tried to reason with myself. *What is wrong with me?* I wondered. *How can this laughter be so painful? How can two, handsome, healthy young people who are attracted to each other cause me this much distress?* But I wanted them to stop. The overwhelming nature of this jealousy was unfamiliar. It wasn't like me. I felt possessed.

Then my Inner Teacher's voice rose up strong within me. *Mary Ann, are you the only person on this mountain? Are you able to think of anyone else but yourself?*

It was true: I had not considered how the other members of our trekking party might be responding to the laughter. I took from around my neck the *mala* (prayer beads) that HE Chagdud Tulku Rinpoche had given me during the Red Tara empowerment, and I blew on it as he had done before handing it to me. In the Nyingma tradition, masters chant the blessings of the great realized beings of their lineages. They blow these blessings into the *mala* as a way of infusing the *mala* with the wisdom of those beings. Rinpoche himself embodied an ancient awakened spiritual energy, which I had visualized entering into my beads when he first blew over them. Though I now sat in the Himalayas, thousands of miles away from him, I felt his presence flow through the red wooden beads between my fingers, and I began to relax.

From Rinpoche I had learned the Tibetan Buddhist practice of *tonglen*. I'd learned to take the golden light of the universe into my *heart-mind* and then send that light back out. Rinpoche also taught us to absorb other people's toxic emotions and to transform that darkness into gold light before sending it back out again with the exhalation of the breath. At first students had recoiled at the thought of assuming others' distorted energy, worried that the practice would make them ill, but Rinpoche had explained, "If you experience revulsion, fear or anger, that is *your* obstacle, *your* karma. It is not other person's. So you must first practice giving and taking on yourself. Purify your mind."

Now, within the cocoon of my tent and the sounds of my fellow travelers around me, I decided it was as good a time as any to practice *tonglen* not only with others, but on myself as well. Late-evening light outlined the tent's zippered door. I concentrated on the light and allowed my *heart-mind* to journey into the other trekkers' tents. I meditated and relaxed into a deep silence. Then I sensed Sam, the anesthesiologist, in his tent, which happened to be close to mine. A strong emotional feeling came over me and an inner knowing came with it. Tanya had told me on the bus that he was here because his second marriage had just failed. I had a vision in which he was holding himself so that he didn't shake. His knuckles were white, his face wreathed in pain. I realized he was an alcoholic going through withdrawal on this trek; he wanted sobriety, and he wanted his wife back. I pulled back from what I saw, pained. I liked Sam, who looked after me in a way, by asking how I was doing at the end of each day.

Laughter still emanated from Hari's tent.

My *heart-mind* moved into Tanya's tent. During our harrowing bus ride into the mountains, she had confided not only that she didn't want to be here, but also that there was a history of suicide in her family and that she had brought both a bottle of antidepressants and a month's worth of sleeping pills. I was afraid for her and felt myself backing out of her tent, for she was holding a bottle of pills.

Hillary was a strong climber, a mountain lady. She lived in a log cabin in the Utah mountains with her alcoholic, abusive husband. It was apparent that she hated her marriage and felt trapped in it. Then I received an unexpected insight: she was in love with Hari! She sat alone in her tent, crying with heartbreak at the sound of Hari and Cathy laughing. The uncharacteristic jealousy that I had felt was not mine at all—it was hers, and I had picked up on it.

Tired tears stung my eyes as I leaned back on my duffle bag. Sorrow and laughter came together in the center of my chest and began to radiate outward. The sword that had pierced my heart with my trekking partner's pain and jealousy was being withdrawn. There were no entrails attached to it. Instead, the steel cage that had trapped my heart for the last year opened. The laughter ebbed, and night shadows crept down the surrounding mountain slopes, dimming the light around our tents. Camp was almost dark, and the thermometer fell quickly.

Painful questions around the nature of ministry now preoccupied my *heart-mind*. Rinpoche had taught me that thoughts have form and that one can sense other people's thoughts. "If you take on thought-forms and feelings of others like they are yours, become attached and identify with mental images not your own, how can you help those around you?" he had said. There was still so much to learn. To fulfill my lifelong intention to be one with God, to find the inner happiness and peace Rinpoche spoke of, and to serve others, I would have to maintain a clear mind and develop a strong sense of detachment. I had wanted to help others for as far back as I could remember. This desire—coupled with the challenges of being overly sensitive, of being different, of being a visionary or a mystic—had felt like both a gift and a curse at different times in my life. To experience self-love and accept who I was, I would need to understand the nature of attachment and the universal benefits and blessings of taking and giving.

Perhaps I should become a Buddhist after all, I thought. But I was a feminist theologian, a scholar of the Judeo-Christian scriptures. Even Rinpoche had said it was too late for me to start again, to learn a new system, a new language, a new set of scriptures, that I should instead be of service to his many students who were wounded, angry former Christians in need of healing. If I served in this capacity, however, I'd be admitting that Christianity was a fraud, that my lifetime devotion to the church had been a mockery. Rinpoche had pointed to the universal validity of all scriptures, but the individuals I'd encountered in my tradition did not see it that way. And I didn't want to be identified with the growing cultural aversion to the Church, for despite everything, I loved it. Yes, I loved the Church! Or, at least, I *had* loved it. Or thought I loved it. Or knew I *should* love it.

I felt trapped within the maze of these questions. As darkness descended and the star-studded sky illuminated our mountainside encampment, I zipped my sleeping bag up to my chin and decided to consider these thoughts in the coming days. Grateful and relieved that the piercing emotions of the evening had been pacified, I fell into a deep sleep.

Chapter 11

APPROACHING NA

Within this earthen vessel are bowers and groves,
and within it is the Creator:
Within this vessel are the seven oceans and the unnumbered stars.
The touchstone and the jewel-appraiser are within;
And within this vessel the Eternal soundeth, and the spring wells up.
Kabir says: "Listen to me, my Friend! My beloved Lord is within."

—KABIR, "Within This Earthen Vessel"

ASCENDING AND DESCENDING several thousand feet daily, moving from mountaintop to mountaintop, we eventually passed the 12,000-foot mark. We needed to make another 2,000-foot gain to reach Na, where we would spend two days acclimating before the final push to our goal. Time took on an altogether different quality as we made our way toward the village of Na, the guardian of the gates to the upper Sacred Rolwaling Valley.

Along the way, my body grew stronger, my speed increased, and my backpack felt smaller and more comfortable. Although blisters covered the soles of my feet, I used a pharmacopoeia of ointments and moleskin to swathe them and, fortunately, experienced no pain.

Through pantomime, Norbu had taught me to fill my large canteens with boiling water after dinner, so that by nightfall they could serve as hot-water bottles. I also took ibuprofen before bed. This nightly ritual, along with the sleep that comes from utter exhaustion, provided me indescribable relief. I awoke each morning refreshed, feeling lighter than the day before.

Two days before we reached Na, Hari walked back to me as I navigated around large boulders. Bright morning light glared off the surrounding stone mountains, and far below was the green of the forest. Hari blocked my path, hands on his hips. As usual, he radiated celebrity good looks, his broad shoulders supporting a huge backpack as if it weighed no more than a feather.

"There is a change in plans," he announced with a broad smile, but he spoke too quickly, his eyes glancing about. "We are coming to a mountain I had intended to circle, but now we plan to go straight up and over it." He shifted from one foot to the other, refusing to look at me directly. "This will be too difficult for you, Mary Ann, so I'll be leaving you with Norbu and a cook." In a rapid-fire burst of words, he concluded, "You can follow the original route. We will meet you in two days." Hari's words slid through perfect white teeth framed by a Cheshire Cat grin—a charm offensive. Then he turned and strode away.

Profoundly hurt that Hari seemed so relieved to get rid of me, I had to lean over my poles to catch my breath. It felt as though I'd sustained a severe blow to the solar plexus. I had finally begun to identify with my fellow American trekking misfits, finding comfort in the embrace of a group I felt I belonged to, which was a new and precious experience for me. Now I was to be forsaken. From the beginning of this journey, from long before this journey, I had dreaded abandonment, and here it was again.

Looking across the canyon, I envisioned my lone pup tent hovering above the green forest far below. *Be careful of what you fear, for you will attract the manifestation of that very fear.* I forced myself to walk forward, although the image of the solitary tent continued to burn in my brain. At one point, I looked across the canyon again, only to see a huge black fiend materialize, red-eyed and howling. The scene morphed into a dark, moonless night in which the apparition prowled through the trees near my floating tent, hungry, eager to kill, stalking, waiting to devour me as soon as I was abandoned and left defenseless.

I spent a few moments trying to catch my breath, then again resumed walking. As I crossed a wide, steep slope slippery with scree, I felt something shatter internally. My consciousness was dominated with horrifying images of that formless dark monster engulfing my small tent. I had no sense of Norbu, who always protected me with an alert constancy and who was, in fact, directly behind me.

Child! Concentrate! Watch! my Inner Teacher reminded.

I meditated on my feet and on my walking poles. My mind seesawed between images of the tent, the vision of the fiend, and my boots gripping their way through the slippery shale detritus. Then the terrifying images faded, and a new set of images arose: there I was, at the end of my two-day abandonment, my ordeal over, the group walking toward me after my days and nights of solitude. I was smiling, victorious, laughing, while the others stared in disbelief and awe. I would do it. I would show them. I'd show the world I could do it. I would get a gold medal for bravery. But I couldn't dwell on these seductive images either. Prideful fantasies were just as distracting as the images of the monster.

Child! Keep your eyes on the terrain ahead of you. This is extremely dangerous! Concentrate. Watch where you place both your poles and your feet. Stay on stable ground.

There was no stable ground. I had to move as quickly as I could over the loose stones. If I paused, my weight would cause both me and the shale to slide down the steep slope. I finally managed to find a relaxed, light-footed rhythm. This sense of delicate control yielded a feeling of excitement, and the beginnings of a smile formed at the corners of my mouth. Around a bend, the group sat on rocks along the trail, balancing plates on their laps, eating lunch. I had successfully passed through the monster's scree.

Hari ambled toward me with his square jaw, straight nose, and muscled body. Was Hari my demon? What did he want now? With a sober expression, he said, "Mary Ann, we have decided to stay together and proceed as a group."

Relieved and profoundly pleased, I joined the others for a trailside lunch, although I mostly toyed with my food. A mild case of altitude sickness had stuck with me since 11,000 feet, making it difficult to eat much. At some indeterminate point in time, the rule of silence had evaporated, and the anesthesiologist, whom I secretly called Dr. Ben, advised me that I needed to eat to keep my energy up. *My energy is just fine, thank you very much*, I thought. More important was whether I could trust any of them. Had they all originally voted to leave me behind? Loss of appetite was not, for me, a cause for concern, but betrayal and abandonment had haunted me for a lifetime.

As I sat there, trying to resuscitate those old fears, I found that they were gone. Instead, while idly poking at the thick lentil glop, I found myself fantasizing about wearing a size ten, or maybe even an eight, once I got home. Home! Perhaps such mundane and materialistic thoughts about getting home safe and sound would help me climb these treacherous mountains. Home! This was the key. Back home safe. For the first time since arriving in Kathmandu, I trusted that I was safe. I no longer sensed demons hiding beyond the veil of the unknown.

The next day, after hiking all morning and a short lunch on the trail, we looked up and saw, five hundred feet above us, camouflaged on a steep, boulder-strewn mountainside, the ancient Tibetan Sherpa village of Na.

Villagers approached us, running, skipping from boulder to boulder, singing a welcome to brothers, fathers, and husbands. The Sherpas had come home. Wood-flute music floated down on soft breezes as Sherpa Dorje's shy but jubilant wife, Tsering, greeted him with their firstborn, a son. We held a collective breath as a radiant Dorje lifted his infant son into the cloudless blue sky, bathing him in golden sunrays. He kissed his baby in greeting, and we broke into applause. Tsering wore the traditional Sherpa garb: an earth-colored, woolen, ankle-length wrap called a *chuba* and an apron woven in stripes of brightly colored wool. Flushed with happiness, Tsering was especially picturesque.

Even as villagers and trekkers stared at each other, absorbing the details of disparate cultures, the village women's fingers twirled constantly about drop spindles with confident skill and speed. We joined the Sherpas' procession into Na, where we later visited their homes and feasted on their famous small potatoes, which were served in pyramids atop chipped platters. In one tiny home, thinly cushioned wooden benches lined the single room, redolent of wood smoke, that made up the total of the stone house. We devoured the potatoes, dipping them into bowls of cracked salt while our hosts and hostesses grinned in approval. Pungent medicinal herbs hung in bunches from indoor rafters; outside, under the eaves, lines of colored corn were strung like Christmas lights.

After our potato banquet, grandmothers—or *anni-las*—retrieved faded photographs and old picture postcards from apron pockets. One *anni-la* and I leaned our heads together to study a worn black-and-white photograph with serrated edges. From the photo stared a dark-haired young man, dressed in a white shirt and dark pants, standing in a nondescript American-style apartment. Another grinning, toothless *anni-la* asked, "Do you know my son? He lives in California." We trekkers admired a postcard of Hollywood and Vine, and tried to explain, to blank faces, that the urban population of Los Angeles numbers in the millions.

At midmorning, villagers passed around large wooden cups garnished with bamboo straws and filled with fermented barley seeds and a potent clear alcohol. We sipped ourselves into a state of giddy inebriation, enjoying ourselves until the party ended, whereupon we nearly had to crawl out the low doorway. With free time before lunch, I made my way to a small rock outcropping that overlooked a vast array of smoky blue mountains and deep-green river valleys.

Hari, in his usual fashion, popped up beside me and launched directly into a monologue. "I have waited fifteen years to become a trek master, and this is my first official trek. I worked a year in Kathmandu putting this trip together. Most treks are harsh and primitive—dried food, no amenities, unpleasant conditions. Most use trails littered with toilet paper and garbage. I knew I could do better—create a unique experience along the lines of a first-class African safari. But I needed ten paying clients..."

I flashed on the moment when the first trek leader I'd signed up with told me to contact Hari. I had hesitated, but Hari was going to have to cancel his trek if he couldn't find one or two more people to join. The implication of Hari's words was crystal clear.

Shocked, I turned to him. "My God, Hari, you accepted me on this trip just because of money?"

He looked away. But before I could say anything more, I apprehended something that caused me to take an abrupt step backward: Hari and I were just alike! My mind recoiled, but the truth was before me. Both of us were compelled to throw caution to the winds of adventure. How many times had I put my life in peril, in ways both commonplace and extreme? Over the years, I had sped on interstate freeways, piloted stunt airplanes, and hurtled down ski slopes rated far beyond my capabilities. And here I was, at the age of fifty, tackling the Himalayas despite all my reservations. Hadn't I outgrown youth's sense of permanence? Was I continuing to take risks out of discontent and, above all, to prove myself worthy?

My Inner Teacher's unbidden, and now unwanted, voice penetrated my mind. *Child, let the one without sin cast the first stone.*

I felt a heavy stone in my hand. I wanted desperately to hurl it somewhere—at Hari, at the mountain, I didn't know where. My heart raced with anger at myself, and I took another unthinking step backward. Hari swiftly grabbed my arms and pulled me back from the edge. Our eyes met, barely inches apart. We locked glares, staring each other down in silence. Then the lunch gong rang. I extracted myself and, on rubbery legs, headed to the mess tent.

As we were finishing what turned out to be a high-spirited lunch, Hari asked from the far end of the table, "Mary Ann, do you think I am ready for the spiritual path?"

I looked at him, and after a choking pause, I replied in a cautious tone, "Do you have any idea what that means, Hari?"

Startled by this unexpected turn in the tenor of the conversation, the group sat abashed, looking first at him, then at me, like spectators at a tennis match waiting for the next smash.

I made an effort to gather myself. I knew just how tricky and devastating the spiritual path was, but I also knew how ecstatic and exhilarating it could be. Hari's karmic path had crossed with mine on this dangerous trek, and I did not want to create additional bad karma between us. Enough was enough.

I submitted to my Inner Teacher, emptied my hand of stones, and finally said, with genuine if hard-won compassion, "When the student is ready, Hari, the teacher will appear."

God, I prayed, *don't let that teacher be me!*

Chapter 12

Guardians
of the Gate

Let the beauty we love be what we do.
There are hundreds of ways to kneel and kiss the ground.

—JALAL AL-DIN RUMI, *The Essential Rumi*

TWO DAYS LATER, JUST BEFORE DAWN, a cup of hot tea and a lantern were delivered bedside. We ate breakfast, then gathered for departure under a strange gray sky streaked with blues and violets. The entire village came to bid us goodbye, walking with us for the first half hour of our climb. Then, after a final round of embraces and farewells, I watched with mixed emotions as our new friends turned back toward Na.

In the first hour, as the altitude increased, I thought that the holiday in Na had worked a secret magic on me, granting me unexpected stamina. In the second hour, however, I was climbing more slowly, and in the third hour my legs felt like deeply rooted tree trunks. Each step was like pulling those heavy trees up by their roots, dragging one leg forward, and then repeating the process. I gasped for air, leaning over my poles every few feet as my oxygen-starved lungs heaved.

At some point, I looked up and saw through my blurry eyes a mound of stones. I looked back down, sucking at the scant supply of oxygen, then groggily looked up again. The mound, about six feet tall, stood at the entrance to a valley. Although I couldn't judge the distances well in the diamond-clear atmosphere, I guessed the valley was a mile or more wide and about two-and-a-half miles long. We were walking on a wide trail bordered by stone tablets, each of which stood about three feet tall. Each tablet and each stone in the tall mound was etched with elaborate symbols. Before me was a valley crisscrossed by winding trails similarly bordered with carved tablets. There were hundreds, if not thousands of them, each inscribed with sacred Sanskrit vowels and consonants. Each flawless mantric syllable appeared smooth and proportionally perfect. I knelt down to run my finger inside one of the deeply etched symbols, and the moment I made contact I burst into sobs.

I had arrived at the sacred valley.

This was the first Thanksgiving I had celebrated without family. I had traveled so long and so far to reach my destination. An entire life! The past fifty years flowed through me as I wept. It wasn't a mental filmstrip of actual events, but the emotions associated with each significant life experience—the bitter and the sweet, the ugly and the beautiful, the despair and the hope. As each feeling arose, I knew precisely which part of my life it represented.

I heard my beloved Inner Teacher's voice. *Child, every choice, every decision you have made in the past fifty years was necessary to get to this place. All the embarrassment, remorse, and regret were necessary. Every hour of your life, all your achievements and losses, all your joys and hopes—they are all sacred, as sacred as these encrypted wisdom stones, and all as impermanent as last night's dreams.*

Until that moment, I had perceived my life as equivalent to the underside of a tapestry. All I had been able to see were the knots and snarls of jumbled yarn, long strands of thread going nowhere, colors mixed and chaotic. Now the tapestry turned right side up, and I saw before me a masterpiece. That was *my life*! It was a tour de force, radiant, intricate, incomprehensibly beautiful.

Norbu touched my shoulder and asked me if I was all right, his voice filled with concern.

Unable to communicate my vision, I looked into his warm, caring, dark eyes. "Thank you, Norbu. I'm okay. Let me be, please." I gestured downhill toward the quickly rising tent camp. "You can see me from there. I need to be alone. Truly, I am fine."

His wise, compassionate expression registered understanding, and he slowly took his leave.

Camp was on the downhill side of the valley, very close to one of the towering peaks of the Mount Everest range. Mountains nearly the size of Everest encircled the valley. Our group, like a busy ant colony, set up tents, drank tea, and socialized.

I stood up and looked out over the whole valley. No one had said a word about this place, other than how sacred it was to the Sherpas. I was totally unprepared for the effect it was having on me. My feet now seemed to float above the ground. I collapsed my poles and stuck them into my backpack, where they stayed for the rest of the trek. My breathing normalized, and I no longer felt weak or heavy. I had never walked with such lightness, smoothness, and ease.

As I strode forward, the letters rose off the stone tablets throughout the valley. They were refined as silver and gold are refined. Carved precisely, sparkling, flashing, dancing through space in every direction, they burned with an exhilarating fire. Each letter was a poem, a prayer, a gate to the splendor of the Divine. Every letter had a road of its own, its own special mystery. They whirled through both my heart and the sky, for there were no trees to obscure my view of these singing, dancing mantric syllables, which streamed from stone to sun, from sun to stone, in an unbroken continuity. I was submerged in an ocean of no boundaries, no time or space. Had I invoked this cosmic libation by merely placing my finger in the stone's etched mantra?

The swirling Sanskrit letters penned scripture, passage after passage, in the space surrounding me, with a limitless light that emanated from the spiritual sun behind our sun. The first words of the Lord's Prayer entered me, but not the version I had learned as a child. Instead, I felt Jesus' words as translated from the original Aramaic: "O, breathing Light, your name shines everywhere." I perceived the three lines of script in three alphabets, one atop the other, in languages I did not know, but could somehow understand: *In the beginning was the Word, and the Word was good, and in that goodness is the Life that is the Light that shines in the darkness.* This knowledge translates in Western scriptures as "In the beginning was the Word, and the Word was with God, and the Word was God." And in this moment in which the Word in its many forms danced about me, I recognized that each of them bore the knowledge and wisdom behind all that was, is, and ever will be.

As I stood enthralled, the words of Isaiah 42:16 filled me: "I will lead the blind by ways they have not known, along unfamiliar paths I will guide them; I will turn the darkness into light before them and make the rough places smooth. These are the things I will do; I will not forsake them." I suddenly knew that Jesus had walked here. I knew that Egyptian Pharaohs, Zeus, Aphrodite had all walked in this sacred valley. Lao Tzu took the first steps of his thousand-mile journey here. The Buddha, Padmasambhava sitting under the Bodhi Tree, Yeshe Tsogyal, Mary Magdalene, and the Dalai Lama had been here. Druids and wizards gathered here for sunrise. Sir Isaac Newton, Leonardo da Vinci. Native American shamans. The Pilgrims, George Washington, Abigail and John Adams, Thomas Jefferson, Benjamin Franklin, Patrick Henry gave birth to American Democracy here. Genghis Khan. Harriet Beecher Stowe. All of them knew of this sacred place. The letters danced their dance and sang their song even as our Earth's star spun its flaming way into existence.

And then I heard a chorus of inner voices sing, *Welcome home, child! Happy Thanksgiving! We have been waiting for you.*

I have no idea how long I steeped in the songs of the magical stones, but when I turned from them to make my way down to the camp, my doubting intellect quickly jumped in. *This is crazy thinking, I told myself. The altitude has muddled your brain. Pull yourself together.*

Doing my best to ignore this critical voice, I slowed down, reluctant to end my divine odyssey and reach "civilization." However, my feet eventually carried me to the mess tent, where lunch was under way. I needed to act normal, but how on earth could I?

Child, listen carefully: Don't DO anything, just BE.

I nodded and smiled, taking part as well as I could in the animated conversation, although I dared not utter a word about my experience, lest my companions think I was a lunatic. As they discussed their plans to head for even more glorious heights the next morning, I learned that I was to stay behind with Norbu and several porters. Though none of us acknowledged it directly, we all understood that I was an absolute non-candidate for this day trip. My heart pounded with anticipation. I would have an entire day in the valley of stones to myself!

I sat in the mess tent feeling edgy, fidgeting with silverware, paper napkins, and salt and pepper shakers in an attempt to act normal. The others, too, were wired with unusually high-voltage tension. Some explored; some drank tea, told stories, planned the next day's agenda. Among my trekking companions there was no talk of the carved stones, no awe or wonder about the beginning of time, evolution, or dancing letters. The general conversation instead embraced the thrills to be experienced on the morrow. I could not trust myself to speak, so I remained silent and contemplated my own agenda, preparing myself for the moment when I could saturate myself in the presence of the Holy Ones, the ancient grandmothers and grandfathers of the valley.

The group left at daybreak, but Norbu let me sleep in, waiting until he saw my shadow moving inside the small tent before bringing tea and breakfast. Throughout the day, Norbu and the porters were gathered around the small cookfire next to the mess tent. I sat in the doorway of my own tent and tried to write, but my words, huge and barely legible, tilted drunkenly across the lined pages of my yellow spiral notebook, which frequently slipped off my lap. All I could manage was to gaze at a towering mountain as my bare white feet soaked in the warm, healing air.

Midmorning I booted up and walked to the stream that ran along the base of that soaring mountain, washing my clothes in the frigid snowmelt. Back at my tent, I lay them over sun-washed stones. I planned to wear these garments the next day, hoping the valley's sacred magic would permeate my very being as we began our descent. I bathed my feet in icy water I had carried up from the stream, then sat mesmerized again by the overwhelming presence of the mountain before me.

There were many small, square, stone dwellings dotting the valley. On the downhill side of the gently sloping terrain, close to my tent, some of these rock cabins were dug into the hillside. Behind each home was a small piece of tilled land. These were likely the gardens in which the villagers of Na, who summered in this valley, grew their famous potatoes. We had learned as we feasted on those potatoes that the villagers used them as currency to barter for all their physical needs. The potatoes, and maybe corn as well, had been turned under. Only a few upright stalks of stiff gray showed evidence of the year's harvest.

As the sunlight began its afternoon slant, a series of visions took hold of me. The sacred valley and its mountains became part of an ocean that surged with waves, that ebbed and flowed. A deafening roar lifted that ocean into a cosmic tsunami. Tectonic plates ground against each other in a cacophony of warring elements and volcanic eruptions. The Great Mother of the Sea was in violent labor. She was giving birth to a new mountain range, to the mountain in front of me. I was a part of that ocean. There were pterodactyls, brontosaurs, Cro-Magnon men, all my ancestors. The beginnings of civilizations. I saw gods and goddesses, white temples, gold crowns, beginnings and endings, constant change in slow motion, a bud slowly evolving into a rose of incomparable beauty. And through it all, I felt a calm, abiding love permeate everything in, on, and around me.

With evening's gentle approach, these precious images faded, and my fellow trekkers returned to camp. They walked slowly, their heads bent forward, and went directly to their tents, miserable with altitude sickness. Those able to eat dinner shared in hushed voices the majesties they had beheld at the pinnacle of their climb. Nauseated, eyes rimmed in red, besieged by migraines, they nevertheless exhibited joy at their day's journey. With a radiance that could not be oppressed by physical discomfort, James and Dr. Ben both affirmed that the trip had been more than worth the suffering.

"I wish we could go back tomorrow," Dr. Ben said.

Hari glowed with the pride of accomplishment. He had led his companions to one of the world's most beautiful locations, and together they had shared a day of bliss that outshone the trials of the journey. Indeed, he had guided all of us to where we wanted to be.

Early the next morning, Norbu rushed into my tent. "Hurry! Hurry! Now! Now, madam. Come!"

I dressed quickly while Norbu waited outside holding an arctic coat with a gigantic fur-lined hood. As I slipped into the red coat's voluminous warmth, I looked up to see that the valley was white with snow. On cue, the sun peeked innocently over the eastern horizon, transforming the snow-covered mountains, valley, stones, ground, and sky into hues of ripe pink and orange. All that was visible was clothed in these ethereal colors. And we humans, swathed in our crimson parkas, gathered in quiet solidarity as the pulsing colors, somehow animate, proclaimed their spellbinding presence. Enveloped in their light, I knew we were all connected, that we were all *One*. We were all spiritual beings learning how to be physical beings, gods learning to be mortals. It was a moment of resonant silence infused with a profound beauty, an unveiling of the great secret of our true selves, an amazing grace.

PART 11

MEETING
YESHE TSOGYAL

Chapter 13

MY SOUL BROTHER

I live my life in widening circles
that reach out across the world.
I may not complete this last one
but I give myself to it.

I circle around God, around the primordial tower.
I've been circling for thousands of years
and I still don't know: am I a falcon,
a storm, or a great song?

—RAINER MARIA RILKE, "Widening Circles"

MY HIMALAYAN JOURNEY sent transformative shock waves through my system. I knew that spiritual experiences could be profound, but was still unaware that such shocks are fundamental to the spiritual path. It is said that Moses' hair turned white after God presented him with the Ten Commandments on top of Mount Sinai. Similarly, though my hair had been graying for several years prior to my trek, it was completely white by the time of my return. My mind, body, and soul were undergoing bewildering revisions that I wasn't sure how to integrate, let alone describe. Even when HE Chagdud Tulku Rinpoche asked about my journey, I could not speak clearly. Jumbled, incomplete, halting sentences emerged from my mouth. Relief from this discomfort came only when my lips remained sealed, as if with wax, when anyone brought up my trek to the Sacred Rolwaling Valley. "It was beautiful, very beautiful," I would say, then change the subject.

My daily life gained momentum, with fulfilling activities crowding my calendar. Over the course of the next three years, each of my three children married, and our nuclear family doubled in size. My Christian ministry continued as busily as ever with my involvement in both hospice and the Methodist Church. And there were more of Rinpoche's teachings to absorb, more empowerments to receive, more retreats to attend.

In early 1992, Rinpoche asked if I wished to participate in his annual Dzogchen retreat scheduled to be held the following year. Dzogchen is the king of all *dharma* teachings: *dzog* means "complete," suggesting that all the teachings of the Buddha are complete within this path, and *chenpo* means "greatest," "highest," or "most exalted." Known as the Great Perfection teaching, it is considered the most ancient, most direct stream of wisdom in the Nyingma school of Tibetan Buddhism. The Dzogchen teachings were brought to Tibet from India by Padmasambhava in the late eighth and early ninth centuries, then transferred to Yeshe Tsogyal, who transcribed them. Dzogchen's unique characteristic is enlightenment in a single moment through the realization of one's luminous awareness. Before I could qualify for this extraordinary spiritual retreat and receive these highly secret teachings, I was required to complete several hundred thousand mantra recitations, circumambulations, and offering practices. Month after month, I fingered my *mala* and recited ancient mantric words of power while at home, walking, or traveling. Only after I had completed a dedicated year of these spiritual practices did HE Chagdud Tulku Rinpoche admit me into his Dzogchen retreat.

Although I did not know it at the time, also at the retreat was the Venerable Chödak Gyatso Nubpa Rinpoche, a highly recognized young Nyingma lama who was to receive the most advanced teachings Rinpoche had to offer. Throughout the early 1990s, extraordinary master teachers who had led the Tibetan Nation into exile across the globe were gathering thousands of students throughout the United States, Canada, and Europe. Teachings were often held in private homes, and serious students were finding ways to finance the establishment of permanent centers. These were explosive years of growth and dedication. Students from all walks of life found healing and enrichment in the presence of these famous masters, and the word spread. Rinpoche's students had requested that he establish a Nyingma center in Napa, and he'd sent for Lama Gyatso to help cultivate the budding spiritual community that had taken root in the area. Thus, a few months after the Dzogchen retreat, HE Chagdud Tulku Rinpoche asked if Lama Gyatso could reside at my home, and since I trusted Rinpoche implicitly, I immediately agreed.

When I heard the doorbell chime on a warm spring afternoon, I hurried to open the front door. There stood a handsome and jovial lama: the Venerable Chödak Gyatso Nubpa Rinpoche. Although he had only his "suitcases"—two brown paper grocery bags—I knew that he was an esteemed Nyingma, and I stumbled over how to address him. Laughing, he replied, "Just call me Lama Gyatso." I welcomed him in, and thus was my "spirit brother" ushered into my life.

As a child, Lama Gyatso escaped Tibet with his family and eventually settled near the Dalai Lama, where he was educated in a monastery school. When he was still a young man, he was chosen to represent the Nyingmas in the Parliament of the Tibetan Government in Exile, becoming well known for his eloquent speeches, devotion, and dedication. As part of his duties, he worked for the Dalai Lama, who sent him as a liaison to newly forming monasteries-in-exile, and thus he came to know Nyingma luminaries throughout India. Despite his diplomatic gifts, however, Lama Gyatso's primary passion was the *dharma*. He eventually approached his primary teacher, HE Chagdud Tulku Rinpoche, who was celebrated for having mastered certain high teachings that Lama Gyatso wished to pursue. Lama Gyatso was Rinpoche's most senior student in Asia, and he followed Rinpoche to the United States to receive these teachings. The master-student bond between them was profound.

On the first morning of Lama Gyatso's residency at the Family Home, Buddhist drum and bell vibrations emanated from his quarters. I waited for him to finish his prayers and join me in the kitchen, where I had prepared oatmeal and tea. I had planned a quiet morning of introductions and a house tour to familiarize him with the location of light switches and the like. As I quickly learned, however, Lama Gyatso began each day with a three-hour practice or prayer session, after which energy shot out from his strong body and bright eyes like meteors. When he finally entered the kitchen, he was an animated whirlwind of enthusiasm. In one hand he held a stack of seven small copper bowls, and in the other he held a plastic bag filled with tiny dark pills. After placing the copper bowls on the counter, he held the bag toward me.

"Mary Ann," he said with merriment, "these are longevity pills that the Dalai Lama blessed just before I came to America."

Although this was no formal ceremony accompanied by ritual instruments and chants—I wore jeans, my hair was rumpled—I was now familiar with accepted protocol, so I reached toward him, left hand atop my right palm and received the pills in my upturned hand. With the effect of Lama Gyatso's drumbeats still enlivening in my blood, I felt tipsy with wonderment that this exchange was happening in my very own kitchen. Sunlight streamed through the green leaves of the tulip tree outside the windows, the pills exuded incense-like aromas, and my golden retriever, Pookie, sat looking at us with his head cocked.

Lama Gyatso filled the sink with warm, soapy water and carefully submerged the copper offering bowls under clouds of billowing white. The bubbles danced within a refraction of rainbow colors. After washing these treasured bowls, he turned them upside down to dry on a clean towel. Later, he would place the shining bowls back upon the bedroom altar he had created within hours of his arrival. Each morning, he washed his offering bowls, prayerfully refilled them with water infused with ritual substances, then floated a rose petal or small flower on the quiet surface. He performed this ritual with great care, precision, and attention, never spilling a drop.

Once he had set his bowls to dry that first morning, Lama Gyatso asked if we could take a walk through the gardens, as he had already figured out where all the light switches, furnaces, and doors were. After I had gone to bed the night before, he had familiarized himself with the house, but had been unable to visit the gardens. I led the way out the kitchen door and into a glorious morning. The Family Home is situated on a gentle hill surrounded by acres of vineyard, where the sunlight illuminates the arching tendrils across distances, giving an impression of green seas surging in the valley. As Lama Gyatso and I toured the gardens, we encountered Francisco, the groundskeeper, pruning a hedge of white iceberg roses. Francisco took off his work gloves and stuffed them into the back pockets of his workpants. Lama Gyatso silently held out his small plastic bag. I pantomimed the proper hand-holding gesture, and Francisco extended his hands, smiling. The three of us chatted until the arrival of Maria, the housekeeper, who I introduced to the lama now in residence and to his longevity pills. After bowing her head in reverence to receive her allotment, she gazed at Lama Gyatso with adoring eyes. Indeed, within minutes of meeting him, Maria had wholeheartedly fallen in love with our new lama. Before long, she geared her menus toward the likes and needs of "the holy man in the house." It was his room that she cleaned first thing every morning.

Lama Gyatso and I completed our excursion, which he thereafter repeated daily as part of his morning ritual of house and garden blessings. Sometimes I joined him on these sunrise walks, and he would explain how and why to touch plants, flowers, and shrubs while quietly chanting prayers of blessing. Sky, clouds, animals, trees, and birds, as well as the many unseen beings surrounding our hill, were enveloped in his prayers and loving gaze. I was elated to be in the company of another who felt as I did about the environment, and I was deeply pleased to have my beloved home and garden purified. Lama Gyatso's formal and educated understanding of the conscious ethereal beings that surrounded us far exceeded mine. Every morning his quiet chants extended an invitation to me and all such beings who lived at the Family Home, seen and unseen, to the celestial realms. Lama Gyatso's large, perfectly shaped, shining white teeth produced a magnetizing smile that beamed youthful vitality. His luminous, gold-flecked, amazingly intelligent brown eyes, infectious laughter, and simple delight in life caught us all unawares at the Family Home. A materialized god, it seemed, had moved into my house.

Lama Gyatso never wavered in his spiritual commitment to a daily three hours of prayer. He chanted mantras and recited prayers from ancient texts in his room. He sat on his floor cushion, holding a bell in his right hand and a *dorje* in his left hand, which he placed next to his heart. At certain points, he played handheld drums. At other times, he played a large, floor-standing drum. The rousing energy that emanated from these instruments penetrated the house with transformative vibrations.

As soon as Lama Gyatso began his practices, Pookie would lift his ears, stand up, pad directly to Lama Gyatso's bedroom door, stretch his body across the threshold, and lay his head on crossed front paws. Pookie had always whimpered with discomfort at the sound of music, but he now appeared to wait expectantly for Lama Gyatso's pulsating chants to arise. When they did, the house went otherwise silent. Repair people, visitors, employees, and students all stopped speaking and followed Lama Gyatso's prayers. Although we all proceeded with our various tasks, our individual *heart-mind*s rose with the cadence of the drumbeat and the ringing bell to higher dimensions. At the soul level, it was as though, after a long journey through the desert, we had come upon a clear blue lake in which we were able to drink and bathe ourselves until we felt light and clean.

During his prayers, Lama Gyatso sat facing a colorful altar, which was the centerpiece of his room. At his request, a student built a low desk, upon which Lama Gyatso placed ritual implements, cherished photographs of those for whom he prayed, statues, and sacred texts. When I saw pictures of me and my children placed there, waves of security washed through my heart.

And so it was that a Christian hospice chaplain and a laughing Tibetan lama began a shared residency that would lead to a singularly powerful and enduring relationship—for me, a relationship more compelling than any other I had known and more transformative than I could have imagined. It was also a relationship that would lead to the creation of a new home, in America, for the Ancient Ones of the Nyingma wisdom tradition.

Chapter 14

TWO CULTURES, ONE HOUSE

I have no wings, but still I fly in the sky.
I have no magical power, yet like magic
I journey through realms of illusory display,
Here and there, in nine directions,
Exploring the connections of my karma.

—HE CHAGDUD TULKU RINPOCHE,
Powerful Lord of the Dance

BEFORE I MET RINPOCHE and Lama Gyatso, I had imagined Buddhist teachers to be exotic, colorfully dressed, humble yogis who sat in the lotus position all day, radiating peace and wisdom. My image of gentle, compassionate, undemanding holy men who drew people into the healing matrix of their presence was accurate to some degree, but woefully incomplete. Although my Nyingma teachers certainly possessed many of these qualities, they were also extraordinarily dynamic and enterprising. Wherever they lived, for however long, Buddhist centers and temples, large and small, sprang up. Students and the curious flocked to them in large numbers, and teachings flourished in rented halls, churches, and homes.

Over the years, HE Chagdud Tulku Rinpoche visited the Family Home on many occasions, and welcoming him was like opening my front door to a hurricane. With Lama Gyatso in residence, preparations for Rinpoche's visits only intensified, becoming even more complex and demanding, and required many long ceremonies to purify our hill, the surrounding lands, and all the beings that inhabited them. Lama Gyatso was devoted to Rinpoche and thus spared no effort, including mine.

Central to the Buddhist tradition is the idea of taking refuge in the Three Jewels: the Buddha (the highest spiritual potential in all beings); the Dharma (the path to enlightenment); and the Sangha (the community of practitioners). For Lama Gyatso, his teachers were more precious than diamonds, sapphires, or rubies. It is one thing to read about the master-student relationship, but quite another to witness it in person. I had never seen one human revere another much as Lama Gyatso revered Rinpoche. Although Lama Gyatso spoke little of this relationship during our early months living together at the Family Home, he expended every iota of our energy to prepare for Rinpoche's visits. By example, he taught me about the devotional nature of the relationship between student and master.

Before one of Rinpoche's visits, Lama Gyatso said, "Mary Ann, we need a large, clear bowl filled with milk to place at the front door for Rinpoche's arrival." When I asked why we needed a bowl of milk, he did not respond. Although he always answered my questions, he didn't always do so directly or immediately. Sometimes, as we ran about collecting wood and branches to burn in fire pujas and smoke offerings, Lama Gyatso would offer straightforward explanations. Sometimes he would seem to ignore or forget my queries, but at mealtime would expound on the very subjects I'd introduced. When Lama Gyatso decided the time was ripe to answer my question about the bowl of milk, he said simply, "In Tibet we honor the arrival of our guests, Mary Ann. We offer the best we have. Now we must find a flawless flower to float on the milk." We searched the gardens high and low for just the right flower. Only a perfect bloom, with no discoloration, in the right hue, with the right scent, would be good enough for Rinpoche.

Each day with Lama Gyatso was filled with activity. People arrived at our front door asking for the lama. They left flowers at his bedroom door or peered through the glass door to the kitchen, hoping to get a glimpse of him. The phone rang nonstop, and soon we needed a second line. People streamed in with children, sick pets, ailing parents or friends, all seeking either counsel or healing prayers. None were turned away.

My birth family was gifted with seemingly unlimited, even hyperactive energy, unable to sit still for long; they moved, talked, drank, and traveled constantly. While Lama Gyatso and Rinpoche were equally active, their energy was purposeful, thoughtful, and dedicated. The meaning of the Tibetan word *gyatso* is "ocean," which seemed apropos, as the visible ocean is constantly moving and rolling, but under the surface, the water can be both still and calm. Although I, too, was highly industrious and engaged in my own demanding responsibilities as a Christian minister, managing the family estate, and helping to care for my ailing parents, Lama Gyatso's cyclonic energy stirred me to unprecedented levels of activity. Thus, my early days with Lama Gyatso often left me exhausted, frustrated, exhilarated, and inspired. Each day was a prayer in action.

Lama Gyatso taught continuously—at mealtimes, on walks,

sitting in front of the fire, while driving. He acted as though time were a limited commodity, as though he had too much to share, too much to do in too little time. His passionate words, stories, and teachings poured out like colorful, mighty rivers springing forth from invisible sources. As his English improved, he was increasingly able to tell me stories. In this way, I became the beneficiary of the Nyingma tradition of oral storytelling, which is passed from generation to generation, with students sitting at the teacher's feet, listening to magical voices spin the Wheel of Dharma, the ancient scroll of wisdom on which is recorded, according to Buddhist lore, all that can be known.

Lama Gyatso seemed to live intuitively, which served as an open invitation for me to do the same. My childhood had taught me that people were not to be trusted, and it took years for me to learn the art of determining whom I could or could not trust. During those early days of rapid and sudden change with Lama Gyatso, the buds of trust pushed through the dormant branches of my heart toward the light.

He was eager to hear about both my nighttime dreams and my daydreams. I began, shyly at first, to share more about my inner world—stories from my childhood, encounters with My Yogi, and the visions that were most vexing or compelling to me. Lama Gyatso always listened very attentively. We openly discussed the alternate worlds and parallel universes that I had never dared to mention to anyone else, but that, as I was finding out, were honored by the Nyingma masters and were in fact part of a huge body of ancient spiritual science. For the first time in my life, I was learning what it meant to truly be myself and to trust someone. Lama Gyatso trusted me as well. We were interested in each other's stories and spent many hours by the fire sharing our hopes and aspirations and pondering our perceived failures. The days and weeks flew by with such speed that I actually had little time to think about it, but little by little trust was becoming automatic.

Lama Gyatso came into the kitchen one morning and said, in the offhand way he had of suggesting significant things, "Mary Ann, do you know who Yeshe Tsogyal is?" He said it nonchalantly, without looking at me, while preparing to wash his offering bowls.

I sat in a chair next to the large window, relaxing in warm rays of sun before the days' activities began, looking out over the garden at the tall tulip tree. I recalled that in my early days of study with Rinpoche, he had given me a Yeshe Tsogyal empowerment, which initiated me into using a Yeshe Tsogyal text to recite certain mantras, to focus my meditations, and to help me engage in visualizations that allowed me to cultivate an awareness of and identification with attributes associated with Yeshe Tsogyal—compassion, knowledge, wisdom. Thinking back on this, I told Lama Gyatso that I did know a little about Yeshe Tsogyal. "Why do you ask?"

He skirted the issue: "Well, I've just got to make sure to teach you the Hundred-Syllable Mantra of Vajrasattva, the Seven Line Prayer, and a few other prayers, or it may be hard for people to believe who you really are."

I looked at him. This wasn't the first time he had referred to me and Yeshe Tsogyal in the same sentence, and the studiously casual manner in he which made these comments stirred my curiosity, but also made me self-conscious. He seemed to be intimating that I had a direct connection to this extraordinary woman, a tantalizing suggestion that made me uneasy for several reasons. First, throughout Western history, women who have claimed spiritual agency have been subject to ridicule and oppression; indeed, in my own ministry, whenever I had managed to achieve some recognition among those to whom I ministered, I had been forcefully embarrassed or rejected by the male clergy, and I hardly welcomed the idea of revisiting that possibility. Second, even though my divorce was a decade in the past, wounds from that public humiliation still felt fresh. I preferred the safe retreat of my home and spiritual practices, away from town and family gossip. I had no desire to be thrust into the public spotlight again. Third, while I had by now received many teachings and empowerments from noted Tibetan Buddhist masters, I was still engaged as a Christian minister. Although I had no qualms about practicing both religious traditions, I wasn't foolish enough to believe others would share my ecumenical understandings of truth. I feared that many would consider my spiritual life compromised and my ever-increasing involvement with the Nyingmas as denigrating to Christianity. Finally, perhaps most difficult of all, was my still wounded self-confidence, which convinced me that I was unworthy of Yeshe Tsogyal's legacy.

All of these thoughts, however, were still inarticulate. So instead of asking Lama Gyatso what he meant by his comment about "who I was," I simply switched topics. I reminded him of our first conversation, in which I had expressed a desire for him to pour all of his knowledge and wisdom into me. I now asked him to teach me the Hundred-Syllable Prayer of Vajrasattva, a powerful mantra of purification. We moved out to the garden, Lama Gyatso taught me this prayer line by line, in the version compiled by His Holiness the Fourth Dodrupchen Rinpoche, and the captivating musical cadence of the words mesmerized me.

Om Vajra Sattva Samaya
Om [syllable of the Vajra Body]! O Vajrasattva Samaya

Manu Palaya
Please grant me your protection

Vajra Sattava Tenopa Tithra
O Vajrasattva come reside in me

Dridhro Me Bhawa
Reside firmly in me

Suto Khayo Me Bhawa
Be pleased with me

Supo Khayo Me Bhawa
Grow within me

Anu Rakto Me Bhawa
Be passionate toward me

Sarwa Siddhi Me Praya-tsha
Grant me all the siddhis

Sarwa Karma Sutsa Me
As well as [fulfillment of] all activities

Tsittam Shreyam Kuru Hung
Make my mind virtuous. Hum [syllable of Vajra Mind]!

Ha Ha Ha Ha Ho
[The laughter of joy in the Four Boundless Attitudes,
Four Wangs, Four Joys, and Four Bodies]

Bhagawan
O Conqueror

Sarwa Tat'hagata
Vajra of all the Tathagatas [Buddhas]

Vajra Ma Me Muntsa
Do not abandon me

Vajra Bhawa Maha Samaya Sattva Ah
Make me a vajra holder, O Great Samayasattva. Ah [syllable of Vajra
Speech, which unites all indivisibly into oneness]!

A year after Lama Gyatso's arrival, spring floods washed away sections of the drive leading to the Family Home. However, a long detour that was free of storm detritus angled through hills and vineyards carpeted in flowering greenery, thus allowing passage for our arriving guests. Red-winged blackbirds rested on trellis wires that anchored rows of pruned cabernet vines. The bold scarlet and yellow shoulder patches of these birds contrasted with the pastel blossoms of wild radishes, poppies, and yellow mustard. Their tumbling songs accompanied Lama Gyatso as he chauffeured HE Chagdud Tulku Rinpoche and other distinguished guests to the Family Home.

The Family Home had been a frenzy of activity for days as the *sangha* prepared for this visit. Inspired by Lama Gyatso and full of my own gratitude, I had begun to invest great effort, time, and expense to honor the teachers who were expanding my worldview in such miraculous ways. No detail was left untended, and by the time our honored guests arrived, the house and gardens sparkled with the promise of spring. Cherry-blossom bouquets brightened every room. Fragrant smells of jasmine tea and rice danced through the hallways. Sangha members greeted our esteemed guests at the front door with the now familiar Tibetan rituals of welcome. Bows of respect and honor accompanied blessings, flowers, and the exchange of *kataks* (traditional silk scarves folded with precision).

Twelve of us sat at the dining-room table for lunch, including HE Chagdud Tulku Rinpoche's honored guest, the Nyingma Rinpoche Lodi Gyari, who was the Dalai Lama's special envoy to Washington, D.C., as well as a close friend of Lama Gyatso. Conversation flowed easily. Then I remembered a dream I'd had about one of HE Chagdud Tulku Rinpoche's main translators and senior students, Emily, who was also seated at the table.

Impulsively, I said to her, "You know, I've been meaning to tell you about a very interesting dream I had about you."

HE Chagdud Tulku Rinpoche put his fork down and became quiet. I had expected that Emily and I would have a private side conversation, but as soon as I mentioned the word *dream*, silence descended. I had never been in company in which dreams, let alone *my* dreams, carried such significance.

Feeling a little self-conscious, I nevertheless proceeded to describe the dream. In it, I was visiting Emily at Rigdzin Ling, HE Chagdud Tulku Rinpoche's *gonpa*, his primary center for Nyingma studies, in Junction City, California.

"You were living there in a house cut into the side of a mountain, but I could not quite get to it," I said. "There was a narrow but deep ravine between your front door and me, and there was no bridge. It was too dangerous to advance. You opened the front door and there were two young boys with you. Then you reached across the ravine and handed me a text." I turned to Rinpoche and said, "You know, a text like the ones we use for our practices. It was rectangular, long and narrow, filled with hundreds of loose-leaf printed pages. This one wasn't like our maroon or blue colored texts, though. This one was luminous yellow."

Rinpoche's face became a question mark as he waited for Emily to translate what I had just said. During Emily's translation, Lama Gyatso and the other lamas sat straight up in their chairs and stared with unblinking eyes into the near distance. The silence in the dining room echoed in my brain. When Emily finished her translation, Rinpoche looked at me. "And so?"

There was one mysterious, but delightful detail still to be shared. This detail felt like the most important and fascinating aspect of the dream. Looking at Rinpoche, I said, "The cover of the text looked very old. There were lines of age running through it, but it was also shiny yellow and brand new. It was both old and new at the same time!" I smiled at Emily and said, "I was so pleased you gave me this text."

Rinpoche and Emily had a brief but intense conversation. "How old were the boys?" he asked me.

I hadn't considered their presence in my dream to be of major importance. I shrugged. "I don't know."

His Eminence leaned forward, eyes blazing into mine. "How old were they? Think!"

Puzzled, I paused so the dream images could resurface, and I did some rudimentary mental calculations. "They were not teenagers, they were younger than that."

HE Chagdud Tulku Rinpoche insisted. "Tell us how old those boys were."

Their ages popped suddenly into my mind. "Seven and nine."

As soon as I spoke, Emily sobbed in an outburst of grief. I was profoundly shaken. A wave of intuitive clarity washed over me that the two boys who appeared on the other side in the dream mirrored a specific reality of loss in her life.

I also sensed that, for the holy men around me, the presence of the yellow text and of those boys somehow authenticated me as a spiritual peer. Although I had not been conscious of it before that moment, I suddenly realized that I had been seeking such validation. And while I had been excited to share the dream with Emily, something else happened when I shared it with the masters who now surrounded me. I was venturing, in a small way, to go public with what I carried within me as a sacred gift. This awareness was bursting out of the confines in which I had kept it either totally secret or limited to confidential conversations with Lama Gyatso. But dreams and visions can be vehicles for divine messages, and it was time for mine to be shared, especially with my teachers.

Unused to what felt like profound public openness, I quickly reverted to shyness and into the role of accommodating hostess. The conversation moved on, bright laughter flooded the dining room, and dishes were passed around the table. But I was in a state of quiet wonder. Something within me was spiraling open. Dreams, teachings, visions, and experiences whose meanings had been partially concealed for years flashed in my mind's eye. I recalled moments when HE Chagdud Tulku Rinpoche and Lama Gyatso had treated me differently than they did their other students. Lama Gyatso had once announced that I was not his student, but his mother, which confused all who were present, including me. Another time, Rinpoche invited me to receive teachings that other students had spent years preparing for, but I had not. On several occasions when I was unable to attend Rinpoche's retreats, he had assured me, "It's okay. You not need to make Rinpoche's retreat. You already make many retreats in past lives." And I had noticed that neither Rinpoche nor Lama Gyatso ever questioned the veracity of my dreams or visions; in fact, both men listened closely and sometimes even asked for my advice.

If only the Christian world, the only world I had known in this life, could feel like the bright light that beckoned me homeward, could welcome me like the Buddhist world did. The tension between the worlds was drawing ever more taut within me. Before that tension could be resolved, however, I would have to learn to see, accept, and trust the essence of my true inner nature—as did these Buddhist masters—as the living incarnation of Yeshe Tsogyal.

Chapter 15

LOVE AND LOSS

Come to the edge.
We might fall.
Come to the edge.
It's too high!
COME TO THE EDGE!
And they came.
And he pushed,
And they flew.

—CHRISTOPHER LOGUE,
"New Numbers"

M Y SPIRITUAL STUDIES taught that we are all electrical beings. Electricity powered my home, but it also fired synapses across the hemispheres of my brain, and it beat my heart. The spiritual expression of this same energy is known as *kundalini*. And just as one approaches electrical currents with caution and respect, one does not engage with more spiritual energy than one is trained to handle. If such energy isn't cultivated gradually, by way of spiritual knowledge, practice, devotion, commitment, and discipline, what is otherwise a redeeming force can be destructive, even deadly. Lama Gyatso and HE Chagdud Tulku Rinpoche brought high levels of spiritual electricity into my home and life, but they did so without rushing me. I was therefore able to ease into the process of aligning my outer reality and ever-intensifying spiritual experiences with a new understanding of my true nature. As long as I was guided, actively learning, and deeply involved in my practice, I could trust this slow unfolding. My relationship with Lama Gyatso and my spiritual practices took root, and the hours of daily meditation and study began to pay great dividends in what the Nyingmas call equanimity.

As challenging events in my personal life demanded my attention, I was grateful for this emerging presence of inner peace, which steadied me as I faced a series of family crises, including the dying process and death of my father. Rinpoche offered valuable teachings on detachment that played a key role for me during my father's last months, a time in which my birth family's theatrical responses to life were especially pronounced. I practiced separating myself from the alcohol-fueled emotional hysteria, allowing my heart to open in a nonjudgmental fashion, and being more fully present in my role as part-time caregiver. Detachment and equanimity also allowed me to see the roles, both good and bad, that my father and I had played over the fifty-four years we had been in each other's lives. What mattered most to me, though, was that in the two years leading up to his death, he demonstrated that he was proud of me, of the choices I'd made; he did so by coming, if only one time, to hear me preach and by relaying to me his friends' praise of my ministry, even though this made Mother angry. Something in me had always known that he loved me, and by the time he died, I felt profoundly grateful for all he had given me. I was blessed to be with him the night he died. After his last breath, I opened the large bedroom window and told him to go, to fly toward the Light, to be free and to relax in knowing that we would do our best to take care of Mother.

Though we had so rarely been able to connect in words, I loved my father deeply. To honor him, I made all the funeral arrangements and wrote most of the service, minus the Eucharistic portion of the Mass. Despite family arguments about whether or not I, as a woman, would be allowed to preach in San Francisco's historic Old St. Mary's Cathedral, my parent's parish, the Paulist fathers of this very Roman Catholic church were most accommodating. They loaned me an alb, similar to the one I wore in the Napa Valley. Two priests compassionately helped me choose the music, notified musicians and cantors, and supported me as a visiting clergy member.

The morning of the funeral was surreal. In Asia, Lama Gyatso performed *p'howa*. I prayed that the Light Beings and Jesus would guide my father through after-life challenges and to Heaven, or what I was beginning to refer to as the *bardo* and Pure Lands of Buddhist cosmology. In San Francisco, before the service began, I carried my fifteen-month-old granddaughter, Sarah, around the church, and together we lit every candle in the cathedral, filling the vast holy space with flickering lights. The walls and the altar of Old St. Mary's were white, and a bright red carpet covered the floor. Most Catholic churches I knew featured Jesus suffering an agonizing death on a large cross, but here the altar held only a diminutive, empty gold cross symbolizing the Resurrection of Jesus. Dominating the cathedral was a spectacular, two-story fresco of Our Heavenly Mother, which soared above the altar. The beautiful Divine Mother was gowned in white, with a dark blue drape, and surrounded by light and angels.

The colors of this church and its fresco—red, white, blue—were the same colors I was learning to use in Buddhist visualizations to move inner spiritual energies. I now perceived Our Lady Mary as a Buddha, similar to Tara and Yeshe Tsogyal, each powerful in her own right and an essential part of the expansive cosmos.

"See?" I whispered to Sarah. "That's Our Divine Mother going up to heaven. See all the little angels? That's what you were before you came into your mommy's tummy."

After the services, a stately recession followed Daddy's casket down the church's center aisle, behind Mother and the rest of our family, and ended at its doors. Outside, my mother, my sisters, and I stood silently atop the worn red-brick steps under the large clock face. A plaque high up on the square bell tower read "Son Observe the Time and Fly from Evil" (Ecclesiasticus 4:23). Daddy's highly polished coffin rolled smoothly into the open back of a long black hearse. Tourists in sneakers streamed along California Street, and delicious aromas drifted up from the large Empress of China restaurant at the end of the steep block. Cable cars rang their bells under a clear blue sky, and we squinted in the bright sunlight, smiling as graciously as possible as we greeted friends and relatives who had come to say goodbye to a man they loved and admired.

While preaching my father's eulogy under Our Lady's towering fresco, my eye was repeatedly drawn to a tall, handsome man and his wife sitting in a pew halfway down the church. They smiled and laughed at my jokes, then dabbed their eyes with handkerchiefs when I related one of Daddy's last escapades. These were Don, who was my father's protégé, and his wife Barbara. They stood out from the crowded surroundings in a singularly powerful way, and were genuinely caring in expressing their condolences. I felt an instant connection with both of them. When we shook hands, however, I experienced no signals warning me that within a few months this lovely, robust woman would die unexpectedly. Or that not long thereafter, Don would become my second husband.

Mother did not take well to widowhood. She suffered unending grief. Half-gallon bottles of vodka emptied quickly and stood blatantly about, broadcasting the drugged anger of a woman abandoned by her best friend, confidant, and husband of sixty-four years. As San Francisco's summer mists rolled in chilly waves outside my parent's Russian Hill high-rise that summer, mournful, long-drawn-out moans emanated from invisible foghorns. The fog stole like a thief through the city streets as Mother prayed for a death she was terrified of meeting.

Mother was still in the grip of mourning when Don's wife died, and she asked me to represent the family at the memorial, which I did, sitting alone at the back of the church. After the service, I introduced myself to Don. As we stood in September's brightly lit street, he gazed at me. His face was as flushed as it had been inside the church when he delivered his loving tribute to Barbara. Don's penetrating hazel eyes conveyed the rigid tension that was evident on his exhausted face. He was dressed sharply, in a dark suit, white shirt, and tie, but he looked lost as the two of us stood engulfed in a vast sea of energy full of discreet meaning. I wasn't sure if he understood who I was, so I spoke more slowly.

"Yes, yes," he said. "I know exactly who you are."

"Mother is sorry she is unable to be here, but sends her love. She wants you to know how important you were to both her and my father."

We said little else, but I remembered how Don had stood out at my father's funeral—tall, silver-haired, square-jawed, handsome. Buddhist cosmology speaks of "emptiness," which refers to an empty fullness, a fecund nothingness, the base of the universe seething with creativity. In that moment, in the mundane nothingness of a respectful exchange, at the most unexpected time and place, I had unknowingly found the love of my life. When the crowds of people exiting the church broke the silent spell between us, I took my leave, but I felt Don's eyes follow me down the block and across the street to the parking lot.

Though my parents never forgave my exodus from the Catholic Church and into the world of Protestants, and though we certainly never discussed my deep relationship with Nyingma and Buddhist culture, Mother phoned after Barbara's funeral with what might have been a degree of concession. "Aren't you some sort of minister who supposedly helps people when they die?" she barked at me over the telephone wires. We had discussed my ministerial role many times, and she perhaps recalled something about my work as a hospice chaplain. "Well, then, why don't you do something useful for once and help Don McComber?" Mother issued statements, questions, commands, and directives in a thick river of alcohol abuse. Under this deluge of confused emotions, however, I could hear her concern. Don had been my father's apprentice. Both had become CEOs of well-known American insurance companies. They had friends in common and shared experiences of rising to corporate power and of the disappearing fame forced on them by retirement. Though Mother had been lost in the depths of suffering since Daddy's death, she truly cared about Don and wanted me to reach out to him on her behalf.

I wrote to Don, letting him know that I was a hospice chaplain and would be available to him should he need someone to talk to. About a month after Barbara's death, we spoke over the phone, and he asked me out to dinner. He arrived at the front door right on time, and we talked for many hours that first date. Every time I tried to steer the conversation in the direction of grief counseling, he redirected.

"You're very beautiful, but so young!" he said.

"I never thought fifty-six was that young," I said softly.

"You are fifty-six?" He looked hopeful. He was sixty-six, and quickly decided that a ten-year age gap was acceptable. Knowing that many ill-fated relationships begin in the immediate aftermath of heartbreak due to divorce or death, I cautioned Don (and myself) that he would need time to grieve, especially since his wife had died so suddenly. But we couldn't be apart from each other. We met every day for dates, picnics, and candlelight dinners.

Given the tumult of my first marriage, I had vowed not to remarry in haste. I'd been single for nineteen years and was determined to enter into matrimony only if I knew exactly what I was getting into. But when I met Don, my intentions dissolved. He was a revelation. Perhaps due to his native self-confidence, he was the first romantic partner to express genuine joy in and respect for what I had accomplished. I was free to be honest not just in my vulnerabilities, but also in the full force of my strengths. He loved me for who I was. Even as he honored my power and my individuality, he somehow also managed to infuse our relationship with gallantry and masculine attentions. Each month a fresh arrangement of flowers arrived at the Family Home, along a with a handwritten card on which Don expressed love and appreciation for our life together. Such generosity was typical. With him came an intoxicating and liberating mix of affirmations—I felt at once beautiful, powerful, desired, and protected. And likewise, my own love and admiration for this man continually deepened.

We married nine weeks after we met. Our secret wedding was just ours. Late afternoon shafts of winter sunlight poured through the windows of the Family Home into the living room, which was filled with yellow and red flowers. A fire blazed, and a Native American shaman declared us husband and wife. Though Don was traditional in many ways, a sense of excitement surrounding the new, the possibly wild, maybe even the forbidden had entered our lives and made us feel like teenagers running away to Las Vegas. We felt deservedly selfish. We felt free and deliriously happy.

But it was still soon after Barbara's death, and her children, who were in their forties, remained lost in deep grief. I would not yet be a welcome addition to his family, so Don and I kept our romantic life private. Together, we talked about our pasts, read aloud to each other in bed, held each other, and made plans for the rest of our lives. These were sacred moments. We decided to do whatever was necessary to keep this intoxicating romance alive.

When the time was right, we formally announced our "engagement." Lama Gyatso officiated at our public wedding while the minister from the Methodist church I preached at and the Native American shaman presided on the lawn outside the family room. God and Buddha were included in our marriage vows: we promised to pay continual homage to the deities of diamond sparks and fireflies as well as to the God I preached about in church. Don hosted the wedding feast at his house in Napa, which he had put on the market. Since he was unable to travel after our wedding, we had decided to celebrate at a Giants baseball game in San Francisco. We left the wedding feast carrying our new stadium booster seats, and the family threw rice, laughing and shaking their heads in amused wonder. En route to the baseball game, Don and I speculated about whether our twenty-nine offspring would get along, then decided simply not to worry about such things, to relish every moment instead, because we knew our years were numbered.

We laughed. We made love. We took ocean cruises and spoiled each other. I called Don Mr. King and he called me his Queen. Don was a natural leader who had risen through the ranks in athletics at Stanford, in the military, and on Wall Street—the all-American kid who made it to the top of corporate America. But he was really a farm boy at heart, and thus embraced life at the Family Home with great joy, driving his treasured tractor every day, mowing weeds, tirelessly collaborating with Francisco to beautify the grounds. Soon after our wedding, he planted a small estate vineyard.

As a couple, we dedicated our time to philanthropic pursuits. We traveled to Central and South America with one of the nation's first micro-lending programs, Women's Opportunity Fund, a flourishing organization that helped the poorest of the poor—women and their children—open small businesses. I'd been involved with the leaders of this program and introduced Don to several board members; when asked to join their board, I declined but Don accepted. While I expanded my ministry and donated time to various humanitarian organizations, Don also assisted in the founding of Queen of the Valley Medical and Wellness Center, in the city of Napa. Together, Don and I developed the hospital's mission—to integrate traditional Western medicine with preventive practices—then helped raise $15 million for the project. Don eventually became president of the Queen's Foundation and a member of their board of trustees. Between our hospital work and our extensive family commitments, we were extraordinarily busy, so we cherished our evenings together, discussing details from our day's activities, viewing sunsets, reading, studying, and watching sports.

Shortly before my father died, Lama Gyatso had moved to Los Angeles to establish his new *sangha*, Thondup Ling. He was deeply immersed in establishing this center, but whenever his hectic schedule allowed time for rest and relaxation, he flew up to visit Don and me, often accompanied by several other lamas and rinpoches. Despite Don's spiritual reservations, he and Lama Gyatso quickly bonded. Both were natural leaders, men of passion and profound integrity who were devoted to those they led. They loved life, laughter, and success, and everything they touched seemed to turn to gold. Don reflected the material world, Lama Gyatso the spiritual, but both enjoyed fast cars, good food, and cowboy movies. They complemented each other, and together they graced my life with an immeasurable abundance.

Despite that fact that I felt unprecedentedly free and powerful with Don, I did not reveal the full extent of my sacred explorations. Don's world revolved around the physical aspects of life, and he showed little interest in spiritual phenomena. As proud as he was of my Christian ministry, he found Buddhism much too foreign to even try to understand. So I downplayed the esoteric aspects of my spiritual journey and especially my role as Yeshe Tsogyal. With these parts of myself, I trusted only Lama Gyatso and a few of my other beloved lama friends.

Yet the wheels of change were turning. The teachers to whom I'd had such close and immediate access were moving on to new horizons. Not only had Lama Gyatso relocated to Los Angeles, but HE Chagdud Tulku Rinpoche had transferred his headquarters from Rigdzin Ling, a Buddhist center in Northern California, to Brazil. Both Lama Gyatso and Rinpoche would continue to guide me, but it would have to be from afar.

Around the same time, my Taizé ministry abruptly came to an end. In 1997, the abbot of the Catholic monastery that was home to our Taizé gatherings informed me that Rome had issued a decree stating that no women were to be allowed on the altar of a Roman Catholic church. I would no longer be able to minister at the services I had started. Recognizing their popularity, however, the abbot decided the monastery would continue to host the services. It was with great sorrow that I relinquished my role in the Taizé gatherings, but in truth, my heart was no longer in the Christian Church. My Good Friday calling now seemed to be a mysterious code for a higher purpose I had not yet fully deciphered.

Though my calling continued to haunt me as I spent more and more time with the Nyingmas, I was in no rush to assume the mantle of Yeshe Tsogyal. Indeed, I wasn't entirely clear what that even meant. It is one thing to be recognized as a *tulku,* or incarnation, if you were born in Tibet or lived among the Nyingmas, where rituals, processes, and a cultural lexicon allow for and celebrate such extraordinary rites of passage. In the West, however, experience and recognition of such possibilities is virtually nonexistent. And there was the fact that I was a wealthy, middle-aged woman whom many still regarded as a Christian minister—that was my public identity. Until I became more settled with who I actually was, my role as Yeshe Tsogyal had to remain secret. I did not want to be flooded with questions I would be unable to answer, and I certainly wasn't ready to face my birth family's inbred cynicism or ridicule. I even feared that if I were to be elevated to such a role, my marriage might be threatened. Therefore, I asked Lama Gyatso not to discuss the topic, except with other lamas and rinpoches, and he assured me that he would protect my secret. He went on to say that should anything happen to him, several masters in Asia were aware of me and who I was. "If you ever need someone to speak to or ask questions of," he explained, "you can visit them, and they will help you." His soothing words always relaxed me.

Above all I needed time, a great deal of time, to explore what it truly meant to be Yeshe Tsogyal. Deepening and strengthening my orientation within the Billion-fold Universe of Buddhist cosmology through meditation, study, prayer, and mantra became my primary joy, comfort, and focus. I now entered a cycle of withdrawal from the world. I immersed myself in a sea of dissolution. So much was new—I was a new wife and an awakening student of the *dharma* and spiritual sciences—and yet it felt like so much of my known life as a minister, activist, mother, and grandmother was dissolving into a mysterious vastness, causing familiar physical structures like my home, church, office, and not least my body to feel fragile and impermanent.

Yet my life was also vibrant and full. Don and I soon had a family of thirty-five, including our children, their spouses, and our grandchildren. Family holidays were large, loud, boisterous rituals, and we treasured them. Our honeymoon lasted, as did the romance. I was profoundly grateful for my marriage, which steadied me as I faced monumental inner shifts, as well as a series of devastating events: my younger sister became critically ill; one of my nephews died racing motorcycles; my older sister was paralyzed with a spinal cord injury she suffered in a horrific automobile accident—and there was still more to come.

Mother lived a very unhappy four years as a widow, but she blossomed when around Don, and my status rose immeasurably in her eyes now that I was his wife. Her lovely apartment was in the Bay Area, close to my younger sister's home and just an hour's drive from Napa, so we often visited and took her to lunch. (My birth family treated me with respect when I was with Don, so I made it a point never to visit them unless we were together.)

Yet Mother's health was in decline, and one day, just after Thanksgiving in 1999, I received a frantic call from her housekeeper. She had suffered a severe stroke. Afterward, she was unable to return home without twenty-four-hour care. Although she had constantly criticized my religious life, I had for years promised to stay by her side and be with her at the moment of her death. She would bow her head, in tears, and thank me. Thus, I spent most of the month of December sitting at her bedside.

On New Year's Eve—indeed, the eve of a new century—Mother turned ninety-one. She sat in her wheelchair looking lost, dejected, and confused. When I asked if she would like to say the rosary together, her entire countenance lit up with a desperate, even frantic eagerness. So I began, "Hail Mary, full of grace, the Lord is with you, blessed art thou amongst women," and Mother clutched her rosary with swollen, arthritic fingers, which she usually tried to hide. She recited with me, her hoarse voice full of despairing devotion. "Holy Mary, Mother of God, pray for us sinners now and at the hour of our death." Afterward, the nurse put her in bed, and I walked down the hall to be alone.

Mother's body began to shut down the next day. My sister Cecilia and two nieces joined me to be with her. Shortly after Mother lost consciousness, there was a soft knock at the door. When I opened it, two gray-haired women, both strangers, stood quietly before me. Both wore plain, somber-colored, worn cloth coats. One of them did most of the talking, while the other woman quietly clutched a brown paper bag. They exuded a calm air of fatigue and loving maturity, but also a pronounced sense of urgency.

As they tried to peer around me, the spokeswoman asked, "How is she?"

"She is dying," I said. I was exhausted from my long vigil.

"How much time does she have?"

"Not long," I replied. "Maybe half an hour. I don't know. Pretty soon."

Upset, the woman said, "We didn't know she was so close to death."

"I am so sorry," I said and stepped aside, inviting them in, but they shrank back and shook their heads.

The quiet woman said, with a great deal of concerned intensity, "It is very important you give this to her! We had such a hard time finding it." She held up the paper bag. "After going to several stores, we finally went to the Rexall Drug Store. The clerk had to get a ladder out and climb up to above the display cabinets to find it. You must give this to her now."

"Right away," said the first woman. Their compassionate gazes moved from me to Mother and then back to me.

I took the bag and asked again if they wanted to come in to say goodbye.

"Oh no," they said in unison. "But you must give this to her now." Then they turned on silent feet and vanished.

Cecilia sat on the opposite side of the bed while my nieces stood at the end, one of them massaging Mother's swollen feet. I encouraged her to stop, to allow Mother to rest, explaining that physical contact and massage might not be helpful during Mother's last moments. She protested, however, and I relented. My niece's gesture was an act of love, and my own Buddhist understandings needed to stand aside.

A heavy silence hung over the room, broken only by the death rattle of Mother's breathing. Cecilia stared at me and nodded toward the door, silently asking what had just happened with the visitors. I shrugged in puzzlement, but handed her the bag. She reached inside and pulled out a bottle of inexpensive pink hand lotion—Desert Rose. Mother had been an avid rose grower her entire adult life, and Cecilia had carried on this horticultural legacy, always sharing the bounty of her own garden with Mother. As Cecilia unscrewed the golden cap, the scent of rose swirled about the hospital room. My sister looked at me, her eyes asking if she should apply the lotion to mother's body. I nodded, and Cecilia slowly smoothed the lotion into Mother's dry arms.

Mother suddenly sat straight up in her hospital bed and broke into a broad smile that lit up her face like a thousand radiant suns. Mother rarely, if ever, smiled! Her eyes shot open as she gasped in joy, beholding a vision of what must have been indescribable beauty and love before she closed her eyes and lay back. As soon as she touched the pillow, her head fell forward and her breathing stopped. Mother died smiling, enveloped in an atmosphere of rose perfume.

When we asked around the retirement home, no one seemed to know the mysterious women who cared so deeply about Mother, who had gone to such trouble to give her the heavenly gift. But my longtime prayers had been answered: my mother had died not only peacefully, but with joy.

After Mother passed, I learned that, according to some traditions, the rose emits the most potent energy field of any flower on earth—rose essential oil vibrates at 320 megahertz of electrical energy, whereas lavender vibrates at 118 megahertz, and the human brain vibrates at a mere 90 megahertz. I also learned that, according to some traditions, angels use the scent of rose as a physical sign of their presence. While I never learned the identities of those two humble women, I will never forget Mother's magnificent smile as she was carried away in the arms of rose-scented angels.

Chapter 16

SHE BECOMES KNOWN

We are the Pilgrims, master; we shall go
Always a little further: it may be
Beyond the last blue mountain barred with snow,
Across that angry or that glimmering sea,

White on a throne or guarded in a cave
There lives a prophet [within] who can understand
Why [we] were born.

—JAMES ELROY FLECKER,
The Golden Journey to Samarkand

A NEW CENTURY HAD BEGUN, and it was the dawn of the Age of Aquarius—a time, astrologically speaking, when upheaval can make room for love, unity, and integrity, if given the chance. We had all survived Y2K, despite worldwide anxiety about whether digital technology could survive the date change. The new year would be filled with divisive events: mass demonstrations in Belgrade led to the resignation of the Serbian strongman Slobodan Milošević; a controversial U.S. presidential election resulted in a Supreme Court challenge; and Hillary Rodham Clinton was elected to the U.S. Senate while still serving as the First Lady.

Don took me to Hawaii for a "second" honeymoon and a chance to recoup my energy, which had diminished during the many months of Mother's decline. But I didn't recuperate as much as I'd expected. Over the next four months, I struggled with increasing fatigue. Once, while driving home from San Francisco, I had to pull off the freeway to sleep. This overwhelming fatigue, however, did have an upside, for it enabled me to surrender my attachments to the mundane world. I just didn't have the energy to hold on to them.

A week after my sixty-first birthday, I was diagnosed with cervical cancer. Though the odds were very high that I would be "cured" with a total hysterectomy, the word *cancer* was upsetting. Buddhist teachings on impermanency arose in my mind. None of us know exactly when or where we will die. I had learned a lot about death as a hospital and hospice chaplain, as a student of Tibetan Buddhism, and as witness to the deaths of my parents, but now I was confronting the possibility of my own. "Death comes to all," I heard Rinpoche's voice repeat over and over as I meditated on my *p'howa* practice and made sure all my affairs were in order.

Don was my shepherd, driving me to doctors, helping me with medical decisions, and handling all the details regarding the surgery and hospitals. Not since childhood had I been relieved of so many responsibilities—it was an enormous gift. The love Don and I shared deepened exponentially. My meditation practices were already second nature, but I slipped into a realm of surprising psychospiritual giddiness and trust, knowing I was in the care of an extraordinary woman surgeon, of Don, of Lama Gyatso, and of Lama Gyatso's primary teacher, His Holiness the Fourth Dodrupchen Rinpoche. At the doctor's office, I was able to laugh and joke. Though the cancer was growing rapidly, I was filled with hope and gratitude.

On the day of my surgery, as I lay on the cold steel table, I prayed to the Blessed Virgin Mary, Yeshe Tsogyal, and the Red Tara to make themselves visible to me. I had heard that some patients have out-of-body experiences while under anesthesia, and I wished to have this experience, too. I awoke after midnight having neither seen the great female deities nor consciously gone out-of-body, but my hospital room was suffused with red light, which made me feel connected to the Red Tara and immediately put me at ease. The next day I checked with the doctors and nurses, each of whom told me there were no red lights outside the hospital that could have filled my room with the red glow that I had basked in.

Recovery took many months. Don and I had a slightly amusing setup in the family room: two recliner chairs on swivels, such that after dinner, he could turn his chair to watch sports (with the sound muted), and I could turn the other way, toward the fireplace, and immerse myself in spiritual studies. Occasionally I shared information I thought would interest Don, and he would listen intently. Astrology and Buddhism used terminology that Don couldn't readily follow, but I had learned to use language he was comfortable with, and he clearly appreciated the newfound knowledge.

In the evenings, I'd retire to the northwest-facing windows of our bedroom to experience the extraordinary, visionary phenomena of light and color that occurred regularly that summer. At sunset, blended swaths of reds, oranges, and yellows illuminated the horizon against the ever-deepening blue of the skies over Mount Saint Helena and the Mayacamas mountain range. The panoramas of color held me in an ecstatic state of joy and love through that entire summer. It felt as if great, silent conversations took place as I gazed out the window. I sat awash in the most pure love I have ever known. I was sure that it was the eternal love I'd heard about since childhood.

During this precious healing time, I informed friends and family that I would be on a house retreat. I needed solitude to heal. I didn't want to go back to the life I had been living. I no longer wanted to rush from one meeting to the next, which felt increasingly frustrating. And as I retreated from difficult family relationships and worldly responsibilities and benefited from the blessings of seclusion under Don's care, something within me began to shift radically. My mystical awareness and understanding was growing, and I needed to expand into it. Lama Gyatso, with whom I spoke regularly by phone, instructed me to write down all my thoughts, dreams, and visions, and send them to him. Through meditation, study, writing, and slowing down, I was ushered ever more deeply into the inner realm of the Divine. Unconsciously, I began to see myself as a new creature, complex, ornate, richly symbolic. On the conscious level, I now called my Inner Teacher "She" in recognition of my familiars Mother Mary and the Red Tara—and soon Yeshe Tsogyal as well.

One evening, during a call with Lama Gyatso, I suddenly heard myself declare in a strange voice, demanding, loud, wrathful, "It's time, Lama Gyatso. She is finished with her silence. It is time for her to speak. She wants to be heard. Now." The voice was decidedly feminine, and it erupted from within me with a force I could not resist. Both Lama Gyatso and I experienced no confusion about who She was—Yeshe Tsogyal bursting forth from the confines of my spiritually impoverished Western mentality. I experienced an instantaneous transformation in my perception of who I was. I knew with inexorable certainty that She and I were One, both emanating from a timeless, eternal realm.

For a brief period, I believed that with this utterance my job was done, that my destiny had somehow, mysteriously, been fulfilled. But Lama Gyatso knew better and set in motion activities that would soon help me solidify my newly emergent self.

Since moving to Los Angeles, Lama Gyatso had transformed Thondup Ling into an enterprising *sangha*. In 2003 he also established Ari Bhöd–Pema Drawa Foundation, known as America's Tibet, on 475 acres of beautiful, forested, sacred retreat lands high in southern California's Tehachapi Mountains. According to Lama Gyatso's vision, Ari Bhöd was to be dedicated to the preservation of ancient Tibetan sacred art forms, with Tibetan artists, writers, doctors, visionaries, and students from around the world invited to partake of the land's blessings and to create a sacred legacy for generations to come. As soon as the land was purchased, Lama Gyatso engineered an auspicious gathering of Nyingma masters to inaugurate and bless Ari Bhöd–Pema Drawa. He informed me that he had also requested their presence specifically to meet me and thereby initiate the complex, layered process of recognizing me as the incarnation of Yeshe Tsogyal. Thus, in September 2003, eight lamas from Sikkim, Taiwan, Nepal, and India landed at the San Francisco International Airport, creating quite a stir in Marin County, where many students came for empowerments and teachings.

On their first day, the lamas were scheduled to offer teachings at the Mill Valley Community Center, then room overnight with my daughter, Aimee, whom Lama Gyatso had come to call his "American sister." As the motorcade of lamas arrived at the community center, Aimee held the hands of her two daughters, Olivia and Emma, and waited to greet them. Two-year-old Emma stood with her cherished pacifier lodged firmly in her mouth. As the cars rolled to a stop and the maroon-and-gold-robed masters emerged, Emma broke away from Aimee, ran to His Excellency Tinkey Gonjang Rinpoche, and prostrated herself. Emma had never seen anyone prostrate before, nor had she ever seen HE Gonjang Rinpoche. Once finished with her prostrations, she raised her small arms and a lama carried her into the community center's makeshift throne room, where the teachings would take place. As soon as HE Gonjang Rinpoche was seated on his throne, Emma was placed on his lap. Without hesitation, she picked up and tried to use the ritual instruments that had been laid out for HE Gonjang Rinpoche's use in the empowerment ceremony. She seemed surprisingly familiar with the proper use of the instruments— from the lamas' perspective, an auspicious beginning to what proceeded to be a transformative visit.

During our dinner at Aimee's kitchen table that evening, high energy animated the conversation, with Lama Gyatso interpreting for the non-English-speakers. At some point, Lama Gyatso caught my eye and gestured toward one of the lamas whom I had just met.

"Did you know that Lama Lubdrub was born in the Sacred Rolwaling Valley?" he said.

My life-changing trek flashed through my mind. I had never described it to anyone, not even to HE Chagdud Tulku Rinpoche. Although Lama Gyatso knew I had been there, I had never shared the details.

"But I was there!" I exclaimed and found myself repeating those four words again and again, my memory drawn to a particular campsite, a valley that overlooked a gentle slope with many stone huts. After that day's long hike, I had sat outside my tent, mesmerized by the towering mountain in front of me when my gaze landed on a single nearby hut. *Go look inside that hut,* said my Inner Teacher. I walked to the hut and found that it was locked and barred. I peered in a window, but could see nothing, so I returned to my tent. *Go back, look again.* In the grip of a strange compulsion, I returned to examine the perimeter of the one-room structure, but again found nothing.

Visions of that mysterious afternoon flooded my being as I now sat in the presence of these spiritual masters. An inexplicable stillness came over me, as though I were awaiting something I could not yet see. I could neither eat nor speak.

"Lama Lubdrub's parents were forced to escape Tibet while his mother was pregnant," Lama Gyatso explained. "They made it across the border into the Sacred Rolwaling Valley just in time for his precious mother to give birth to him. He and his parents lived in a small stone house from the time he was a baby until he was two years old. After his second birthday, his parents left the Sacred Rolwaling Valley and carried him to the top of the largest mountain overlooking the valley where His Holiness Trulshik Rinpoche has a monastery, Thupten Chöling. Lama Lubdrub lived with His Holiness Trulshik Rinpoche on that mountain and now serves as his Vajra Master."

HH Trulshik Rinpoche was a renowned spiritual leader and Supreme Head of all the Nyingmas, most notably serving as one of the Dalai Lama's primary teachers. In the role of Vajra Master, Lama Lubdrub acted as the hands and feet of HH Trulshik Rinpoche during liturgies. While HH Trulshik Rinpoche sat on a throne before an altar adorned with holy implements he used to empower those in attendance, Lama Lubdrub was entrusted with the complex ritual of bringing each instrument forward to be blessed. Every movement in the ritual, even down to the forms made by the hands, known as *mudras*, was choreographed. The ceremony represented on the physical plane HH Trulshik Rinpoche's energetic gestures on the spiritual plane. Lama Lubdrub, like all Vajra Masters, was charged with serving as the conduit of his teacher's spiritual power.

As Lama Gyatso spoke, my mind stopped. I bowed my head in silence, internally bridging that scene fourteen years in my past—the voice urging me to investigate the stone hut, the magnetizing energy that emanated from the mountain, the uncanny sense of being observed by someone atop that mountain—with the present company around Aimee's dining table. I simply could not play hostess with these holy men, not with the magic and mystery of my experience in the sacred valley swirling through my consciousness. What could I say when all I had were questions? Did the lamas know I had been in the Sacred Rolwaling Valley? Had they perhaps known it even at the time, when I was actually there? I could not be sure. Anything felt possible. All I could comprehend was the pure joy that beamed forth from their faces as they gazed reverently at me.

I had met Lama Lubdrub only a few moments before dinner started. He knew no English; I knew no Tibetan. Yet in that brief span of time, it had become clear that our lives were intertwined.

The visiting lamas performed a powerful healing ceremony at the Family Home the next afternoon. Afterward, we relaxed on the lawn garden, which was graced with the delicate scents of roses and herbs. The lamas strolled quietly, absorbing the beauty of the landscape, and I sat in a chair set within in a circle of chairs, gazing out over the vineyards toward Stags Leap, the valley's sunrise mountain, to the east. An energized peace prevailed. Eventually, the lamas sat down with me, Lama Lubdrub and the Venerable Lama Nawang Thogmed taking seats opposite me.

I suddenly found myself sitting upright. Between Lama Lubdrub and Stags Leap behind him, I saw the vast apparition of a colorful Light Being that seemed to radiate from deep within my psyche and fill the early evening sky. The top half of this wrathful being was fierce, horrific, yet also somehow farcical, with red-orange hair flaming out and around her head in a stiff cloud of fire. Her mouth was split open in a devouring leer that should have been frightening, but to me her antics were comic, as though she had gone to great lengths to appear in her Halloween costume, and I laughed. Wanting desperately to convey this vision to Lama Lubdrub, whose name I could no longer remember, I waved my arms and hands in a drama of enthusiasm, resorting to body language and vocal theatrics in an effort to overcome the language barrier. Lama Lubdrub smiled beatifically and leaned over to Lama Thogmed to ask for a translation. I was jolted out of my altered state. Why didn't he understand me? I was speaking a universal language, wasn't I? Disappointed, uncertain, I slumped down in my chair for a few puzzling minutes and then got up.

Lama Gyatso charged several lamas to remain by my side in order to attend to what I was saying and doing. I dimly sensed that the gathered lamas were forming a perimeter around me, as though they were guarding me. I still wore the alb that I'd donned for the healing ceremony that HE Gonjang Rinpoche had led earlier in the living room. Now I wanted to change into my regular clothes, so Lama Gyatso also summoned several women to escort me to my dressing room so they could report to him anything I said or did. After putting put on casual pants and a large white overshirt, I returned to the lawn, gripped by a forceful inner energy that directed me to the vegetable garden. I found myself walking with a determined gait, but Lama Gyatso stopped me in the prayer garden.

"Sit down, Mary Ann," he said.

Normally, the prayer garden is an invitation in and of itself, with its flagstone terrace, arbor, and fountain. But I bridled at Lama

Gyatso's command, driven by an incomprehensible yet compelling need to get to the vegetable garden on the other side. Despite my impatience, Lama Gyatso's strong arms gently seated me in a wrought-iron chair beside the fountain. The lamas surrounded me and began to chant. HE Gonjang Rinpoche produced a thick package of sacred texts from somewhere deep in his robes. He repeatedly tapped the top of my head with this sacred text in cadence with the chanting of the lamas, which I assumed meant that he was calling in the blessings of the deities, paying tribute and acknowledging their protective presence. Agitated and restless, I tried to stand up. The urgent calls from my inner self increased, and I knew it was very important to get to the vegetable garden, but Lama Gyatso continued to restrain me with a firm hand on my shoulder. Only after HE Gonjang Rinpoche had completed the blessings was I free to move, which I did quite abruptly.

The hillside garden burgeoned with the autumn harvest. White iceberg roses and blue cat mint lined the wide stone path. Terraced vegetable beds overflowed with tomatoes, chili peppers, bell peppers, onions, string beans, cucumbers, melons, and eggplants, as well as a surplus of giant orange pumpkins. The lamas remained at a slight distance. Lama Gyatso watched me from closer by. All were quiet.

Something was calling to me. I stopped by the bed of tomatoes and swept my hand over the plump red globes, frustrated and confused, attempting to explain to those who were near me that these were heirloom tomatoes.

No, not the tomatoes.

I strained to hear this powerful feminine interior voice as I turned to inspect a large watermelon.

No, no, she said. *Keep going.*

And then I saw eggplants the color of nighttime, and stopped.

Yes, the eggplants! Look carefully at them.

Lama Lubdrub was standing next to the garden. I twisted a large eggplant free and turned to him. I looked at the precious fruit in my hands, then at Lama Lubdrub, then back to my offering.

Yes, that's it. Give it to him.

I handed it to him, trying to explain the metaphorical significance that I sensed. "See the color? It's the color. It's deep, dark purple. Do you understand? It's the color of the womb, of the Great Mother. She guides us day by day along the path to liberation."

He looked at me through loving, calm, beneficent eyes, yet was still uncomprehending. Desperate to communicate with him, I felt an inner tugging and, looking back at the eggplant bush, was drawn to a tiny eggplant. Lamas and family members had gathered nearby. They remained outside the vegetable garden, however, and very quiet.

This is the mother's child. Show it to him.

I laid the baby eggplant next to its mother in Lama Lubdrub's large, callused hands. As he and I stared at the eggplants, we went instantly into a deep trance. Our minds now somehow unified. We journeyed to a silent, peaceful, nonhuman place.

When two minds unify, they enter a space where an extraordinary level of communication can take place, not in human language, but in a language beyond words, an angelic language of Light. Light is indeed a language; it speaks to us. In this place, the deeper self emerges. From this deeper self, I was able to convey to Lama Lubdrub a truth that I was completely unaware of on an intellectual level, but that my ordinary self was now beginning to embrace: that this interior voice represented the very essence of my Being. Indeed, in that moment, what I would eventually call my Buddha consciousness had spontaneously raised Lama Lubdrub's consciousness into the realm of union. There, in that Pure Land, we both experienced unequivocally that I was Yeshe Tsogyal, the Mother of All Tibet.

As I began to return to common reality, I was stunned by the expression of recognition on Lama Lubdrub's face and took a step back. His eyes had flown open, and we looked at each other. Then he turned his gaze in a silent stupor upon each individual lama. I felt a tremendous wave of joy. He understood! Finally! As the vast feminine sacred consciousness within me fully expressed herself, she was met with comprehension.

I looked around. Don stood next to HE Gonjang Rinpoche at the edge of the vineyard. The other lamas were spread across the hillside. Aimee sat on a large stone. I felt extraordinary relief, believing that my mission was now over and that life with Don would once again resume its quiet, predictable routine.

Breaking the transcendent silence that permeated the garden, Lama Gyatso shouted, "Save everything she touches. We will bring it all to Ari Bhöd."

The Nyingmas consider objects held by an individual during an entrancement to be powerful divination tools that provide the lamas access to the individual's *mindstream*. I wondered if these items would be used as part of the formal recognition process, which I had learned that HE Chagdud Tulku Rinpoche had initiated ten years before. I sensed that the lamas would need every tool available to them, given that I was an American, a woman, and a former Christian minister. In most ways I existed outside institutional Buddhist structures, so garnering formal recognition of my status was up to the lamas and rinpoches.

For my part, I now knew unequivocally who I was. There was, however, the task of learning how to grow into the extraordinary legacy of Yeshe Tsogyal. The eruption of such visions, the things I heard myself say, the enormity of this transformation remained surprising. I had always aspired to be like the quiet, passive, prayerful Virgin Mary, but Yeshe Tsogyal possessed me with a dynamic, animating intensity. Her presence was an irresistible insertion into my personality, one that simply took charge at times. I never knew what to expect next. All I could do was wait for the next chapter to unfold.

Chapter 17

PILGRIMAGE TO SIKKIM

Your life's journey has an outer purpose and an inner purpose…. Your outer journey may contain a million steps; your inner journey only has one: the step you are taking right now.

—ECKHART TOLLE, *The Power of Now*

IT WAS FEBRUARY 2004, and I was destined for Chorten Gonpa, monastic home to the renowned abbot His Holiness the Fourth Dodrupchen Rinpoche, as well as to three thousand monks and nuns, ages three to one hundred. I had been invited by Lama Gyatso to participate in Losar, the annual Tibetan New Year religious celebrations. I yearned to be with the lamas and to commune fully with the altered states I had been experiencing since my visions in the vegetable garden. I was being called deeper into such spiritual experiences, whatever challenges that might involve.

As the plane tilted momentarily to the right, the mountain deities of the Himals appeared below us, and once again I felt the majestic embrace of their sharp peaks and glaciers, within which were enfolded monasteries, prayer flags, and the rhythmic beating of ritual monastic drums. I was returning to the land of snow and Tibetan Buddhism, where bells had rung harmonies of compassion, strength, and courage across mountaintops for over a thousand years. As I gazed through the ice crystals ringing the plane's oval window, as I had done fifteen years before, the allure and challenge presented by the massive forms of stone and ice called to me. Hidden between those frigid mountaintops lay my destination, the ancient Kingdom of Sikkim—and, I was convinced, My Yogi, who continued to appear to me in visions.

I disembarked and merged with the flow of arriving passengers, following signs that pointed the way to passport control, baggage and customs, and finally the terminal's reception area. The usual sea of name-signs, printed in a variety of foreign alphabets, bobbed up and down. A handsome young man with café-au-lait skin, shining dark eyes, and black hair held high a sign bearing my hand-printed name. This was Tensing, who did not speak English. He wordlessly picked up my suitcase and carried it to a dirty, battered, and apparently bullet-riddled Jeep in the parking lot. An implosion of anxiety vaporized my euphoria. Who was this man? Was he really expecting me to climb into this wreck of a Jeep? Did he actually know who I was? Did he know where I was going or at least where I was supposed to be going? I refused to get in the Jeep until we had signed a few key words like "Sikkim," "Gangtok," and "Chorten Gonpa," and I was reasonably convinced that he was indeed my appointed driver. Tensing hopped into the driver's seat, gunned the engine, and off we went.

The Jeep jerked its way into altitude, through impossibly green tea plantations, past mud-plastered huts with straw roofs, through jungles inhabited by chattering monkeys, through rhododendron forests, past rock slides, around crater-sized potholes. I stared straight ahead, too fearful to peer into the bottomless ravines with their nearly vertical sides. I prayed for the length of the narrow, twisting road to Sikkim. *God help me, what have I done this time?* At one point, sweating with uncertainty, I poked Tensing's shoulder, pointing ahead and asking, "Sikkim?" Tensing turned to flash me the high sign of adventure as we skidded around a huge boulder, tires inches from the edge of yet another infinite drop to nowhere. I decided not to distract him again.

Although I had originally planned to make this journey with Lama Gyatso and his entourage, I had abandoned that plan due to illness. I disliked traveling alone, but whatever challenges I had experienced while traveling on my own had always, in the end, increased my self-confidence. Leaving my world behind to follow these lamas halfway around the globe seemed natural at the time. I was confident that my motives for this journey were well-advised. Nonetheless, I deeply missed Lama Gyatso's competent, firm, charismatic presence and was anxious to reach Chorten Gonpa, where I would reunite with him and the seven other lamas I had not seen since their extraordinary visit to the Family Home and Ari Bhöd the prior autumn.

Reassuring myself that Tensing and I would reach Chorten Gonpa soon enough, I leaned against the cracked, dusty vinyl seat of the Jeep and relaxed. We drove for several hours on serpentine roads, past sheer cliffs and jagged gashes of ravines, eventually passing through picturesque Gangtok, a town-city built into the steep cliffs of the 28,000-foot Mount Kangchenjunga. Homes, shops, stalls, and vendors lined ancient footpaths that now were roads, although barely wide enough for modern vehicles, on the mountainous terrain of the world's third-highest peak. Ear-popping altitude increased until at last we reached Chorten Gonpa, which lay on the outskirts of Gangtok. I gratefully exited the Jeep.

I began the final ascent on foot amid hundreds of weather-faded prayer flags. I climbed to the beat of drums, cymbals, long horns, and short horns, as thousands of seekers gathered above to chant in Losar, the Tibetan New Year. The air rolled in waves of rainbow light, a radiance that seemed to reflect off prisms encapsulated in each atom of the purified air. Here, mountains and glaciers met sky.

"Mary Ann, you are here!" Lama Gyatso's jubilant bellow filled the air as he walked toward me, grinning widely.

With moist eyes, I responded, "Yes, I have arrived."

"Come," my friend said, as he led me toward the monastery complex. "His Holiness is waiting to bless your arrival. It is always best, Mary Ann, to enter the mountain in silence." During our silent approach into crystal blue skies, a rush of joy swept through my body.

Divining the chaos Tibet was to experience, His Holiness the Fourth Dodrupchen Rinpoche had fled Tibet in October 1957. The semi-independent Sikkimese government, thrilled to have such an illustrious rinpoche take up residency in Sikkim, granted HH Dodrupchen Rinpoche this spectacular mountaintop for the monastery that came to be known as Chorten Gonpa. Over time, HH Dodrupchen Rinpoche had become one of Tibetan Buddhism's greatest living saints and leaders, a renowned spiritual and administrative leader for all Tibetans. "Even the Dalai Lama requests teachings from His Holiness," Lama Gyatso once whispered reverently.

As Lama Gyatso and I walked through the resplendent light that bathed Chorten Gonpa, we were joined by his childhood friend Khenpo

Chowang Rinpoche. The three of us entered a central courtyard, surrounded on three sides by buildings. Children darted about through wisps of incense smoke as dusk approached, and young male monks walked hand-in-hand with family members they saw only once a year. Many of these monks were in fact still boys. Their spiritual training required that they go for long periods without seeing their families of origin in order to cultivate detachment from their home lives and to form attachments to the family of monks. The nostalgia triggered by family visits can interrupt the flow of monastic spiritual energy, reconnecting to which can take much time and effort.

We approached a series of five *stupas*, which are mound-like structures that serve to house relics and facilitate meditation.

"We will circumnavigate the largest first," said Lama Gyatso.

"Each *stupa* represents a different facet of the mind. We have spent fifty years building them," Khenpo Chowang Rinpoche said with pride.

As we circled the largest *stupa*, which represented the enlightened mind of Tibet's great saint Padmasambhava, Lama Gyatso must have noticed my exhaustion. "After your exciting trip, maybe your mind needs a little calming, yes? We all need to visit the *stupas* after driving up the mountain." He began to laugh. "Do you know the Indianapolis 500? Some of us believe that in their last lifetime maybe our drivers raced cars there!"

I joined in the merriment and gentle laughter, breathing in the crisp evening air as the sky darkened. Khenpo Chowang drifted away and Lama Gyatso led me to a dilapidated green wooden bench.

"Every year," he said, "we drive all our Jeeps to Bhutan, then ferry the Bhutanese back here for Losar. It's a three-day drive and involves navigating one of the world's most dangerous, terrorist-filled roads, and, yes, those were bullet holes you saw."

I was surprised, for I had not mentioned my observation to him.

"The Bhutanese are so devoted to His Holiness," he continued, "they risk their lives annually to come here and again to return home."

"Are any killed along the way?" I asked, suddenly nauseated.

Ever the artful dodger, he responded, "We will go see Khandro-la now, Mary Ann."

Lama Gyatso explained that Khandro-la was the wife of His Holiness, speaking of her with such devotion that I knew he held her in the highest esteem. Khandro-la and His Holiness accepted every fleeing Tibetan, Sikkimese, and Bhutanese who made it to Sikkim and Chorten Gonpa. Some took monastic vows, while others worked elsewhere in the large compound.

In addition to the monastery's usual population of monks, nuns, and refugees, five thousand pilgrims had gathered for the Losar celebration. Despite the presence of this multitude, calmness enveloped the monastery grounds in a profound sense of quiet discipline. We walked past huge cauldrons filled with the staple food for those gathered: boiling water and rice mixed with smatterings of chopped vegetables and small portions of meat, which were included whenever it was available. Then, entering a glass shelter, we were surrounded by hundreds of burning butter lamps whose flickering tongues carried skyward the pleas and prayers of the grateful, the hopeful, and the suffering. Nuns, glowing with perspiration, stirred melting coconut butter over open fires, then filled and refilled the lamps as the mountain sky became radiant with twilight hues of orange, blue, and purple.

"The lamas have kept that row of butter lamps burning for your safe arrival, Mary Ann," Lama Gyatso told me while we stood inside the hot enclosure. All the years I had spent feeling invisible in my birth family and first marriage and marginalized within the Christian church hierarchy seemed to disappear in the all-consuming love that surrounded me.

We headed toward the buildings at the far end of the courtyard, where a line of about a hundred people stood waiting quietly. Throughout the next several weeks, this line was constantly replenished with silent men and women who held to their hearts gifts and offerings for HH Dodrupchen Rinpoche. Lama Gyatso spoke in a hushed voice. "The people standing there are Bhutanese devotees of His Holiness. He greets and blesses each person, hour after hour, week after week, until attendants need to hold his fatigued arms up. Attendants ask him to rest, but His Holines always replies no. He's seventy-nine years old, you know."

Lama Gyatso opened a door and ushered me into a small square room containing a bed and several chairs. On the bed sat an elderly Tibetan woman dressed in worn clothing, a threadbare knit cap partially covering her unruly gray hair. The bed was layered with pillows and blankets as old and mussed as she was. Here, nevertheless, was a widely revered spiritual figure. She was surrounded by lamas and engaged in a lively discussion. Unaware of her great mystical accomplishments, I sat next to her on the bed and wondered what the subject of their discussion might be. They paused to smile at me and then resumed. By this time, I had already spent many an hour with the lamas and was accustomed to this process. My silence allowed me a few moments to take in the new and exotic surroundings.

Eventually, a nun in maroon robes entered with an offering raised over her shaved head—a small china plate bearing an apple pierced with toothpicks, each of which held a small square of soft orange cheese. The nun bowed reverently and offered this simple yet elegant gift to

Khandro-la, who received it with outstretched arms, then offered it to all. The plate passed from hand to hand. I have never seen a lama eat a bite of food without praying, as these lamas did now, cheese cubes resting on their open palms. I was deeply moved and humbled.

Soon Lama Gyatso turned to me. "Come, Mary Ann. It is time for you to receive the blessings of His Holiness." The lamas stood, exuberance radiating from their faces due to the knowledge that I would now meet their beloved master. I bowed and bid Khandro-la farewell.

As I took leave of Khandro-la and prepared to enter the chamber of His Holiness, the air seemed electrified, and my body was charged with adrenaline. My introduction to His Holiness was of tremendous personal import to me as a student of Buddhism and because I was holding out hope that he might be My Yogi. I also knew that I was being presented as a living incarnation of Yeshe Tsogyal, as one who had consciously experienced her enlightened Buddha nature. I assumed that, as an American female Christian minister, I was a controversial figure for consideration. Had Lama Gyatso put his credibility on the line? Was I under any particular scrutiny? Would my conduct serve as evidence of my qualification and authenticity? Wouldn't a true Buddha be expected to proceed through such meetings and ceremonies with instinctive proficiency? Nyingma rituals are often quite precise and elaborate, and Lama Gyatso had taken pains to prepare me on how properly to present my offerings: a *katak* and an envelope with a cash gift. Simple enough on the surface, yet I remained conscious of all that would be conveyed in the exchange.

Lama Gyatso stood next to a pair of weathered green doors that led out of Khandro-la's room. He held one door open, gesturing for me to open the adjoining one, as each door was so narrow that both had to stand open in order for a person to pass through. I hesitated, then pushed it open, feeling the profound import of what lay beyond those doors. The passage we entered was dim and filled with the shadowy outlines of consecrated Buddhist ceremonial objects like *phurbas* (ritual daggers) and *dorjes* (ritual scepters), which rested on tables and hung from walls. Lama Gyatso hurried me along the passage. From beneath the curtains ahead, streams of peach and golden light flowed toward me, as though in greeting. Lama Gyatso motioned me to approach the light. Together we stepped into the warm radiance of HH Dodrupchen Rinpoche's chamber.

What happened next isn't entirely clear. Although I was apparently successful in making my offerings, I don't remember doing so. All I remember is being drawn spontaneously to my knees at the feet of His Holiness. As I did so, this incomparable jewel, whose boundless compassion for all sentient beings was legendary, laid his warm hands upon my head, held them there, and prayed. The gentle, calming imprint of his palms seeped into my body, where it flowed like a timeless fluid throughout my being as my heart joined with his. My mind emptied. I knelt immobile, caught between the spaces in the web of the eons, beyond origination and cessation.

During those moments of welcome and blessing, I forgot about my search for My Yogi. Whoever My Yogi might be, HH Dodrupchen Rinpoche represented all that I yearned for. He was a living reflection of the Nyingmas' astounding body of indestructible wisdom, a great master of the mind, of mysteries and miracles. He taught others how to transform themselves, how to help themselves and others navigate sorrow and increase happiness, and ultimately led all beings toward enlightenment. Wasn't this exactly what I sought?

Chapter 18

LOSAR

The Ancient Masters were subtle, mysterious,
profound, responsive.
The depth of their knowledge is unfathomable.
Because it is unfathomable, all we can do is
describe their appearance.
Watchful, like men crossing a winter stream.
Alert, like men aware of danger.
Courteous, like visiting guests.
Yielding, like ice about to melt.
Simple, like uncarved blocks of wood.

—LAO TZU, *Tao Te Ching*

FOR CLOSE TO A THOUSAND YEARS, during the days leading up to Losar, worshippers throughout Tibet have devoted themselves to prayer to pacify negative karma brought forward from the preceding year. This ancient and much-loved celebration persists, as well, throughout the Tibetan Nation-in-Exile.

When I entered the temple with Lama Gyatso on the first day of pre-Losar rituals, he said, "Mary Ann, I have reserved a seat for you close to me and next to Khandro-la. Come now, hurry along." We deposited our shoes and sandals atop a huge pile of footwear and entered through a glass door. Feeling both self-conscious and exhilarated, staring straight ahead, I followed Lama Gyatso to a faded red plastic chair, which I grew to cherish, not only because it saved me from the physical challenge of sitting on the floor, but because it represented Lama Gyatso's efforts to take care of me. Once seated, I was consumed by the energy of the moment. Muscular lamas clashed heavy cymbals to generate fiery sparks of invitation to the invisible beings who inhabit the realms of the Ten Directions described by the Nyingmas. A storm moved overhead. Thunderclaps roared off the mountaintops as though the chariots of the deities were cresting the icy winter peaks in answer to the chanted summons. Sikkim's guardian dragons—lightning, thunder, and wind—sucked oxygen from the temple. What enemies would have dared threaten our gathered assembly in the face of these fierce protectors? These roaring sky dragons merged to become the one mighty Protector Dragon of Sikkim: rain.

The heavenly waters felt as if they were sent to wash away all obstacles to HH Dodrupchen Rinpoche's devotees, purifying the mountaintop home of the Holy Ones. Maroon-and-yellow-robed monks beat a steady rhythm on drums of many sizes. Horns, long and short, straight and curved, cried the ancient chants as Lama Gyatso's students from several continents sat gracefully in the lotus position. My lama's radiant smile enlivened me while howling, darkening skies alternately dimmed and brightened the temple light of burning butter lamps. Lightning bolts shot past temple windows as the ceaseless beat played hour after hour. The rising cacophony helped to release our bodies into timelessness and our minds from all artificial constraints.

I began to sense the presence of the sky dancers known as *dakinis*, energetic beings who take female form to evoke pure potentiality by moving energy in space. These ethereal presences joined the temple throng of swirling primary colors in a wild, careening dance. Awe had arrived, holding all of us in its thrall of hurtling diamond arrows, which pierced barriers to compassion and opened the view to the Pure Land. As with all the Nyingma rituals I'd experienced, the liturgical sounds, colors, and aromas immediately gentled me into a hypnotic trance, and my body became a harp of ten thousand strings playing the song of eternity.

The cadence eventually slowed, and silence overtook us as the day ended. The lamas removed their yellow, rooster-tail-shaped hats. Smiling monks arrived carrying large baskets of consecrated snacks, and they showered us with cookies, candy, citrus, and nuts. Toothless, giggling *anni-las*, beloved grandmothers, surrounded me, trying to catch the goodies, which quickly disappeared, stuffed into faded cotton *chubas*. Imitating Khandro-la, who I noticed was transferring her own treats into the gnarled hands of the *anni-las*, I too passed my treats to the precious human beings crowded about me.

Each morning after breakfast I joined the temple crowds, leaving my shoes among huge piles of plastic go-aheads and Western footwear. Inside the colorful temple, we sat from dawn to dusk, participating in the cleansing rituals for the days leading up to Losar. Following Nyingma tradition, we began with confessionals and purification rites, calling in the pain of the cosmos and transforming it. After the gathering of blessings, embodied in the food and drink, we sat motionless through the day, absorbing the electrical currents of mantric syllables, while monks, hidden in their cells, supported us with their spiritual rituals, meditation, and fasting. Through fasting, the monks sought to cultivate an altered state of mind, not unlike going up in altitude, in which through greater clarity they were better able to project their minds and thus escalate the intensity of divine energy for the benefit of those in attendance and everywhere. Such magnified energy opens hearts to profound spiritual insight, so that all beings might move past suffering and attain enlightenment.

Thus the days passed in the temple. The masters rolled out their robes for us. Following maps only they could see, we took weightless flights into mysterious realms. At day's end, once home from the land of omniscient wisdom, unconditional love, and enlightened power, I would stand up, legs cramped and numb, my back in spasms, to hobble my twisted body toward the guesthouse, where I would collapse, shaky with exhaustion. HH Dodrupchen Rinpoche, however, would be carried out of the temple back to his throne room, where he would continue to bless the patiently waiting Bhutanese, one by one.

Along with the intensification of energy came an increasing number of devotees, who arrived in a steady stream over the course of the retreat. Then, for the final day of Losar, which begins and ends at dusk, huge numbers arrived all at once, the crowds swelling from three thousand to five thousand during the night's vigil. The Bhutanese and Tibetans around me, old and young, catnapped on the floor and snored until their neighbors poked them in the ribs. Children slept nestled in parent's laps. During these last twenty-four hours, we remained inside the temple, the monks relieving each other in shifts in the long lines of horn and drum players.

The conclusion of the retreat unfolded as a grand finale of butter lamps, instruments, and incense until the golden dusk bowed her way off the temple stage into an absolute and magical silence. The sunset illuminated thousands of faces filled with pure, unfettered adoration, each turned toward HH Dodrupchen Rinpoche. My heart skipped several beats. I then turned my gaze toward His Holiness, and in another heart-stopping moment I realized that this humble saint had sat throughout the retreat, maintaining an elevated state of meditation in complete silence. Without saying a word, he had transformed the people gathered before him. I suddenly understood what it meant to be in the presence of a higher being, one who possessed enough patience and control over the cosmic power flowing through him to empty the ocean drop by drop with a blade of grass. Until that moment, I had not experienced the exalted spiritual presence of such a being in human form.

From the perspective of my Western mind, I was witnessing a miracle. The hours I would spend preparing just one twenty-minute sermon back home—the research, the logic, the attempts at intellectual discourse—had never come close to invoking the spiritual ecstasy that now surrounded and filled me. But here, through the enlightened use of color, sound, aromas, sacred art, and mantric vibrations, the vast congregation had been transported to a new level of consciousness. The collective essence of the congregation shone outward, suffusing the temple with sensual and mystical radiance. Although deprived of sleep, I felt strangely alive, rested, and composed. I was in love with His Holiness, with Khandro-la, with everyone and everything that surrounded me.

Chapter 19

THE WILD-HAIRED YOGI

In the history of humankind, never before has there been a less spiritual age. Never before have we paid so little attention to the human soul. Never before have we been more obsessed with the material world and less connected to the spiritual one. The result is a generation of unhappy people who disguise their melancholy with the quest for power and material wealth. The question of who we are cannot be asked without first asking who we were. Not to do so is walking away from past knowledge that has future implications.

—M. J. ROSE, *The Reincarnationist*

MY HAVEN BETWEEN temple sessions during the retreat was a weather-beaten green bench, the sole piece of furniture in the courtyard of the *stupas*. As I sat there one day, I was surprised to see a barefoot man with untamed hair, dressed in a short, threadbare *chuba*, bound up the steep hill to the *gonpa*. I assumed he was Bhutanese. Yelling and gesticulating at whoever crossed his path, he arrived at the monastery's magnificent gold-domed *chorten*—a monument reflecting the perfect proportions of the Buddha's body—which was surrounded by a six-foot-tall wrought-iron fence. He strained against the bars, but they pressed back, so he bent down to extend skeletal arms through the fence and scoop up coins tossed there as gifts to the Buddha. He was stealing money offered in supplication and gratitude by the devotees! He grabbed all the reachable offerings and stuffed them into the fold of his *chuba*. Before long, a wide swath circling the interior of the fence around the *chorten* was stripped of offerings. I watched him with raised eyebrows, appalled by his impropriety. Why was no one stopping him?

Then the wild-haired yogi climbed the fence, agile as a monkey, lightly dropped down on the other side, and rushed to the *chorten*. He embraced the statue, covering it with joyous kisses. His laughter proclaimed what I assumed to be paeans of love. I'd never seen a public display of such pure, undefiled, passionate devotion. This exuberant thief captivated me.

He climbed down from the statue, scurried over the fence, and accosted everyone in his immediate vicinity, yelling and pointing. Was he lecturing or proselytizing? I wanted to avoid his gaze and his ranting. I pulled my sun hat low over my face and donned my sunglasses in an effort to make myself small, obscure, and hopefully invisible, but I was a white-haired, middle-aged white woman standing five feet ten inches tall. I must have looked like a silly ostrich trying to poke her head in the sand.

Over the next few days, the trodden path about the famous statue became the wild-haired yogi's temple. He held court. Whether he was inside the fence sweeping up his dues or outside the metal enclosure, people accepted both the man and his apparent lunacy. He did not join the temple crowd inside the large hall; he looked so feral I doubted that he frequented the interior of any building.

He repeated his noisy circumambulations each day, and I continued to evade him until one afternoon I noticed a group of boys who I thought were taunting him. Without thinking, I jumped up from the bench, grabbed my ever-present walking poles, and waved them at the boys.

"Stop that!" I yelled. "Don't you hurt him. How dare you show such disrespect!"

The wild-haired yogi stared at me.

I turned away and saw Lama Gyatso standing by my bench, an unreadable look on his face. Embarrassed, I apologized.

"I don't know what made me do that, Lama Gyatso."

Casually, he said, "Mary Ann, let's take a walk, have a little chitchat. Nothing important."

"Chitchat," of course, meant that a teaching was imminent.

As we strolled, Lama Gyatso asked, "Do you know what a *beyul* is?"

This word was new to me, but then again I was surrounded by what seemed new, yet at the same time wasn't. While I had never heard the Tibetan word *beyul*, I had a feeling this word and concept would open doors to a primordial past with which I was deeply familiar, if only at the level of the subconscious. These masters regularly thrust me into new planes of awareness that destabilized the cherished psychological structures that I'd inherited from family, church, and nation. Their teachings acted like lightning bolts, swiftly striking down ignorance and years of false emotional belief systems. Frustration would follow, shooting a barrage of merciless arrows into my brain and *heart-mind*, driving me uncomfortably along the path of discovery.

But such experiences were just as often sublime. Walking with Lama Gyatso, I remembered a summer evening with HE Chagdud Tulku Rinpoche, not long after we met, when we stood together in the family garden and looked over the moonlit valley below.

"Rinpoche, is it right for me to be a Christian minister, a hospice chaplain, and a Buddhist?" I had asked. "I don't want to compromise the scriptures of either tradition. I don't want to mislead or confuse people."

The fragrant evening was bright with stars, and the dazzling, near-full moon hung over the heavy-leafed August vineyards below. Heavenly aromas of jasmine, honeysuckle, and rose wafted softly on the air.

"Look at the moon," he said and pointed his finger at the silently drifting lunar goddess. "Look. See laser beam go from finger, shoot path straight to moon?"

I pointed, too, and a path of silvery light from my finger connected me to the moon.

"See light from my finger? It goes straight to moon also, yes? So which is true path to moon? Yours or mine? Now see people all over the world pointing to moon like you point, like I point. Many pathways, yes?"

Rinpoche continued to point at the moon, and I envisioned the sky filled with silvery highways, with people from all walks of life, from all nations and religions, standing and pointing to the same moon.

"Your path, my path close, not same, but close. Both true. Many paths authentic. Not all, but many."

At Chorten Gonpa, in the shadow of Mount Kangchenjunga, walking head bowed, I slipped my hands into the sleeves of my down coat and waited. I knew that Lama Gyatso would offer no definitive, intellectual analysis of my interaction with the wild-haired yogi from Bhutan, but would instead provide clues or hints to help me find my own way.

"Mary Ann, Lhatsun Namkha Jigme, or Fearless Sky, was a wild-haired yogi who spent years meditating in caves," Lama Gyatso began. "He received a vision showing him where certain sacred scrolls were hidden. He went to this place near Chorten Gonpa, up there," he said pointing to the mountain. "Then he dug them up out of the earth. These cryptic yellow scrolls contained accounts of *beyuls*, remote Himalayan valleys where plants and animals have miraculous powers. The scrolls spoke of hidden places where aging halts and enlightenment can be quickly attained."

"Lama Gyatso, are you saying Shangri-La exists?"

He disregarded my question. "Lhatsun Namkha Jigme left his followers behind and crossed the Himalayas in the year of the Fire Dog, guided by a *dakini* in the form of a white vulture. Fearless Sky crossed the face of an ice-fluted wall. He descended into a maze of mist-shrouded ravines beneath Mount Kangchenjunga, searching for the door to the innermost realm beyond the *beyul*. Weeks passed, and Fearless Sky's disciples assumed he had perished. They began to build a cairn to honor his passing. Suddenly, they heard the shrill blast of his *kangling* echoing from those cliffs up there." Lama Gyatso gestured toward the high passes. *Kanglings* were ritual instruments made from human thighbones. Their purpose was to sever one's attachments to the human body and to outdated forms of thought by replacing them with sudden, momentary glimpses of truth or flashes of inspiration.

Eyes unfocused, staring at someplace far away, Lama Gyatso continued, "Fearless Sky's disciples heard the very same sounds we are hearing now, coming from this very same mountain, from a spot near where we are standing. Soon after, the wild-eyed, wild-haired yogi emerged from the banks of fog, bringing tales of his experiences at the heart of the *beyul*. He wanted his disciples to share in the experience, but he found he was unable to return there when they were with him." Lama Gyatso paused, letting his words sink in. "The hidden realms remain sealed from the outer world not only by towering mountains, dense forests, and glacial passes, but also by veils placed there by Padmasambhava. Only those with the karma to do so can enter the depths of these hidden lands."

We stood motionless, transfixed, the astral light of this holy place flowing through both of us. Lama Gyatso's words seemed to externalize his extraordinary mental state. Rarely in this life have I felt such intimacy with another human being as I did in that moment with Lama Gyatso, whom I called my brother and who called me the Mother of All Tibet.

As we walked back to the temple, I paused and looked intensely at the wild-haired yogi from Bhutan. Perhaps, like Fearless Sky, he had visited the realm into which so few gain entry, the sacred space of enlightenment, which fundamentally transforms the individual, where human concerns about "right" behavior fall away. Those who return from such places act spontaneously, outside norms. They simply respond to their higher selves, unpredictable to those around them. They are the divine clowns of God.

On the day after Losar, the pilgrims started their long trek home. Chorten Gonpa returned to relative silence and calm, but our beloved Lama Gyatso still had many surprises planned for me and for his students over the next few days in Sikkim. He wanted to take us to small fabric shops filled with exquisite brocades and wool in Gangtok. He wanted monastery tailors to measure us for new outfits. He had arranged for feasts at restaurants and for tea with the Sikkimese princess who had financed his first trip to America. We were to visit HE Gonjang Rinpoche's monastery, joining him and his beautiful wife, Semola, a Bhutanese princess, for a post-Losar luncheon. Lama Gyatso also planned for us to make a pilgrimage to a statue of *Guru Rinpoche* that had been built under the auspices of HH Dodrupchen Rinpoche.

However, Lama Gyatso's health had been compromised by his efforts during the retreat, leaving him so weak it frightened me. He often experienced periods of extreme debility after events into which he had poured his energy for the benefit of others. Knowing that his charismatic youthfulness disguised serious health issues—resulting from his childhood in refugee camps, which involved years of inadequate diet and exposure to hepatitis C, which had severely damaged his liver over time—I visited him in his bedroom to attempt to dissuade him from pursuing the plans he had made. He slept on the floor. Only a thin mattress separated him from the damp chill of the concrete ground. Lying there unable to move, yet with incredible faith, devotion, and gratitude, he whispered that I was not to worry, as His Holiness was performing special prayers for him.

I remained concerned. I left him to rest, walked to the glass hut where the flickering butter lamps burned, added my prayers for his improved health, and went to meditate on the green bench. As I contemplated Lama Gyatso's troubling health crisis, praying for his recovery and reminiscing about our friendship, I noticed the wild-haired yogi walking from the large gold-domed *chorten* in uncharacteristic silence. He was heading straight toward the green bench where I sat.

No, I prayed, *I'm not ready for this. I'll sit still, I won't move a muscle, I'll do anything, just don't let him come any closer.*

My prayers went unanswered. He approached and sat at the other end of the bench. Rigid, I slid as far as I could without falling off.

Don't come closer, I thought. *Please stay where you are.*

He inched his way toward me. I stared straight ahead, trying to ignore him. He laid his head on my shoulder and curled his body, childlike, next to me, half sitting on my lap as though I were his mother and he my child. An unexpected warmth of spirit flowed through me as my body relaxed into a marvelous experience of—love! Yes! A maternal wave of joyous love swept over me. He and I sat like mother and child, utterly still, when the head nun approached and handed the yogi his Losar gift, a number of paper bills. (Gifts of food, necessities, and cash are traditionally made during Losar.) The yogi's arm shot out like a lizard's tongue to grab the money, which he stuffed deep inside his *chuba.* He put his head back on my shoulder, and again I fell into a deep state of relaxation. The nun remained, observing us with curiosity.

At that moment, I looked directly at the vast countenance of the brilliant sun shining behind the nun and I heard my inner voice exclaim, *Well! Here we are once again—just the three of us, together after such a long time.* I doubt the Mother Superior lost her composure often, but as my Inner Teacher spoke, her lips parted and her eyes widened. I was sure she had heard my silent voice. The three of us remained motionless, bathed in the brilliant, canary-colored light of the daytime star, and time stood still. Regenerated by the solar force, I was filled with exultation at this reunion. I was ecstatic. We had been separated for lifetimes, I understood, but now we were reunited. I continued to gaze directly at the sun and the nun.

After a mysterious period in no-time, the nun departed toward the rooms of Khandro-la and His Holiness. Not long after she disappeared, four other wild-haired yogis bounded up the hillside from the same direction. I'd seen none of them before that moment. My wild-haired yogi was multiplying before my eyes, dressed identically in worn-out *chubas*. The yogis laughed as they swerved around our bench. Playfully, they slapped and seemed to congratulate my wild-haired yogi, then cried out teasing words and gestured toward the parking area. I assumed they were saying, "Come on, the Jeeps are leaving. We have to go." For a split second, I thought my wild-haired yogi would ignore them and choose to stay with me. He let them run ahead, but then he lifted effortlessly off the bench and chased after them. They wove their way downhill in an undulating line of flying, dancing leaps.

My heart plunged. I wanted to cry. I stood up and reached out my arms. *Don't leave yet. Please don't go. Don't leave me again!* But they disappeared in a flash. I sat down, put on my sunglasses, and pulled my hat brim low to hide my profound feeling of loss. The grief I felt at the departure of the wild-haired yogi felt somehow connected to my grief at the likelihood that Lama Gyatso, too, would soon depart, a possibility I had yet to fully acknowledge. I had become increasingly dependent on Lama Gyatso's friendship and guidance on the spiritual path, and the prospect of his death was painful. In the midst of my sorrow, however, was the realization that that strange, skinny Bhutanese yogi had taken me to a deathless eternal space and shown me an everlasting home in the world beyond, where consciousness abides. From that experience I understood that impermanency relates only to the physical body and that my connection with Lama Gyatso would never die.

Chapter 20

VULTURE BEAUTY AND THE TWENTY-ONE TARAS

The simplest but highest and deepest teachings and training in the Nyingma is the Great Perfection meditation, known in Tibetan as Dzog Chen, a meditation for bringing the mind to the ultimate ease, the natural and undeluded state. It is the swiftest and most extraordinary means to dissolve the phenomena of mental fabrication into the absolute nature, Buddhahood. Great Perfection practitioners are remarkable for their attainment of the result. They train themselves through natural means to achieve the ultimate state in a short time. Those who are trained in this meditation, in addition to being normal, simple, and easy to be with, possess clairvoyance, miraculous power, and wisdom of bliss and emptiness. Many who have attained the realization of this practice dissolve their mortal bodies at death without leaving behind any remains. This is a sign that they have attained the fully enlightened state of Buddhahood.

—TULKU THONDUP, *Hidden Teachings of Tibet*

For the next twenty-four hours, a group of monks sat with Lama Gyatso. Joined with His Holiness's *mindstream*, they prayed for my beloved soul brother's recovery and the restoration of his energy. I, too, prayed fervently for his health. Happily, Lama Gyatso's condition did improve, dramatically. Once he was restored to his normal energetic self, he met me in the courtyard by the green bench, where he described his plans for the American contingent's day trip to the statue of Guru Rinpoche.

"Before construction of the Guru Rinpoche statue began," he said, "His Holiness spent months preparing meticulous architectural and engineering plans. Minute attention to the smallest of details consumed His Holiness and lama-artists for months, even before the first shovel of dirt was moved." Lama Gyatso spoke emphatically, seeming intent on conveying something of significance.

It was difficult to reconcile the physically weakened man who had barely been able to speak two days ago with the vibrant man in front of me. Still inundated with the visionary events of the retreat and with the circumstances surrounding Lama Gyatso's illness, I had a difficult time attending to his high-spirited remarks.

Lama Gyatso's muscular body was tense and his eyes penetrated mine, looking far past my state of mind. "Originally, His Holiness selected a certain small statue to replicate in the creation of the much larger Guru Rinpoche statue, but after studying it closely, he decided it would not do. He had found a small imperfection and told the engineers and architects, 'If we copy this statue as it is, this small imperfection will be magnified many thousand times. This flaw will be an obstacle to those who gaze upon it. We must find another prototype.'"

I tried to concentrate and look interested, but we had already seen many statues. Another statue was, it seemed to me, just another statue.

"Mary Ann, if we are to preserve these ancient sacred art forms of Tibet at Ari Bhöd–Pema Drawa, we need to pay attention to all that His Holiness does. You and I have a profound purpose and must concentrate on the meticulous details just as His Holiness does, even though most observers will rarely be conscious of such minutiae. It is our responsibility to ensure there are no obstacles created to block the paths of spiritual seekers who come to us at Ari Bhöd."

The mountain slopes and streams of Ari Bhöd were dedicated to housing and preserving Tibet's ancient sacred art forms, which otherwise were disappearing along with the great masters who carried their secrets. These art forms—including *stupas*, *thangka*s, painted mandalas, and three-dimensional mandalas—all serve as representations of the human mind, as artistic maps designed to lead seekers into meditative states, as aids to help to unlock the deepest reaches of consciousness. While I clearly understood the importance of preserving these artistic guides to our sacred inner landscapes, I was surprised to hear that this would be my responsibility. I now finally gathered myself to pay strict attention to Lama Gyatso, but he had already said what he had needed to say.

The day of the outing dawned clear and warm. We American students of Lama Gyatso were relaxed, happy to be wearing casual clothes, and giddy with expansive Losar energy as we piled into our vehicles for the trip, which routed us around one of the many mountains surrounding Gangtok and Chorten Gonpa. We drove past patches of snow still clinging to narrow dirt roads. We bounced and jolted through tea plantations, forests, and small farming endeavors.

Along the way, we experienced multiple mechanical breakdowns. These were social, communal moments. All the Jeeps stopped, and the drivers gathered under lifted hoods, conferring, pointing, and pondering until they could agree as to what next needed jury-rigging. Inside the Jeeps, we Americans peppered Lama Gyatso with questions and gawked at snow-capped mountains just over the Tibetan border. We were in no hurry.

At midmorning we disembarked and crossed the torn-up terrain of a construction site. After we had walked a short distance, an extraordinary statue appeared, four stories high and as wide as a city block. Guru Rinpoche. I stopped in my tracks. How could HH Dodrupchen Rinpoche have built something this size in the middle of nowhere? Were we supposed to build something like this at Ari Bhöd? Lama Gyatso, born and trained as a leader, thought in terms of abundance, but my cosmology, in terms of projects on this scale, was more limited, more directed toward spiritual and material poverty than toward abundance. Still, the words of Helen Keller came to mind: "Life is either a daring adventure, or nothing. One can never consent to creep when one feels an impulse to soar." Lama Gyatso was born to soar, and given the events of the preceding days, I was waking up once again to the fact that I was too.

The statue, which appeared to grow ever larger as we approached, stands as a symbol of the fact that all sentient beings are, at some level, conscious of a universal language. Guru Rinpoche represents our higher selves, our own Buddha nature, yoked to the *mindstream* of all enlightened beings, past and present. Lama Gyatso and I simultaneously and spontaneously recited mantras as we walked the promenade that encircled the huge statue. I felt miniature by comparison. Yet I sensed a living presence radiate from the statue, reminding me of who I was, who I was capable of being, who we all are capable of being. *Is this who I am? Can I activate this sort of majestic power within me?* There is a teaching about how the vibratory energy of one ocean wave, when it strikes the land, however large or small that wave might be, sets into motion vibrations felt throughout the universe. That statue set into motion an opening of my mind that continues to expand, even to this day.

Off to the side was a small, tastefully built cabin. When we reached it, Lama Gyatso explained in reverent tones, "This was built for His Holiness as a place to rest and pray during construction. Sometimes he stayed overnight here. We will go inside for tea and rest ourselves. Only rarely is anyone allowed to enter." How fortunate we felt as we single-filed into the tidy, whitewashed, sparsely furnished room. His Holiness's bed, a rustic affair of ropes and wood, stood against the far wall, leaving a floor space large enough for our group to sit cross-legged in a circle. Lama Gyatso's family, along with several other lamas and attendants, were with us. There must have been a kitchen, because Lama Gyatso's wife, Linnea, and the attendants served us hot tea in cups and saucers, along with a plate of biscuits. "Whenever someone comes to visit, always offer the gift of food," Lama Gyatso had taught me.

The *sangha* sat in silence as we sipped our tea and nibbled on biscuits. Suddenly and without warning, my body became rigid and I was thrust upright. I entered into a clairvoyant and clairsentient state: before me was the vision of two infants. I lifted my cup and in an elated voice said, "I propose a toast to the newest members of our *sangha*." The lamas recognized that I was in a condition of entrancement, and I was pleased they understood. The others, however, looked at me with uncertain expressions. "The twins have been born!" I said and laughed. "They are fine! They are fine! Aimee is fine! They are all fine!" I later learned that my beloved daughter Aimee was, at that moment, successfully giving birth to twins, a boy and a girl, each weighing over eight pounds. Like me in my state of trance, the twins were "out of their bodies" in the moment before birth and were visiting me, as my other grandchildren had done before they had been born.

"How do you know this?" asked one of Lama Gyatso's students.

"Know what?" I asked her.

She looked at me, confused, and replied, "Know that the twins have been born."

"I can feel them! I can sense them. They are fine! Everyone is fine! The twins, they are right here!" I laughed again, watching their spectral forms float about His Holiness's room. Then, as I returned my cup to the floor, my head flopped to my chest like I was a ragdoll, as often happens after I have been in trance.

We returned to the promenade encircling the Guru Rinpoche statue, again reciting mantras. I remained in a daze, but was aware of Lama Gyatso telling someone, "Follow her. Do not let her out of your sight. Listen to everything she says." I drifted over to the porch railing that surrounded the statue and looked into the steep ravine at a village below, thinking, *How fortunate the people in that village are to live in such a shadow as Guru Rinpoche's.*

A flock of hawks hovered over the village. I had great respect for these messengers of the gods, who often brought news of death, transformation, and change. Playfully but silently I called to them, as was my habit back home. The birds lifted up and out of the ravine, higher and higher as I called. Staring deeply into the dark green space of a mountainside, I slipped back into trance.

The next thing I knew Lama Gyatso was gathering us at the foot of the Guru Rinpoche statue, where we offered a long practice of thanksgiving prayers and enjoyed a late-afternoon picnic in the refreshing, cool sunlight. When dusk's crimson and orange curtains folded over the day, we piled back into the Jeeps to head toward Gangtok. On the outskirts of the city, Lama Gyatso, energetic with excitement and joy, stopped the caravan at a two-story dwelling with a ground-floor bakery to make a telephone call. The rest of us got out and stretched. When Lama Gyatso returned, he carried a bag of fried, sugared bread wrapped in white paper—a delicious Losar treat. I happily joined Lama Gyatso in a high-calorie celebration of our visit to the Guru Rinpoche statue, although I knew that this visit signaled the final days of my pilgrimage to Sikkim and Chorten Gonpa.

Weeks later, back in Napa, Lama Gyatso asked me about the birds. "You remember the large birds you saw at the Guru Rinpoche statue? Did you know the birds formed a line as they neared the statue and in their line they circled the statue three times before they left? There were twenty-one of them."

"Twenty-one? Are you sure there were twenty-one?" I asked, astonished. "The Twenty-One Taras?"

"Yes, Mary Ann, twenty-one vultures!"

"Vultures?" I said, dismayed. "I thought they were hawks." Vultures were unappealing to me. Surely the lovely Tara would not manifest in the form of carrion-eating buzzards.

But Lama Gyatso felt differently. "Vultures are sacred to our tradition. Don't you remember me telling you how a *dakini* in the form of a white vulture led Lhatsun Namkha Jigme, the wild-haired yogi, on his vision-quest to the *beyul* hidden in Mount Kangchenjunga?"

As Lama Gyatso described the vultures circling Guru Rinpoche's head, I flashed on a small statue called the Little Monk, which I had placed next to the stone waterfall in my prayer garden. This sweet figure is depicted sleeping, resting his head on a large, round bundle as big as he. The story goes that Little Monk spent his life walking village to village, listening to people's woes and struggles, to their pain and sufferings. People would ask, "What is in your bundle?" The Little Monk never answered. One day he decided that the queries had gone on for too long. He set the bundle down and opened it. The people, who had been expecting treasures, were aghast, for the bundle was filled with trash. One worn shoe, a ragged piece of clothing, broken trinkets. The villagers were shocked. "This is what you carry with you all the time? Junk? Refuse? Why?" The Little Monk replied, "This way I know where all the garbage is!"

Suddenly it was clear to me that the vultures, like the Little Monk, transformed that which was potentially destructive into nourishment. I shared this with Lama Gyatso as we stood there. At a formal dinner that night, when a guest asked him, "Who *are* you?" he threw his head back and gleefully responded, "I am a garbage man, yes, I am a trash collector for the city of Los Angeles!"

During the first five years of their life, the twins were often visited by a small flock of vultures. Whenever the birds arrived, the children would become very excited and call the entire family to come watch them sitting on the garden fence.

Chapter 21

IN THE PRESENCE
OF A MASTER

*What lies behind us and what lies before us are tiny matters compared
to what lies within us.*

— HENRY STANLEY HASKINS, *Meditations in Wall Street*

O N THE EVE OF MY DEPARTURE from Sikkim, I was still
wondering how many years it would take me to find My
Yogi. I had arrived at Chorten Gonpa wondering if he might be
HH Dodrupchen Rinpoche, but found that I had a different, albeit
wholly enriching, experience of His Holiness than I had anticipated
with My Yogi. There was, however, one other candidate: His Holiness
Chatral Sangye Dorje Rinpoche, a lay yogi who was nevertheless
widely revered as the only lineage holder (*chödak*) of the famed
wisdom *dakini* Sera Khandro. I had once seen his photograph and
been stunned by his resemblance to My Yogi. A burning desire to
meet him had welled up in my heart. This longing had persisted, yet I
did not know how to find him. Now the Losar ceremonies at Chorten
Gonpa were complete and the day trip to the Guru Rinpoche statue
had become a memory. My journey to Sikkim was nearly over.

Two nights before I was to return home, Lama Gyatso and I sat in the lobby of my guesthouse. With a sigh of resignation, I said, "I am leaving soon for California, Lama Gyatso, and I am beginning to doubt if I will ever meet HH Chatral Rinpoche. Twice I've come to the Himalayas searching for My Yogi, and yet it is time to go home again. I risked my life searching for him fifteen years ago, and now this incredible retreat with Dodrupchen Rinpoche is over. I have had powerful mystical and visionary experiences here in Sikkim because of your kindness, but I still haven't met the one man I believe is the celestial yogi of my meditations."

Lama Gyatso was concentrating on a stack of papers in his lap. "Please do not worry," he said. "I have already arranged for you to visit with His Holiness Chatral Rinpoche. Khenpo Chowang has scheduled a driver to meet you here at the guesthouse first thing in the morning. You will be driven to His Holiness's temple tomorrow and to the airport the next day."

Pleased with himself, Lama Gyatso looked sideways at me with a mischievous smile and twinkling eyes. This was enormous news! Relatively few people would ever have the amazing good fortune to meet HH Chatral Rinpoche, as he reserved his attention almost exclusively for his most senior students, yet I was soon to be among those few. In fourteen hours I would be sitting at the feet of the world's oldest and most revered Dzogchen master, the saint many considered the protector-grandfather of the Nyingma tradition and a highly realized yogi in his own right. And after fifteen years, I might finally meet My Yogi in person.

HH Chatral Rinpoche was born in Amdo, Tibet, in 1913 and is known as a "secret yogi." He began his life as a vagabond-ascetic, leaving home at age fifteen to dedicate himself to the practice of *dharma*. During his decades of wandering, he was given the name

Chatral, meaning "one who has abandoned mundane activities" or "hermit." I felt a deep connection with this powerful lay yogi. Since first seeing his portrait, I had read about him extensively, and my mind contained a jumble of images from his life as I envisioned it: traveling on foot across Tibet's wide expanse of mountains and plains; during years of solitary retreat in caves, practicing tantric yoga and learning to unveil his body's inner energy currents; passing quietly through sacred forests, staying in hermitages, caves, or his own little tent.

The papers in Lama Gyatso's lap turned out to be my letter of introduction to HH Chatral Rinpoche. As he composed his missive, the beautiful, mysterious Tibetan script flowed from his pen. I loved to watch him write. Each letter penned in black ink had a unique but veiled life of its own, each completed dispatch being more a work of art than casual message. Lama Gyatso finished writing and looked at me. He handed me a red envelope containing crisp new bills of Indian currency and a beautiful silk *katak*. Together we folded the white offering scarf according to custom. As I held one tasseled end, he held the other, and with quick, practiced movements he accordion-pleated the slippery fabric until the fringe was tucked into a neat, narrow rectangle. If presented properly, the scarf would unwind and flow open like a graceful white river of fine silk.

"Mary Ann, you are to carry these offerings into His Holiness's Throne Room and make three prostrations. First offer your scarf, then your remaining gifts." He explained precisely what my offerings, greetings, and deportment should be in the presence of HH Chatral Rinpoche. My deportment would be of great significance for both Lama Gyatso and me. At a personal level, my history of rejection in the Christian Church had left me with a deep fear that I would be rejected again, this time perhaps by My Yogi, whom I loved so deeply. And I didn't want to disappoint Lama Gyatso or damage his credibility. He always emphasized perfection, constantly exhorting students about the correct way to do things, and I imagined the stakes were especially high for those who had been recognized as Buddhas, who were expected to have an innate knowledge of the mantras, of past lives, and of ritual conventions. The pressure I felt to live up to Lama Gyatso's recognition of me as Yeshe Tsogyal only intensified at the prospect of entering another monastery.

I pestered Lama Gyatso with questions and concerns. "How do I hold the offerings and the *katak* while making graceful prostrations at the same time? Do I give the gifts directly to His Holiness or to an attendant? I'm not sure I can get down on and up off the floor without stumbling." Wanting to make an impression worthy of Lama Gyatso's immense kindness, I listened closely to his answers, but I knew I would simply have to trust myself in the end.

I tried to lighten the moment. "Lama Gyatso, you know the Buddha with a thousand arms?"

He was once again focused on the letter, but answered, "Yes, Mary Ann, he needs all those arms to help the many suffering beings."

"Well, he is definitely Buddhist because one needs a thousand arms and hands to carry so many objects as gracefully as you do in circumstances like these."

Preoccupied, he ignored my attempt at humor and said instead, "Be sure that His Holiness gets this letter. The letter is very important." He repeated this injunction while he folded the heavy stationery three times and placed it into a matching envelope. "Do not lose this!" He held his hand atop the envelope in my hand and said one last time, "Mary Ann, do not lose this letter."

Perhaps to try my patience and dedication, fate would have it that the next day my driver took me to two wrong addresses, consuming several hours in a surprising blast of pre-monsoon heat. We finally arrived at a pair of metal gates, recently painted mustard yellow, where the driver helped me out of the Jeep for the third time. He indicated he would wait down the road where there was room to park.

The gates stood slightly ajar, so I slipped in, clutching Lama Gyatso's now sweat-soaked letter and my damp, crumpled offerings. Weary, my face was streaked with perspiration while my woolen mountain clothes stuck to my body and itched. I entered a large, dusty, empty courtyard and walked around looking for something like an office. Before long, a tall, handsome monk approached me. In polished English he asked why I was there, then confirmed that, indeed, at last, I had arrived at HH Chatral Rinpoche's monastery.

Threats against HH Chatral Rinpoche's life were common and a recent assassination attempt had intensified security concerns. I understood that his attendants would not volunteer much information, so not knowing what else to do, I simply thrust the sweat-stained envelope into the monk's hands and mentioned Lama Gyatso. Tibetans knew Lama Gyatso by another name, however, so I could not be not sure that the monk knew of whom I was speaking. He took the envelope and left me in the courtyard under the hot noonday sun. I closed my eyes, relieved to have made it, and waited for the monk to return. When he reappeared, he gestured me toward a flight of outdoor stairs. My legs were shaky as I climbed the painted wooden steps to an upper landing, where I was again instructed to wait. Soon, another attendant opened the door and drew back a cotton curtain.

I stepped slowly into what turned out to be HH Chatral Rinpoche's throne room, a large, austere space filled with the rays of the sun, which were softened by thin white window curtains. Refreshing cool air greeted me. A regal old man dressed in white sat in the lotus position upon a simple wooden throne. I could not see him clearly because of the sunlight enveloping him. Trembling, I tried to remember Lama Gyatso's instructions. I placed my offerings on a three-legged stool beside the door, performed three prostrations in the direction of the throne, then walked barefoot across the polished wooden floor. With each step, my heart beat harder against my ribcage. I saw HH Chatral Rinpoche more clearly now, with his long, wispy white beard, thin white hair, and weathered, ancient face, lined like a map to the Pure Land. I dropped to my knees, touched my head to the floor, and entered an altered state of consciousness.

It was him, the yogi I had envisioned in the days before my Himalayan trek. My Yogi! He had sat waiting quietly for me all these years, and I'd finally found him. Consumed with an exhilarating love, I straightened up impulsively and, before he could speak, blurted in a surprisingly loud, commanding voice, "I've come to thank you for saving my life."

There was a pause as HH Chatral Rinpoche conferred with an attendant-translator, who then said, "His Holiness would like to know when did he save your life?"

I envisioned myself in the Himalayas, at the moment when, confronted with the slippery log that would serve as my bridge across the tumultuous Bhote Koshi River, I had dropped into a trance, an alternate reality in which all fear dropped away and only beauty remained. I remembered how, again and again during that journey, my Inner Teacher had emerged to rescue me. I said simply, "On my trek to the Sacred Rolwaling Valley."

After another conference with HH Chatral Rinpoche, the translator asked, "How do you know it was His Holiness who saved your life?"

Irrationally surprised by this question, I answered quickly, "Because I know him. I saw him every day for a year before I made that trek."

"His Holiness would like to know when that was," the attendant continued.

In the grip of disorientation, I found myself wondering, *Why is he asking me these questions? Doesn't he know me? Surely he knows me as well as I know him. Doesn't he?* So I paused, trying to locate myself in real-world time and space. Finally, I figured it out. "Fifteen years ago. Thanksgiving, nineteen eighty-nine."

"His Holiness asks what did he look like?"

Now my voice came out in an odd, husky, deep, drawling, ancient, rumbling masculine tone. "He is ooooold ... verrrrrrrry verrrrrrrry ooooooooooold."

I observed myself as if from a distance. I had to prove to His Holiness, the translator, the monks gathered in the room, and myself that Chatral Rinpoche was indeed My Yogi. But how was I to do that? I had an idea that, to my altered psyche, seemed reasonable. *If I can swivel my head around enough to peer at the back of his head,* I thought, *then I can see if he has long wispy hair down his back. If he does, then he is My Yogi.* This movement was clearly impossible, but I tried anyway. The instant I made the attempt, a powerful force instead pulled my head down to my shoulder. I could not lift my head, no matter how I fought the force.

Then I heard HH Chatral Rinpoche, now a hazy vision of light and white, say in a voice of gentle, compassionate authority, "Just relax."

On recognizing the voice, I relaxed, paradoxically, into a rigidity that held my spine erect. There I was in My Yogi's celestial abode, a space of liberation. There was nothing there. It was empty of all things material. Nevertheless, I experienced the rapturous phenomena of the most improbable joy, music, song, and luminescence one can imagine. No, it is beyond the imagination. As I lifted into this state of ecstasy, the mundane evaporated.

I have no idea how long this lasted, but it ended when I heard the attendant ask, "Would you like something to drink?"

I was not pleased at being brought back to the earthly realm so quickly and so rudely. With a pronounced frown and an audible, adolescent sigh of resignation, I rolled my eyes. If Emily Post had written a treatise on proper Tibetan monastic etiquette, I'd have just blown every rule in the book. I had gone home to the beautiful realm of My Yogi for a moment, but here I was, once again in a foreign monastic environment and culture, at the feet of one of the most revered saints in the world, acting like a fool.

As I accepted a white ceramic cup of orange soda from the attendant, who was smiling despite my behavior, my body, arms, and hands appeared to be quiet and relaxed. The cup, however, began a shaking dance upon its saucer. Gathering the remnants of my usual self, I pleaded with the dancing cup and saucer, *Please! No more! Stop! Don't do this in front of His Holiness.* But they continued to rattle, and my secret shamanic self, oblivious to proper etiquette, continued to burst out of her lifetime cocoon.

Until this moment, whenever the Mother Yeshe Tsogyal had emerged, I had been under the protection of Lama Gyatso, who knew me and seemed to understand me more than I understood myself. Beginning with the first incident—when I found myself declaring, "She wants to be heard!"—the spontaneous pronouncements of Yeshe Tsogyal had erupted with ever-increasing intensity. In each of those episodes, Lama Gyatso's devotion and love for me was so powerful and reassuring that I was able to trust the experiences as they unfolded, however intensely dramatic they were. Now, though, I was alone with HH Chatral Rinpoche and thoroughly unsure of my reception.

I found myself speaking in an unnatural rumble of a voice, pouting, shaking, and now discomposed by uncertainty. Although I desperately wanted to pay homage to this great *siddha* sitting before me, who I had been so sure was My Yogi, I now felt too overwhelmed to think. Convinced that I had ruined this audience, I decided that I was wasting HH Chatral Rinpoche's time, so I prepared to exit.

HH Chatral Rinpoche spoke to me again. "Relax, just relax."

Immediately I did as he said and traveled in my mind to that wonderful pure place where I never felt anxious, fearful, or unsure. I rested in that place until HH Chatral Rinpoche asked, loudly, "Why isn't Lama Gyatso here?"

The letter! Where was the letter?

I stammered, "Yes! No! I mean, yes, you are right, he isn't here." I struggled again to locate my rational mind. "But I have a letter from him. He explains everything, it's all in the letter, you know?"

HH Chatral Rinpoche sat quietly on his throne, just inches away, watching me.

I had lost the letter! It had vanished. I searched my clothing, left side, right side, all the while explaining, "I had it right here, I carried it all the way down the damn mountain. It's for you. Lama Gyatso wrote it, and it is important. It will tell you everything."

I was near tears when HH Chatral Rinpoche finally said, "I have the letter."

After visiting the realm of My Yogi, I hadn't been able to bring my mind back to the throne room fully. Indeed, I had not wanted to return, but this interaction broke the spell. I found myself in the real world again, both mystified and mortified, having forgotten that I had given the letter to the attendant in the courtyard. With rational consciousness restored, I now experienced what felt like a full-blown identity crisis. I was thoroughly unsure of myself, of who I was, who I had become, who I was supposed to be. And it was obvious HH Chatral Rinpoche was not, in fact, My Yogi. I wanted to escape immediately.

Then it dawned on me. *Wait a moment. His Holiness just spoke to me in English?* He has the letter? As I thought about this, His Holiness spoke to the attendant, who left the room. I resolved to restrain my outbursts. I heard my reassuring Inner Teacher. *No one is judging you, Mary Ann. Why are you judging yourself? The experience is strange, exotic, and new, perhaps, but judging yourself when no one else is judging you is foolish.* My body finally relaxed, and I gave up trying to understand what was going on.

The attendant returned carrying three items. First, a ceremonial *katak,* which HH Chatral Rinpoche placed around my neck. *How kind,* I thought. HH Chatral Rinpoche is known for his loving-kindness, and it was true. He was offering gifts despite my behavior, perhaps even to make me feel better. I'd failed in so many ways, so many times throughout my life, and now I had failed again. Worst of all, I had failed Lama Gyatso, but I didn't at that moment have the energy to feel shame or guilt. I hoped I could leave soon, go home, far away to California, and forget this debacle.

HH Chatral Rinpoche placed a white conch-shell necklace around my neck. Painted on the shell was a delicate red dagger called a *phurba.* Noticing it, I snapped into presence. Something important was happening. Something very unusual. My Inner Teacher spoke. *Pay attention! You are being recognized as a Buddha!*

HH Chatral Rinpoche was conferring a great honor upon me, but I felt numb. I understood that a Buddha or an "awakened one" is someone who has awakened from the sleep of ignorance, who has come to recognize things as they really are, that there are different levels of the enlightened mind, but in that moment I was unable to see myself as such a person. Given the language and cultural barriers, the term "Buddha" seemed to have multiple unfamiliar definitions. From plastic bouncing blue Buddhas glued to the dashboards of taxis to elaborate pieces of sacred artwork, Buddhas were everywhere. HH Dodrupchen Rinpoche was one of the world's most highly evolved spiritual masters and known as a living Buddha, as was HH Chatral Rinpoche. How could I possibly compare myself to them?

During one Losar outing, Lama Gyatso had taken us to visit HE Gonjang Rinpoche's mountainous monastery, which overlooked Gangtok. At lunch, I overheard several young Western women who had gathered about me as we walked the grounds: "I hear she is a living female American Buddha!" The women later arranged themselves at my feet to ask about astrology. I answered their questions as well as I could, but I was flustered by the attention. It was one thing to be recognized as Yeshe Tsogyal by a small circle of lamas I had known for so many years, but quite another to travel across the world to a place where this had become public knowledge among the larger *sangha*. To have strangers treat me with reverence was disorienting. On some fundamental level, I was still integrating this profound spiritual identity which had suddenly "gone public."

It was now HH Chatral Rinpoche himself who was recognizing me, and my heart felt as though it had stopped beating. I could not brush this process aside. His Holiness took up the handful of crisp Indian bills. Fanning them out like a deck of playing cards, he contemplated them deeply, conversing with an invisible and exalted part of himself. After a short time, he handed them to me, one by one.

"No!" I protested. "I don't need the money. I gave those bills to you, I don't need them. You keep it."

I had so much in terms of material wealth and assumed, incorrectly, that he had none. And I didn't understand why, immediately after gracing me with the *katak* and the conch necklace, he had decided to return my gift. Had I done something wrong? Was it a veiled insult? Flooding with painful emotional memory, I thought of how resoundingly the Christian Church had rejected me for the ministry. Each time I had stepped up in good faith to offer myself in service, I had unknowingly crossed institutional and personal boundaries and then been betrayed or abandoned by trusted mentors. I could not bear the possibility that I might open myself to the honor now being extended—the opportunity to step into my spiritual power in full public view—only to risk repudiation once again. At the same time, I felt as though I were surrounded and enveloped in a profoundly sacred space of unconditional love and acceptance. Love and loss were deeply intertwined. I didn't know how to respond.

To the right of HH Chatral Rinpoche sat his daughter, Tsemo Saraswati, the most beautiful woman I had ever seen. She was dressed in summer-weight white cotton trousers and a loose white tunic, and her wavy black hair glistened as it tumbled over her shoulders and down her back.

Turning to her, I asked in a choked voice, "Why doesn't he want my gift?"

She smiled at me, enjoying this immensely. With great love and respect in her voice, she said, "He is making a gift to honor you."

"But I don't want it," I replied. "I don't need it."

I stared at the money in my hand. Then, thinking myself inspired, I said to the beautiful Saraswati, "Here you take it." I held the money out.

"No," she laughed. "His Holiness is honoring you, he is making offerings to you. He is very glad you have come to visit us!"

I looked around the sun-filled throne room, at all the lamas and attendants. Each was smiling and bowing to me, looking at me with great joy and love, yet I remained disoriented and could think of nothing to say. I was simply too overwhelmed. Head swimming, I rose from the floor—usually no easy task for me, but I lifted up like a bird. As I walked to the door, however, I moved like a drunk on stilts. I again attempted to give the money away, this time to the attendant at the door.

"Here, you take it!"

"No," he laughed. "That is His Holiness's gift to you. He is honoring you."

A group of monks walked me to the gate, trying to help me. I insisted I was fine, that I needed no help, but in their loving, humble manner, they formed a protective circle around me and walked me down the road to the parked Jeep, where the driver stood holding the door open. Before long, I was on my way down the black ribbon of asphalt, holding my new necklace close to my heart.

Since my trek to the Sacred Rolwaling Valley in 1989, my life had changed in ways I could have never predicted. Despite having been granted many honors and such good fortune, however, I had continued to identify more with failure than with success. Nevertheless, Lama Gyatso and the Nyingmas were gracious and persisted in responding to my strengths rather than to my perceived weaknesses. After my visit with HH Chatral Rinpoche, however, once I had regained my composure, I found that I was finally and effortlessly able to see myself through their eyes. In the Sacred Rolwaling Valley I had understood that I was a beautiful tapestry that I had created over many lifetimes, a unique work of art. But now, in an instant, I believed it.

The trip to the hotel passed in a blur. I kept my hand on the conch-shell necklace hidden beneath my shirt, HH Chatral Rinpoche's *katak* tied around my neck. I left the money for Lama Gyatso, requesting that he give it to HH Chatral Rinpoche for distribution among his monastery's charitable programs.

Lama Gyatso followed me down the mountain the next day and stopped by His Holiness's monastery to pay homage to his beloved master. Later that night, he told me, "His Holiness was pleased he met you. Everyone you met there was happy and honored that you visited them." I knew Lama Gyatso's words were true. With great humility, I trusted and believed him. My life had been filled with wonders, but nothing compared to the honor I received that day from HH Chatral Sangye Dorje Rinpoche.

"Mary Ann," Lama Gyatso continued, "His Holiness told me that not far from the Sacred Rolwaling Valley is an old man who lives at a very high altitude. This old man is almost two hundred years old."

I leaned back in my chair and closed my eyes. Was His Holiness saying My Yogi lived in the Everest region of the Sacred Rolwaling Valley? It was clear that HH Chatral Rinpoche was not My Yogi, however much I had wanted it to be true. It seemed as if I would never meet this solitary mountain yogi in person, but in that moment I suddenly understood that My Yogi in fact inhabited the same *mindstream* as HH Chatral Rinpoche, who I *had* been blessed to meet. My vision in the Sacred Rolwaling Valley showed me that we were all part of the same sacred whole. My Yogi was not separate from either me or HH Chatral Rinpoche. Sitting there, enjoying the last few moments of my visit with Lama Gyatso, I felt an indescribable peace and understood in some strange and mysterious way not only that My Yogi did exist somewhere for me to one day meet, but that it was I, too, who was my own yogi. And that it was time to go home.

Chapter 22

BETWEEN TIME ZONES

It is again a strong proof of men knowing most things before birth, that when mere children they grasp innumerable facts with such speed as to show that they are not then taking them in for the first time, but remembering and recalling them.

—MARCUS TULLIUS CICERO, "On Old Age"

As I STOOD OUTSIDE the Delhi International Airport on my way back to California from the Losar celebrations, my mind danced between the worlds I had visited at Chorten Gonpa in Sikkim and at HH Chatral Rinpoche's monastery in Darjeeling. I was now walking in ways contrary to those of the world at large, on the proverbial road less traveled. Busy international airports, however, are not safe places for suspended minds. *What goes up must come down*, I thought and comforted myself with the understanding that the spiritual powers of mystery and magic that I'd experienced at the feet of two of the greatest Buddhist masters alive were also right here at the taxi stand, everywhere around me, even inside the cacophony of the airport. Fortunately the practicalities of security checks, ticketing, and passport controls helped settle my thoughts.

After waiting at the departure gate for two hours with fellow travelers in turbans, saris, business suits, and backpacks, I finally boarded the plane. The giant silver bird rose gracefully off the tarmac and into the skies over India, toward towering cumulonimbus clouds shining with the bright, reflected light of the Indian subcontinent, where the colorful silk saris and the dusty, spicy aromas of Delhi had combined with noise, sweat, poverty, and smoke to awaken all my senses. As the plane climbed above India's dusty heat and the miles upon miles saturated with life, I felt steady in the knowledge that whether or not I returned to Asia or saw HH Dodrupchen Rinpoche or HH Chatral Rinpoche again, my spiritual bonds with them would endure.

I pushed my seat back, reflecting with wonder on the events of my trip. At the level of my Higher Self, I experienced little uncertainty about being Yeshe Tsogyal, but at the level of intellect, of everyday psychology and ever-changing emotions, I had yet to catch up with my new sense of identity. Indeed, as Lama Gyatso later told me, HH Dodrupchen Rinpoche warned him that it would likely take years for me to grow into a full understanding and acceptance of the essence of who I was and had been for so many centuries. For what did it really mean to be the living incarnation of this remarkable woman sage, mystic, and Mother of Tibetan Buddhism? I wasn't at all sure how to integrate my visionary episodes into ordinary life— my marriage, my family, my ministry. Among the lamas, I had been given full rein of self-expression, freely speaking to things that only I could hear and see. It was still remarkable to me how my entire way of being could change, the register of my voice lowering dramatically, my personality becoming animated by an intense, piercing energy of unity and love that overwhelmed normal social interactions. It was impossible to accurately describe what I saw or heard in the magical clarity of awareness I experienced in trance. These considerations felt as vast as the skies outside my window.

Passengers began settling in for the transatlantic flight into the nighttime skies. Cabin shades were pulled, blankets and slippers and warm washcloths distributed. After dinner, I opened my journal on the fold-out table and waited. Peace settled through my body as I listened for the very small voice arising from that older part of my brain. A slip of paper fell from my journal. On it I had copied His Holiness the Fourteenth Dalai Lama's Prayer of Aspiration, which was written by Shantideva, an eighth-century Buddhist scholar from India.

> May I become at all times, both now and forever,
> A protector for those without protection,
> A guide for those who have lost their way,
> A ship for those with oceans to cross,
> A bridge for those with rivers to cross,
> A sanctuary for those in danger,
> A lamp for those without light,
> A place of refuge for those who lack shelter,
> And a servant to all in need.

These beautiful and sagacious words resonated with a fiery force within me. We are all capable of benefiting others simply by virtue of being members of the human race, but for some of us, this emerges as a kind of imperative, a conscious and purposeful mission. For me, it was as though the ideals of Shantideva's Prayer of Aspiration had been inscribed in my physical being from the day of my birth. As a child, however, I had neither the maturity, the skill, nor the inner resources to implement this ideal state of compassionate love.

I tried to alleviate pain and suffering wherever I encountered it, beginning right at home in response to my parents' alcoholism and the verbal and physical abuse it unleashed on every member of my family.

As the loving little girl I had been, I possessed the great beauty of pure motivation, but of course did not know how to accomplish a task so formidable. As I grew older, I strove to live in accordance with the principles of love, but I had also in some way felt that the true practice to fulfill such aspirations—in essence, to become Jesus—was akin to heresy. I could certainly try to live by Jesus' teachings, but there were dreadful and powerful prohibitions against assuming that I, a woman, was kindred in spirit.

Now, in this tremendous moment of rapprochement, I understood that while the Christian tradition had emphasized Jesus' forgiving presence, it had also taught that he was separate from me. The Nyingma teachings, however, allowed me to actually take the helm of my own spiritual journey. I was powerful in my own right, and to embrace knowledge, wisdom, and spiritual accomplishment was neither arrogant nor shameful. In fact, it was essential. No one had had to make me into a Buddha. I had come into my mother's womb, as we all do, filled with the flaming seeds of Buddhahood.

Even more, I now understood that I carried the essence of the Prayer of Aspiration forth from previous lifetimes. Yeshe Tsogyal was in my spiritual DNA. I had been recognized by HE Chagdud Tulku Rinpoche, whose very own mother was another incarnation of Yeshe Tsogyal, as well as by HH Chatral Rinpoche and all the lamas who had been present at the Family Home and Ari Bhöd, including the Venerable Lama Gyatso Rinpoche, HE Gonjang Rinpoche, His Eminence Namkha Drimed Rinpoche, Lama Lubdrub, the Venerable Gelong Kalsang Rinpoche, and the Venerable Lama Nawang Thogmed. These spiritual mentors helped to diminish my psychological and cultural limitations and to raise my self-confidence. What a slow, stubborn, stumbling Western student I had been! I had needed the guidance of each of these masters of wisdom and compassion to reawaken within me the true nature of my inherent spiritual qualities and to "recognize" me before I could either recognize or name myself.

Tucked cozily into the tight quarters of my seat on the transatlantic flight home, I began to flash on the events of a lifetime of awakening. As in the Bible, in which "naming" factors into the creation story, one of my first questions as a girl was "Who am I?" Before I could receive my first Holy Communion in the Roman Church, I had to memorize the answer from the Catholic catechism: "I am a child of God." Thus was planted a deep-seated belief that while God created me, I was not *of* God and thus needed to be saved by a force outside of myself. When I was twenty, I married, changed my name, and tried to change my attitudes and behavior as well, then repeated the process on becoming a divorcée. Then HE Chagdud Tulku Rinpoche and Lama Gyatso called me Yeshe Tsogyal, suggesting yet another name. My new name, Yeshe Tsogyal, had unleashed a tsunami of emotional and inner upheaval, but ultimately led me back home, to the sacred place within, in every cell of my body and in my *heart-mind*.

As we flew over the starlit waves of the ocean waters far below, unexpected revelations danced like silvery, flying fish. I envisioned an inlet at the north end of a mountain lake and stared into the dark, boggy shallows as words from the Book of Job bubbled to the surface of my mind: "Out of the north comes golden splendor." The north refers to the unknown, to the darkness, to the Hades underworld of hell-beings, to those buried parts of the subconscious mind one fears to enter. As I peered into fetid swamp waters filled with rotting plant and animal remains, I also saw a teeming, evolving mass of new life. If I were to put even an infinitesimal amount of that swamp water under a microscope, millions of swarming, swimming entities would be revealed in their evolutionary journey through existence. Atop the swamp waters filled with seeming decay, an expanse of gently swaying, extraordinarily white, translucent, and pure water lilies rose above floating green pad beds—these are the flowers that the Buddhists call lotus blossoms. Though they had emerged from the murk, these blooms were cosmic works of art. From the swamp's womb, a ceaseless number of entities transformed themselves from beings of darkness into elemental Beings of Light.

This vision offered profoundly different explanations of the nature of suffering, depending on whether one looked at it from a Christian or a Buddhist point of view. My Christian theology and the belief system of my birth family had been informed by the cross that bore the bloody body of a crucified Christ, by a religious perspective which seemed to idolize suffering, that worshiped the pain body itself. I had been raised to honor the biblical injunction in Matthew's Gospel, "Blessed are those who suffer... for theirs is the kingdom of heaven," which my family understood as an argument for suffering as an end in itself. I unconsciously embraced the holiness of suffering, even though my true self had always been driven to purify, pacify, transform, and alleviate suffering.

Everything I learned from my Buddhist guides and from my spiritual studies taught me to see that the true purpose of suffering was not to experience suffering as its own reward, but to experience it as a means for spiritual transformation. We passed through Good Friday to get to Easter Sunday, of course, but I had for so long been unable to see what that suggested: that suffering and painful karma can be the very birthing conditions for a direct experience of personal transcendence, for new life in this very lifetime. I could now embrace the truth that I am blessed not because I feel pain, but because I can transform it for the benefit of all sentient beings. I can turn the lead of my unenlightened personality into the gold of a risen woman. I could now revere the concept of the empty cross, that is, the journey each individual can make through forgiveness, reconciliation, redemption, and resurrection into Buddhahood.

In my vision, the inlet merged with a clear-water lake; neither was separate from the other. The lotuses were interconnected with, inseparable from the teeming womb of the swamp. The lake waters lapped against rocky shores, and I saw beyond, to fields and mountains, forests and cities, temples and cathedrals. Everywhere I looked, life, death, and rebirth bloomed just like the lilies. These interconnected layers of decay and growth held the full spectrum of suffering, from karma to transcendence, from darkness to light. Sandra Scales's book *Sacred Voices of the Nyingma Masters* includes a teaching, from one of the most important *tertöns* in Tibetan Buddhism, Jigme Lingpa (1729–1798), that describes how suffering and karma inform one another.

When a bird flies high in the sky, no shadow is seen. Only as the bird nears the earth does its shadow appear. Karma has the same dynamic. As we move through this lifetime, we don't see our own karma at first, but as we age, our karma, our shadow, becomes increasingly evident. We must remember that the problems and sufferings in our lives and in the world don't just appear without causes or conditions. The suffering we experience is not created or imposed on us by another person. If we search for the source, we find it to be the mind. Karma depends on the mental attitude that accompanies our actions. When we experience suffering, it is because negative karma that we have created in past lives is now ripening and it will follow us though our many lifetimes until we choose to mitigate it. That is why we must master our own minds.

Scales also relates a tale about Katayana, one of the great disciples of the Buddha, that conveys the significance of this idea. Katayana was invited to a great king's palace where he was entertained with music and dance all day. At the end of the festivities, the king asked Katayana if he had enjoyed the entertainment. Katayana, who had maintained a state of meditation throughout, said "Was there entertainment? I didn't see anything at all." The king did not believe such a thing was possible, so Katayana asked the king to summon a prisoner from the dungeon and to entertain him with music and dance the next day. He said to the king, "Give the prisoner a container filled to the brim with oil, then tell him he must carry it around the banquet hall all day without spilling a drop or he will be executed." The king did as he was asked, and the prisoner spent the next day carefully circling the hall and spilled not a drop. Afterward, the king asked the prisoner if he had enjoyed the entertainment, but the prisoner had been so focused on his task that he, too, had seen nothing beyond it. Katayana asked the king, "Do you understand now? This man didn't notice the festivities because he was worried about being executed and so was tremendously vigilant. Similarly, I did not perceive the entertainment because I am afraid of being reborn within the wheel of life, *samsara*, and thus pay absolute attention to my meditation."

Sitting on the plane deep in contemplation, I suddenly flashed on my interactions with HE Chagdud Tulku Rinpoche. Although he always listened to me, he also performed his practices at the same time, turning the pages of his texts even as we spoke. Like Katayana, he sustained a permanent state of meditation, as did all the other great lamas I had met. For the first time, I understood Jesus and the Crucifixion on an esoteric level. Jesus absorbed the karmic suffering of humankind and transformed it by directing his consciousness inward toward his Father in Heaven, or in Buddhist terms the Pure Lands of Dharmadhatu. He modeled for all the transformative power of purifying and calming the mind by focusing on the Divine. Once again, Nyingma teachings had unlocked for me a deeper understanding of the Christian scriptures I had studied for a lifetime.

Every moment of my life now reverberated with new layers of meaning. As a child, I always experienced the Eucharist as the calling in of the great high spirits to heal us, the parishioners. The priest didn't just call in God's presence—he supplicated Jesus' presence along with those of the prophets, saints, angels, archangels, cherubim, seraphim, and thrones. I experienced the healing magic of that moment when heaven and earth became one in the elements of bread and wine, and believed that *only* there, on the church altar covered with a starched white altar cloth, between two burning candlesticks, could this magic occur. *Only* then and *only* there. To heal others, I had believed, I would have to be ordained so that I could legitimately perform the sacred rituals of bread and wine.

But now I saw that this was a calling that *I remembered how to do from many past lifetime practices.* I hadn't been called to priesthood in the church. I needed to build a temple within both my physical body and my *heart-mind*, an interior but universal safe place where I could consciously commune with and become One with my Buddha nature. The voice that said *This is what you will do* during that long-ago Good Friday Eucharist was my Inner Teacher calling me to transform myself at an elemental level, to awaken and become an enlightened being. And was is exactly what I had been doing all these years. This was the spiritual path!

As I revisited these memories high above the Pacific Ocean, I felt for the first time a deep compassion and love for all of our evolutionary journeys—including mine. In this all-encompassing awareness, I sensed Yeshe Tsogyal gain a subtle ascendancy. She was now emerging and expanding within me as a distinct presence, one I could consciously recognize and turn to for protection and guidance, as I had been doing for years with my Inner Teacher and the beloved figure of My Yogi.

Yeshe Tsogyal and I were like two sides of the same coin. She was the unchanging Mother I'd known for a lifetime—as the Virgin Mary who had comforted me as a child, as the Inner Teacher who spoke to me and guided me, as She who wanted to be heard by Lama Gyatso, as the inner urge that guided me to the Mother-Child relationship of the two eggplants in the vegetable garden at the Family Home and whose beauty and compassion engulfed both me and Lama Lubdrub as we stood silently awash in a divine connection. At times, She had felt both feminine and masculine in tone and presence, just as I had been both mother and father to my children when raising them as a single mother. These moments, along with countless others, were invulnerable, invincible, indestructible, and authentic. No one, nothing, no institution, no experience had or could tarnish my visions and experience of this presence of the Divine in my life.

This knowing ennobled me, and it empowered me to relive many painful memories with an expanded and more merciful perspective. I envisioned the picturesque Methodist church in St. Helena that had once been a church home to me. This image enlarged to encompass the other five traditional Christian churches in St. Helena, all built along Oak, Adams, and Spring Streets. My adult religious journey from the Catholic to the Episcopal to the Methodist Church took place in the equivalent of one square city block. I'd moved from one church to another, then on to becoming a hospice chaplain and a spiritual director, to working with those without church homes, to officiating in many churches.

I now remembered that when I'd applied for ordination twenty years before, I had said to the bishop and his committee, "I am not seeking a parish ministry. I want to be a spiritual director and help those who have no church, but who need a spiritual friend." And when the bishop could not ordain me, he'd said, "Go home, Mary Ann, and build your own church where you will be free." Despite my initial shame at having failed to become ordained in the Episcopal Church, at having to resort to ordination through the Universal Life Church, people trusted me and came to me for help anyway. No one seemed to care where I had been ordained. Some even told me they came to me precisely because I had not been ordained in the institutional church. I had, in fact, become exactly what I said I wanted to be—a bridge for people without churches, a bridge between the individual and the Divine. I had become an ecumenical minister in a church with no walls.

And now I understood: the church I sought was me.

PART III

LIFE
AFTER DEATH

Chapter 23

IN SICKNESS AND
IN HEALTH

Om mani padme hum—*which you've seen inscribed everywhere on rocks, prayer wheels giant prayer wheels—although it calls upon Avalokitshvara, the bodhisattva of compassion, as holder of the jewel and the lotus, its deeper meaning is the cosmic vision of union.* Om mani padme hum *declares that everything is perfect in every atom in every instant, that compassion and wisdom are present everywhere, that love is present everywhere. Bliss emerges from everything everywhere. There is nothing to fear. Even when it looks like hell in front of me, I can just embrace it and it will turn into a bed of roses.*

—ROBERT A. F. THURMAN AND TAD WISE,
Circling the Sacred Mountain

EVERY YEAR ST. HELENA has a homecoming parade. Family members of the current crop of St. Helena's high-school students line Main Street, shopkeepers come outside to join the fun, and kindergarten students sit on the curb waiting for the fire engine to begin the parade with a blast of its siren. Marching bands, crêpe-paper floats, and high-school princesses escorted by handsome princes open nostalgic windows of reminiscence that set cameras clicking and arms waving.

But no marching bands greeted me upon my arrival home from India. I didn't need them. Don was there waiting for me—my prince charming, consort, husband. Grinning like a high-school boy, Don drew me into his arms for a prolonged embrace. When we arrived home, he carried my luggage into my dressing room, where he had taken a bar of soap and written across the mirror, "I Love You!"

We spent the next few months taking short trips together, and I let myself slip into the peaceful depths of our love as well as my newfound sense of being one with the field of Buddhas that surrounded and included Yeshe Tsogyal and me. There was time to consider what all of this would mean, how it might affect my choices, and how I might serve this burgeoning identity, so I concentrated on my spiritual practices, Don's embracing love, and the support of Lama Gyatso.

Several months after my return from Sikkim, however, life took an unexpected turn. Don began to slow down dramatically and experienced intermittent stomach pain. In September 2004, at the age of seventy-five, he was diagnosed with pancreatic cancer. Undaunted, he shifted his leadership skills into high gear, polling doctors at the Queen of the Valley Medical Center in search of the foremost expert in pancreatic cancer. He was a popular patient, bringing our Napa Valley wine to the hospital and talking sports and politics with the oncologists. Laughter poured out of examination rooms.

After several weeks of preliminary diagnostics revealed the tumor to be small and well located, Don entered Stanford Memorial Hospital to have the malignancy removed. The surgery took over six hours. While Don was in recovery, the surgeon approached me in the hall: they had found that the tumor was actually quite large and that the cancer had metastasized throughout Don's body. A smothering cloud of grief enveloped me as I stood in the hospital's spacious hallway numbly watching the surgeon walk away. The hall balcony overlooked a lobby where a pianist played a classical sonata on an elegant grand piano. There were sounds, but I heard no music. Given our ages when we married, we'd made the most of our time, knowing that our years together would be limited. Still, I could not believe that less than eight years would be the extent of our honeymoon, that our life together in this world was quickly nearing an end. How was I to surrender such a comforting love as ours?

For a while after I received this news, pain gripped my heart, bending me over so that I walked like an old woman, but I was also seized by a longing to draw on the inner strengths and powers I had discovered in full force during the previous year with the Nyingmas. Like there is an oak tree inside every acorn, an extraordinary woman lived within me. I focused on her with as much might as I could muster. Slowly, my inner strength surfaced, and it empowered Don and me to navigate the rough terrain that followed. Don had taken care of me as his wife and loved me as no man had before—now it was my turn to take care of him, and I committed myself to helping him die as comfortably and peacefully as possible.

Lama Gyatso organized ongoing prayer support at the monasteries of HH Dodrupchen Rinpoche, HH Chatral Rinpoche, and HH Trulshik Rinpoche. Between these three great Nyingma masters and their monks and nuns, many thousands of devotees were offering up their prayers and practices for Don's well-being. Lama Gyatso, the Venerable Gelong Kalsang Rinpoche, Lama Dorje, Lama Thogmed, Lama Lhundrup, and our Los Angeles *sangha* were also performing long-life practices in

California. Church congregations and friends in Napa, in St. Helena, and at the Queen of the Valley Medical Center sent many more prayers. The energy generated by all these prayers cushioned the emotional and psychological challenges we faced during the early days of Don's journey with pancreatic cancer.

Somehow I remained connected to the ancient Himalayan stillness, affirmations, and blessings that I had received during Losar in Sikkim. I wasn't alone anymore. A new "me" had emerged. True, when people hugged me and offered their condolences, they may have felt they were wrapping their arms around a granite pillar, for I was in an outwardly frozen state. Within, however, I felt balanced and quiet. This strange contradiction lasted several months.

Postsurgery, as soon as Don was able, we met with the head of Stanford's elegant new oncology center. Notices announcing seminars on end-of-life issues and advertisements for hospice and home-health providers were posted in the hallway that led to individual consultation rooms. The posters felt like an assault even though I knew they were intended to be helpful. Don's oncologist told us that ninety-five percent of all pancreatic cancer patients die within three to six months of diagnosis or surgery and that some, only a few, live a year. The physician's hollow voice seemed to echo off distant and alien planets.

Don sat stoically upright in his plastic chair, now forty pounds lighter than he had been before his diagnosis, and stared past the cream-colored walls into the void. When the doctor finished speaking, we all stood. Don shook the doctor's hand, thanked him and his attendants for all they had done. I felt sick and unsteady. We walked through the waiting room and past a giant aquarium filled with large specimens of brightly colored tropical fish. We walked past patients in wheelchairs, on walkers, with canes, some using portable oxygen tanks.

As we waited for our car at the hospital entrance, young students bathed in the golden sunlight of an Indian summer afternoon busily traversed the Stanford campus, exuding an excitement about the myriad new experiences that awaited them. A hundred years earlier, my paternal grandfather, a stonemason and contractor, had helped build Stanford's stunning campus. The university had become the alma mater of my father, my sister, Don, and Don's daughter, Dana. For me, Stanford had long stood as symbol of success, power, football championships, regional pride, and family history. Now, however, it signified only death, loss, and grief.

The following week we returned to the Queen of the Valley Medical Center to meet with an oncologist and had a radically different experience. This doctor rolled his stool up close to Don and started right in. "I know what you have been told about pancreatic cancer and what you have probably read on the Internet and heard from friends and relatives. Forget all of it. Just forget it. Let it go! Men and women are living up to three and four years with cases of pancreatic cancer far worse than yours. They are living good, productive lives, driving, socializing, and going out."

The doctor maintained a powerful force of eye contact with Don as he described the treatment program, which was to begin once Don had fully recovered from his surgery. From that moment on, Don knew he was going to beat the odds. He looked at his situation like a football game. "The Big Game," he called it. He never got angry at his illness, but instead smiled and proudly told everyone, "I am going to win this battle," even as we all gently tried to explain otherwise.

As chairman of the hospital's board, Don visited the Queen of the Valley medical center every day, walking the halls, chatting and joking with the medical staff, and visiting with the hospital president. He was elected Trustee Emeritus of the medical center, an honor never before bestowed, and he attended trustee meetings even in his wheelchair. At home, he drove his tractor, watched football, read about politics, played bridge and dominoes with business friends he had known for fifty years, and entertained family.

I tended to Don, kept him company, entertained, and cooked for him while I maintained my spiritual practices, studies, and meditation. We waited for lab results that measured the cancer's growth or decline. The lab tests would be good for several weeks, and Don would smile. Then the tumors would reappear, sending Don into survival mode. He'd call the doctors to discuss new experimental protocols, which worked for short periods before debilitating side effects set in again. Chemo-induced diabetes required radical shifts in diet. Don's balance became increasingly unsteady and required constant vigilance.

For years, I had ministered to the ill and the dying and knew the difficulties that elders and the infirm faced, but secondhand knowledge can't generate the same sort of empathy that direct and ongoing caregiving does. Don rallied through a number of small strokes until Memorial Day, 2009, when a major stroke temporarily robbed him of coherent speech and made him dependent on a walker. Yet Don remained upbeat, as active as possible, and positive, despite countless visits to the emergency room, imaging center, and chemo lab.

I, on the other hand, felt increasingly fatigued. Whenever the dark, threatening edges of exhaustion or sadness closed in, I'd reflect on my own recovery from cancer during those mystical sunset evenings I now called the Summer of Love. The shifting, vibrantly alive red, orange, and yellow of all those sunsets continued to be rich reservoirs of comfort and strength that I could tap into whenever I felt down or fatigued. Those sunset rivers of blended color spoke to me of awe and wonder.

The Nyingmas believe that the sky, clouds, and rainbows carry consciousness. It certainly felt as if the colors I communed with were beings, emanations of the eternal divine connecting me to all of creation and to Don. These presences consistently reminded me to cherish every moment of our lives together and that I would never lose the love that bound us. The magnetizing sunset rivers of love represented the essence of the real Don, not his physical body. These same streams of light consciousness would always connect me to Lama Gyatso as well. In fact, this vibrant flow connected me to all beings, visible and invisible, throughout the universe. There was no need to hold on to or possess this timeless, endless, beginningless river. It just was, and so was I, and so were Don and Lama Gyatso. We were all One in this exuberant river of eternal light, life, and love.

Chapter 24

THE TIGER MOTHER

May all embodied beings hear
The sounds of Dharma without cessation
From birds, trees
And the lights and sky.

—SHANTIDEVA, *Bodhicaryavatara*

DECEMBER DAYS AT THE FAMILY HOME can begin and end with sharp, angled sunrays. Such a day was dawning when Lama Gyatso opened his Ögyen Dzambhala retreat in Southern California during the winter holidays. The Buddha Ögyen Dzambhala is, among other things, the great protector of wealth. According to tradition, his wealth is self-existent and thus cannot be taken away. His territory is increasingly vast because, having no need to own it, he continually gives it away to all.

Lama Gyatso was always exuberant about these retreats, which led into the New Year, and was particularly energized in 2007. For a decade, he had painstakingly edited His Holiness Orgyen Kusum Lingpa Rinpoche's newly translated Ögyen Dzambhala text, the Prosperity Accomplishment Sadhana of Ögyen Dzambhala. As a *tertön*, HH Kusum Lingpa discovered new *termas* relative to this ancient text and entrusted these texts to Lama Gyatso. In a voice bursting with elation, Lama Gyatso explained to me that he was "opening" for the first time the newly completed Ögyen Dzambhala practice. Stressing the importance of that year's retreat, he specifically requested my presence, as I had developed a close relationship with HH Kusum Lingpa. Regretfully, a bout with vertigo prevented me from traveling, so the morning of New Year's Eve found me sitting on a hillside bench at the Family Home, keenly aware that Lama Gyatso was opening the Ögyen Dzambhala retreat. I concentrated on joining my mind to his in support of his endeavors.

Savoring Napa Valley's sunlit winter skies, I yielded to the day's magnetizing allure and let the celebration of luminosity pull me outside for a short walk. While Don sat inside enjoying the holiday football games, I walked downhill to the rusty iron bench overlooking glistening acres of bare vineyards. Coolness from the bench's metal bars seeped through my jeans as I sat quietly beneath tall, silent Monterey pines and Atlantic cedars, one of which housed an owl's nest. Red-tailed hawks circled above while ravens black as midnight chased about the windswept blue sky.

High in the trees, I sensed, was the ethereal presence of Garuda, a Tibetan animal deity in the form of a sacred bird who spits jewels from his beak and sits among the leaves and branches of wish-fulfilling trees. Sitting there, I fell into trance, and for the next three days, while Lama Gyatso taught HH Kusum Lingpa's Ögyen Dzambhala text, I journeyed through transcendent realms. During those wintry days of reverie, it was nevertheless easy and natural to care for Don. I drifted in and out of altered states of consciousness, and everything seemed sacred, even dirty dishes. Each morning I returned to my rusty bench and let magical beings open doors to the mystical experiences emanating from Lama Gyatso's retreat.

On that first day, I was sitting on the bench as the December sun moved toward its midday station when I suddenly found myself in a monochromatic landscape somewhere in my inner world. Everything in the surrounding terrain was pearl gray. Whether I looked up or down, to the left or to the right, all I saw was gray. This gray light was neither depressing nor bland, but instead undulated with the blended energies of all the colors of light, streaming down from an invisible sun and radiating potential figures of the greatest variety.

Ahead and to my left in the gray landscape, a tiger of cosmic proportions was emerging from another dimension. White with black markings, she leapt into the visible realm like a circus tiger breaking through a ring of fire. I sensed a bright light, like a white sun, surrounding the tiger as she bounded into the gray landscape where I was standing. In this first vision, the tiger did not completely exit the place of light behind her or fully enter into my soft, gray world. I was aware only of the land that I stood upon and of half a tiger materializing from some other sphere of reality.

After lunch on the first day, I returned to the bench and watched squirrels leap from tree to tree, branch to branch, showing off their acrobatic skills. Again, somewhere in the greenery above me, the Garuda bird sang its jeweled siren songs, inviting me into my next vision, which delightfully came when I called it. I saw the tiger immediately. She and I were still in the same gray landscape, but she was now fully present, and this time was lying down. The ground beneath us was nothing more than a wide, cloudlike mantel. The tiger lay with her huge front legs hanging over its edge. Peering over the gray-light ledge, I saw the blue planet Earth far below us and thought I must be in outer space, but the space contained no sun, moon, stars, planets, or asteroids—only beautiful Earth.

My attention shifted from Earth's round sphere back to the outstretched tiger, who was deeply engaged in some sort of project. The Tiger Mother, as I thought of her, appeared to be unaware of my presence. There was no verbal communication between us as she concentrated on her task. When I looked over the ledge again, her vast, furry paws were busily drawing, each of her long, sharp claws acting like pens, issuing black ink as she traced lines throughout the space below. I was fascinated but puzzled by these lines. What were they exactly? Why was she drawing them? It didn't occur to me to ask her, because I was too absorbed in watching the mysterious extraterrestrial project unfold before me.

Then I saw what I thought were the Philippine Islands. As I watched, a devastating tsunami swept over the land, killing huge numbers of people. I was horrified and reacted instantly. "Stop it! Stop doing that! You are hurting innocent people!" I cried. The Tiger Mother continued, unperturbed, undeterred by my outburst. Beside myself with wrath and fear, I rushed toward her, then kicked and pummeled her with clenched fists. "Stop doing that!" Kicking her was like kicking a stone mountain. I felt no physical pain, but the immovable resistance of her body shocked me into silence.

She did not blink or move. Finally, she spoke. "It is not I who creates disaster, pain, and suffering."

My internal argument ceased abruptly, and I turned once again to look below. I saw that her array of black lines were drawn some distance above Earth's surface. They were not in direct contact with either Earth or the victims of the tsunami.

She continued: "Actions generate consequences."

I wondered how such a thing could be. Whose actions, what karma, could possibly have caused a disaster of this magnitude?

Our vibrant gray surroundings appeared to be alive. Radiant currents branched out in large, living swirls. The Tiger Mother's black lines, likewise, were moving and pulsing, creating an intricate geometric matrix that enveloped the entire body of space below. This network of circuitry, although black, appeared to be formed by streams of cosmic light forces.

I knew the Tiger Mother had spoken the truth about actions and consequences, but my heart ached to think that karma—immeasurable and mysterious—could result in as much devastation as the tsunami occurring below. Although I couldn't comprehend the interconnectedness of all I was witnessing, I accepted the Tiger Mother's words as heartbreaking unconditional truth, as *dharma*. Somehow I knew I was in the company of superhuman power. Divinity. My heart softened and was lifted to love.

In the fading light of the day, I felt winter's chill creeping down Napa Valley's western hills and watched the sun slide behind Mount Saint John for the last time in 2007. I stood, stretched my stiff limbs, and climbed slowly back to the house. Everything around me felt quiet, beautiful, mysterious, and holy.

Visions of the black-and-white Tiger Mother continued the next day. Communication now flowed between the two of us, as did an increasing sense of familiarity. Transfixed, I gazed into the Tiger Mother's unfathomable, vibrant green eyes, listening closely as she explained the arrangement of lines she was drawing through the gray space below. "I am expanding this template because knowledge, information, and communications are increasing at such a rapid pace that the old pattern needs to be redesigned and the matrix expanded." As she spoke, I turned my gaze to the matrix, trying to understand.

Feeling less intimidated by her presence, I inched toward her until I finally sat right beside her. Gingerly I reached out to touch her thick, long, bristly hair. Then, leaning against her gargantuan but inviting body, I relaxed. Her long, thick tail curled around, and she used it to keep both of us warm.

Eventually, I climbed onto her broad, powerful back, and together we flew swiftly through space. A gentle warm breeze blew through my hair, caressing my scalp, opening and liberating an inner universe of joy. Our speed slowed before we settled again upon the gray land, in a place identical to the one we had left. I slipped off her back, and we stood together in comfortable silence.

After a while, though, I felt an inner twang of anxiety. With some trepidation, I asked her about the future. "Will I be okay after Don dies? Will I be strong enough to carry on? Will you stay with me?" Instantly, she reared high on two colossal hind legs and roared a thunderous bellow. The Tiger Mother's roar caused me neither pain nor dizziness, but filled me with deepening waves of self-confidence and inner peace. In that moment, I knew love and unity would always be there for me to access. Despite whatever hardship might lay ahead, I would never feel alone.

Sitting on her haunches, the Tiger Mother now dipped her paws into the cloudlike, gray-light ground. Then she lifted them both and streamed the gray substance upward like a Venetian glass blower pulls streams of molten glass to create a vessel. She drew what soon looked like a palm tree. The tree's majestic crown of fronds rose and fell like a celestial water fountain. I was enthralled. Perhaps this was how, before time existed, the original palm tree was created. Did archetypes and prototypes originate within the gray matter we were standing on and surrounded by?

The Tiger Mother finished her artwork, smiled at me, and said, "Now you do it!"

"Do what?" I asked.

"Make a palm tree," she said, still smiling.

I laughed at such an absurdity and said, "I can't do that. I have no idea what you just did or how you did it." I shook my head and shrugged my shoulders, trying to communicate the sheer state of helplessness I felt in the face of her request.

"Try, Mary Ann," she said, "just try. Don't give up before you even try!"

I could not resist her invitation. I yearned to create something, anything, as she had done. I rolled my eyes and thought, *Well, here goes nothing*. My hand disappeared as I lowered it into the gray-light cloudstuff. I pulled up some fog and then became utterly absorbed in the process of creating a palm tree. I was astonished. And while the crooked, spindly, three-dimensional tree I drew looked like a child's rendition of a palm, I could have cared less. I produced a wobbly trunk of medium height with four scrappy fronds that made me laugh with pure joy and love. I had just performed a feat far beyond my human capabilities or understanding and was thrilled with my accomplishment. And to have created a tree out of what? Nothing? No. The gray clouds were *something*, even if I couldn't identify what.

"The next time your palm tree will be the same as mine, " the Tiger Mother said.

To celebrate my act of creation, I laughed long and loud. I loved what I had done, and I loved being in this place with my Tiger Mother. In fact, I was experiencing an extradimensional, universal love that included everyone and everything. Warmth filled my chest, then expanded to fill my entire being. What I wanted most at that moment was another tiger ride through space, so I climbed onto the Tiger Mother's back and off we flew, her thick rudder-like tail jutting straight out behind. I threw my head back, closed my eyes, and enjoyed the sensual pleasure of soft, warm wind streaming over me.

I let my mind drift back to the black lines the Tiger Mother had drawn through space. Did they form a sky map replicating in some way the lines of energy running through our bodies, such as the meridians of acupuncture? For the matrix indeed resembled neural circuitry, and I knew this cosmic network served a vital purpose. Through my Tiger Mother, I seemed to have made contact with a fundamental substance of creation, a power that transcended all concepts of good and bad. I had merged into union with the primordial force from which everything arises, and once again I had returned with direct experience of the deathless realm of the immortal self.

After the retreat, Lama Gyatso visited the Family Home to present me with the strikingly beautiful Ögyen Dzambhala text. He beamed as he did so, saying, "Your copy sat on the altar throughout the entire Ögyen Dzambhala retreat." The text itself was a piece of sacred artwork, handcrafted, each page edged in gold, with a gold-embossed cover of exquisite, textured yellow silk. It was the yellow text from my dream!

Fourteen years before, at the luncheon with Lama Gyatso, HE Chagdud Tulku Rinpoche, and the visiting lamas, I had shyly described that dream, the one in which I stood beside a ravine separating me from Emily as she handed me a yellow text across the dangerous abyss. Now I held another yellow text in my hands. My fingers ran over the thin, silken, finely crafted pages, slowly turning over one loose leaf, then another. Lama Gyatso described how through the blessings of Ögyen Dzambhala we can restore the outer universe and the inner inhabitants back to an original state of splendor and vitality. Through our own charity, generosity, and contact with the resources within our own pure nature, we can maintain this flow of wealth and prosperity. Continued practice can eventually lead to the ultimate prosperity of sublime and ordinary spiritual accomplishments, as well as to the ability to guide all beings to the state of pure awakening.

Within the pages in my hand were multiple references to a tiger—an affirmation of the Tiger Mother visions I'd had at the time of the retreat. Sixteen years of visions and dreams coalesced in my mind as though they were many tributaries emptying into one large river. My mind flooded with images of the yellow-text dream and of my Tiger Mother, images that seemed to stream directly from and into the revelations that HH Kusum Lingpa Rinpoche had incorporated into the ancient Ögyen Dzambhala text. I saw HE Chagdud Tulku Rinpoche and all the extraordinary masters whose abundant blessings of love and compassion I had received. Their gold-and-maroon-robed wisdom-presences imbued the yellow text I now held in my hands as I gazed into the eyes of my soul brother, the Venerable Chödak Gyatso Nubpa Rinpoche. For sixteen years, this amazing being, along with our Ari Bhöd lamas, had either masterminded or was present at each unfolding that opened the rose of my true nature, petal by glorious petal.

Chapter 25

FAREWELL, MY BROTHER

O Noble Child, listen to what I am saying with full attention. There are six states of life, three of which you experience after death. The first of these three you experienced at the moment of death, and now you are going to experience the other two, which are the reality of the mind, and rebirth. Pay undistracted attention to me as I read this to you. Death has now come and you are departing from this World, but you are not the only one, as death comes to all people on Earth. Be willing to release any connection with the life you have been living and release the people with whom you have associated. Whatever fear or terror that might come during the experiencing of the reality of the mind, keep these thoughts in your consciousness and go forward. "Visions may appear to my consciousness, may I recognize them as creations of my own. May I know that these are natural apparitions of the mind and come from my previous lack of responsibility for my previous states of being. May I not fear the beingnesses which will appear in my consciousness, but recognize them as thought forms of my own previous states of being."

—ROBERT THURMAN, *Tibetan Book of the Dead*

IN 2008, LAMA GYATSO'S nine year old son, Rigzin, was recognized as a *tulku*—a realized being who has reincarnated specifically to serve as a spiritual guide for others. Lama Gyatso and his wife spent much of that year engaged in the emotionally challenging process of preparing Rigzin for entry into HH Dodrupchen Rinpoche's monastery. In November, Lama Gyatso and his wife,

Linnea, traveled to Chorten Gonpa, where Rigzin received his monk's robes and laughingly had his head shaved. Rigzin would live in auspicious circumstances, in apartments next to HH Dodrupchen Rinpoche and with access to private tutors, including His Holiness's head scholar, Khenpo Thinley Rinpoche (now formally known as Bhikshu Thinley Dorji). Still, Rigzin's parents grieved as they said goodbye to their only child and made the lonely journey back to California.

Lama Gyatso had planned a return to Chorten Gonpa several months later, but instead his life took an inexorable turn into illness. Following his return from Sikkim, Lama Gyatso was unable to recover from jetlag. Two of his students were a husband-wife duo of accomplished physicians. They ran several tests, and the results were not good. Lama Gyatso, like thousands of other Tibetans, had acquired hepatitis in the refugee camps where he had lived as a boy. His liver had been weakened as a result, and for years he had endured spells of illness. Now his liver was filled with inoperable, terminal cancer tumors. Students offered their own livers for transplant, searched India, America, and Europe for medical advice, and offered to mortgage their homes to help pay the exorbitant cost of transplant surgery. Lama Gyatso decided to undergo experimental chemotherapy in Los Angeles, but the procedure, though excruciating, did nothing to abate the swift spread of the disease.

Due to the dire nature of Lama Gyatso's condition, HH Dodrupchen Rinpoche traveled from Sikkim to his retreat center outside Boston, where Lama Gyatso flew as soon as he was well enough. Aimee and I, Lama Gyatso's sisters, and his senior students traveled to be with them. Noticeably thinner and leaning on a cane, Lama Gyatso greeted us as we arrived at the old, unpainted farmhouse where he was residing.

Lama Gyatso believed the retreat center to be one of the most sacred spots in the United States and spent hours with His Holiness every day for several weeks. The *sangha* met with him during the late afternoons and each dinner hour to discuss ongoing treatment possibilities, the costs of liver transplants, possible donors, hospitals, and surgeons throughout the world, but there were no truly viable options that would ultimately sustain his life. Lama Gyatso decided to stop all treatment and return to Los Angeles.

Despite his pain and the daunting health decisions to be made, Lama Gyatso remained resolute in his role as teacher of the ancient, transcendent wisdom of the Nyingmas. Even as he faced his own death and dying, Lama Gyatso practiced *tonglen*, knowing that the extreme amount of energy presenting itself to him through his suffering and pain could be transformed into empathy, to the ultimate benefit of all sentient beings. In this practice of supreme selflessness, we take another person's pain into our heart, mind, and spirit, transform this darkness into golden light, and send it back into the world to help others. It is a powerful ritual that helps us transform our own suffering and the suffering of others around us. It also helps us to overcome the fear of suffering and thus dissolve the tightness of our hearts.

When I first learned *tonglen*, with HE Chagdud Tulku Rinpoche, I and the other students had many questions and concerns. "Rinpoche, won't absorbing all that toxic negative energy into our minds and bodies cause us illness?" Rinpoche had replied, "That is not a problem. You might come face-to-face with your own fears or resistance. If that happens, begin doing *tonglen* for your own fears and for millions of others experiencing fear just like you at that very moment. Breathe in the terror, revulsion, and anger and allow your heart to open. Relax and offer the relief and happiness a space to enter into."

Lama Gyatso affirmed the power of *tonglen* by practicing it throughout his final days. One day, observing my own pain as I witnessed his suffering, he inspired me to do the same. "This is what we do as lamas, Mary Ann," he said. "We can transform the sufferings of the world by assuming the pain of others. We transform that dark energy and send healing light back into the world as wisdom, and the world suffers that much less. Mary Ann, this is what you and I do. This is the Vajrayana path of the Nyingmas."

After returning from Boston, Lama Gyatso and Linnea made the long drive to Napa for one last visit with Don, who was now confined to a wheelchair. The family room was bright with late summer afternoon sun and bouquets of orange, peach, and pink roses from the bushes that grew outside the window. Lama Gyatso commented on them as he greeted Don in his reclining chair. The two old friends embraced each other, while Linnea and I sat quietly on the large, gray-green sofa.

"Well," Lama Gyatso said, "it seems we are both dying." He held several sacred texts wrapped tightly in yellow cloth, which he quickly unwrapped. "This will probably be our last visit, Don-la," he said. He placed the texts on Don's head and conferred a number of blessings. In that vibrant, rosy afternoon, in the midst of the joy these two men shared, in the light that flowed from Lama Gyatso's blessings, even the idea of death assumed the rose-colored hues of otherworldly beauty.

"I have been very lazy regarding religion and the spiritual path, Lama Gyatso," Don said when the blessings were complete. "I've wasted my life in that regard, and now I wish I had done things differently. I'm not afraid to die, but I don't know what will happen to me after I do."

"Don't worry, Don-la. There is nothing to worry about," Lama Gyatso said. "You are already prepared. All you have to do is relax and, when death comes, continue to relax." He looked deeply into Don's eyes. "Let me tell you a story about a fly. There was a terrible storm and the fly was sitting on a piece of shit. Raging waters swept up the piece of shit the fly and the fly held on to for dear life. The turd with the fly was carried off by the strong currents of the flood. Then the piece of shit and the fly began swirling around a *stupa*. A *stupa*, Don-la, is a statue filled with holy relics and blessings of the *dharma*. The shit and the fly circled the *stupa* three times. Because the fly was exposed to those blessings, when it died it immediately recognized the Light and was liberated."

Don's eyes were fixed on Lama Gyatso. For the five-and-a-half years of his illness, Don had been waiting for the teaching and understanding he received now. Lama Gyatso poured forth the last vestiges of his human strength and energy, transforming his own pain and suffering into a compassionate light of inspiration and hope. This was the extraordinary power of *tonglen* in action.

"Don-la, you have been living here at the Family Home with Mary Ann for almost thirteen years. Mary Ann is what we call a *dakini*. She has taken care of your spiritual needs and will continue to do so. You have hosted great, enlightened Nyingma rinpoches. You have dedicated your life to helping others by building the Wellness Center and growing Queen of the Valley into a medical center. Don't worry, Don-la. Because of your pure motivation and generosity, you have nothing to worry about. All you have to do is relax."

Don never expressed feelings of love to anyone except me. After Lama Gyatso told the fly story, however, Don looked at him with eyes full of gratitude and love. Don trusted Lama Gyatso with both his life and his death. Although he was not religious, Don was a man of faith, and he believed his friend the lama. After Lama Gyatso left, Don bowed his head and sat in a private inner space for many hours.

Several weeks later, I flew to Los Angeles for the day to say a final farewell to my best friend and soul brother. It was a heartrending visit. A *sangha* member met me at the Burbank Airport, and we drove the short distance to the Thondup Ling Center, which was also home to Lama Gyatso and Linnea. The center was a maroon stucco house located in a residential area and had been open to the *sangha* for ten years. I had come and gone from this home many times, when presented to visiting rinpoches hosted by Lama Gyatso and Linnea. Lama Gyatso and I had sat across from each other countless times, discussing our families and *dharma* activities in the airy room that was now dominated by a large hospital bed.

Lama Gyatso was in control, but in great pain. I pulled a chair close by his bed. Linnea and Lama Gyatso's sisters, Tsewang and Sherab, sat quietly on the floor close by, always tending to his comfort and needs, wiping his face with scented water, feeding him, helping him sip water. Soon I would no longer have either friend or spiritual confidant, yet I could not speak for fear that conversation would be too difficult for him. I suggested that we just sit and be quiet together, which we did, but he had things he wanted to tell me.

He placed in my hands one of his treasures, a small crystal pyramid. "Look into it whenever you need guidance," he said, "for it has been blessed by the many great masters who have gazed into it. If you have any question, look into the crystal and the answer will come to you."

My fingers closed around this precious gift. Long-repressed, silent tears flowed down my cheeks as I mutely bowed my head.

Amazingly, Lama Gyatso found the strength to lead one more student retreat before illness finally conquered his body, and those who attended marveled at the power of his presence. Afterward, he was flown with a nurse, who was also his student, to Sikkim and to Chorten Gonpa to be with his master HH Dodrupchen Rinpoche and his son Rigzin. Also with him during his last days in this incarnation were Linnea, Tsewang, Sherab, and his best friend, HE Gonjang Rinpoche.

Lama Gyatso was only fifty-seven years old when he transferred his consciousness, in October 2009. I was told that he was ecstatic, describing the *dakas* and *dakinis* that surrounded him. Four thousand friends, monks, lamas, and grieving students flew to Sikkim from around the world to attend his cremation fires and final rites. In Dharamsala, India, where the Fourteenth Dalai Lama resides, the departments and offices of administration for the Assembly of Tibetan Peoples closed that afternoon after an hour-long prayer session. Our beloved Lama Gyatso—the Venerable Chödak Nubpa Gyatso Rinpoche—had served there as chairman of the 10th Assembly of Tibetan Peoples Deputies, from 1988–1990, as the elected representative of the Nyingma School of Tibetan Buddhism.

As these services took place, on the other side of the world, Don was rushed to the hospital with yet another stroke. He spent many hours on a small metal gurney in a cold cubicle, waiting for a hospital room to open up, but even there, in the gray of the emergency room, Lama Gyatso's smiling, almost tangible presence was so intense that Don and I felt as though we might be able to touch him. The sense of Lama Gyatso's familiar happiness and joy gentled the long day.

Chapter 26

LOVE IS ETERNAL

If I speak in the tongues of men and angels, but have not love, I am a noisy gong or a clanging cymbal. . . . If I have all faith to remove mountains, but have not love, I am nothing. . . . Love bears all things, believes all things, hopes all things, endures all things. . . . Love never ends. . . . So faith, hope, love abide, these three; but the greatest of these is love.

—Paul's first letter to the Corinthians, Corinthians 13

A FEW MONTHS PRIOR to Lama Gyatso's passing from this world, I had a dream that provided a powerful and fortifying spiritual jolt to my attitude toward Don's death, which I believed would take place within months. In the dream, I was in a landscape that had a horizon and sky, yet everything was gray, quite like the luminous gray space where I'd met the Tiger Mother. I was standing on the ground of this cloudlike place when thrilling electrical vibrations rippled up and down my spine. I focused this energy on the area between my shoulder blades, then became airborne. (I'd had dreams of levitation and flying since childhood, and this was always the manner in which I took flight.) I flew through the sky headfirst, like a bird, until I arrived at a large canyon, many times the size of the Grand Canyon. Not thinking much about it, I flew to the other side before I turned back. I was exuberant about my journey. I met Don back at my starting point, coming in for a perfect landing beside him. High on an adrenaline rush, I said, "Don, you have to come with me and see it. You won't believe how much fun it is. Trust me, you will love it!"

Don hesitated and pulled back. "I can't fly."

I couldn't allow him to miss out on this exciting adventure. "Yes, you can. I will help you," I said, but he remained fearful. "Honey, all you have to do is hold on to my arm. I can do it for both of us," I said. He vacillated, but eventually agreed. He gingerly took hold of my right arm, and off we went.

It was a magnificent flight. I can't recall what Don's reactions were because I was so thrilled with our airborne victory over the laws of gravity and human limitation. We soon arrived at the canyon and began to cross its bottomless gray abyss. I hadn't noticed the canyon's depth or inherent dangers on my first flight, but as soon as we neared canyon walls, strong drafts began to pull Don downward. I had to use more and more energy and concentration to maintain the forward direction of our flight. I grew concerned, as I was running out of the energy and power I needed to ferry him across the canyon. Don grew increasingly heavy, and I yelled to him, "Try! Try harder!"

We were now sinking, and I became first weary, then exhausted. It wasn't my body or muscles that were tired, but an inner fatigue that was becoming frighteningly pronounced. I knew that if we dropped below the edges of the canyon walls, we would never muster enough strength to rise back up to the flat lands on the far side of the canyon. We sank rapidly as we approached the canyon walls. I focused, relaxed, and then increased my focus again, surrendering and forgetting about downdrafts, anxiety, and Don's weight. With a tremendous amount of concentrated energy and a relaxed mind, I managed to get us to the other side.

I woke up and realized that we had done it, my husband and I. I felt convinced that the dream was prophetic, telling me that the months ahead would be very difficult if I lost my concentration on the *dharma.* If I maintained a relaxed focus on the sunset river of love, on Lama Gyatso, HH Dodrupchen Rinpoche, and the other great Nyingma masters whose blessings I carried, then Don would make a successful transition when he died. I felt profoundly relieved and incredibly thankful for this insight.

In December 2009, two months following Lama Gyatso's death, I was visiting Aimee's home for a family celebration when one of Don's stepdaughters phoned, her shrill voice charging out of the speaker. "Don just called and said he was going to die. He said that nothing we said would change his mind. He has chosen to die!" I had no idea what she was talking about. Don had seemed fine when I left, and the house had felt so calm, the Christmas lights on and a fire burning away December's winter chill.

I ran to the car with my cellphone glued to my ear, but kept getting a busy signal. I put the phone in my purse and started the engine for the long drive back to Napa. An hour later, I pulled into the garage and hurried into the family room, where a slightly grinning Don sat in his usual chair. J.P., Don's caregiver, stared at me, white-faced and speechless.

The Christmas tree lights were now off, the embers of a dying fire barely glowed in the fireplace, and the winter sky draped an opaque blackness behind the room's large windows. It was close to the winter solstice, the darkest and longest night of the year.

I sat in my chair, trying to maintain a calm demeanor, and observed Don, the table between us laden with pills, a heart monitor, medicinal drinks, and a black telephone.

"Don," I said, "I got a strange telephone call down at Aimee's. What's happening?"

Full of confidence and assuming his "in charge" voice, he said that he and his physicians had decided to end chemotherapy. "I am tired of ambulances, hospitals, and wheelchairs. This is not how I want to live. Nothing you say, sweetheart, can change my mind. I've decided to die. The doctors told me that I will die within a month of discontinuing my medications and have assured me that they will help me die when the time comes."

I fell back into the chair. I could not grasp that he would die so quickly. I could not breath. But he had already called each of his children to inform them of his decision and to tell them he loved them, and I knew that he would have his way.

Don wanted to die in the Family Home overlooking his beloved blue-green hills, the giant oak trees, and the valley of vineyards. We transformed the bedroom into a shrine filled with *thangka*s, butter lamps, flowers, and HH Chatral Rinpoche's precious gifts. Lama Gyatso's smiling portrait laughed from Don's bedside table. Comforting pictures of HH Dodrupchen Rinpoche, HE Chagdud Tulku Rinpoche, HH Chatral Rinpoche, and HE Namkha Rinpoche adorned the altar.

In late February, three of Lama Gyatso's senior students drove the six hours from Ari Bhöd and arrived at the Family Home with their sleeping bags and toothbrushes. I opened the front door for them just as I had opened the door to the charismatic, laughing young Lama Gyatso so many years before. "We are here," they told me, "for as long as is necessary."

They sat quietly with Don twenty-four hours a day. They sang softly, in three-part harmony, the melodious and hauntingly beautiful chants from the Shitro Peace Practice, so special to Lama Gyatso and to our *sangha* at Ari Bhöd. Indeed, our precious Lama Gyatso seemed vibrantly alive and present, his picture smiling not only at Don-la, but at all of us gathered around the bed.

Friends and family came in a steady stream to thank Don for the gift of his life. Don did not stop smiling in those days before his death, and for as long as he could talk, he acknowledged the gifts of friendship he had shared throughout his life with those dear to him.

Aimee was in Sikkim, at Chorten Gonpa, with her daughter Emma, but her husband, Greg, brought Olivia and the twins, Tommy and Cricket, to the Family Home to say goodbye to Papa Don and to celebrate the twins' sixth birthday, on February 24. Greg asked that I give them a teaching before they saw Don, as they had never seen anyone dying. So I told the twins the story about the day they were born and how they had visited us at the Guru Rinpoche statue in Sikkim. Olivia, my beautiful granddaughter, immensely compassionate and mature beyond her years, sat with her father in the armchair.

"Today you are having a birthday, and so is Papa Don," I said. I described how they had been able to travel great distances in their spirit bodies moments before their birth. "So now Papa Don will leave his physical body and begin a great journey in his invisible spirit body. He will be able to fly anywhere in an instant, like you did before you were born. He will be able to fly through walls, doors, mountains. Anything!"

They smiled and seemed to understand. One of them asked if Papa Don had an invisibility cloak like Harry Potter's.

"Yes, but remember how Harry Potter's invisibility cloak didn't hide his shoes? Well, Papa Don will be totally invisible to most people."

"What do you mean, Nana, most people? Will some people be able to see him?"

"Yes," I said. "In dreams and visions we will see him. How do you think I saw you at the Guru Rinpoche statue?"

After their visit with Papa Don, there was cake, ice cream, and a birthday serenade for the twins, followed by boisterous rides on the swing and a somersault contest. Early spring flowers bordered the half-circle lawn, along with tall stands of pure white iris. The magnolia tree bloomed magenta, and in the valley below us the mustard blooms colored the landscape yellow under magnificent cerulean skies and towering cumulonimbus clouds.

Don died on the morning of February 26th, three weeks shy of his eighty-first birthday. During his final days, Aimee and Emma were still at Chorten Gonpa's Losar celebration, but Aimee and I remained in phone contact. Soon after Don's last breath, monks at HH Dodrupchen Rinpoche's monastery began to transfer Don's consciousness by performing *p'howa*, while I read the Bardo Thodol to him, sitting close and speaking into his ear. Family and *sangha* members covered his body with white lilies and roses they had collected from a beautiful flower arrangement gifted by my son Tom and his wife, Colette. Thus, before his final departure from our Family Home, Don and I began a journey through the bardo, that space of time between death and rebirth. Helping Don in this way brought me great comfort, inner joy, and peace amid the tears that poured down my face and shook my body. Two hours after Don passed away, long-awaited rains began in earnest. The three years of drought that California had endured were over.

Don had asked that Lama Gyatso and I officiate at his memorial service. The three of us had planned to have Tibetan long and short horns, drums, bells, and prayers, along with the Western music and liturgy. As it turned out, our talented family of musicians and singers performed their farewells and paid touching tribute to Don at the Grace Episcopal Church on the corner of Spring and Oak Streets in St. Helena. Grace Episcopal Church was now church home to my son Jim, his wife, Stephanie, and their children, Sarah, David, and Jonathan. As part of the service, a Scotsman played the bagpipes, and the United States Coast Guard offered a moving trumpet tribute. When the American flag was formally presented to me, those who who had served in the military stood at attention and saluted while a Coast Guard officer knelt before me and read a special proclamation in gratitude for Don's military participation. Knowing how honored Don would have been by this tribute, I shook with sobs. As I walked out the church doors, I smiled at the realization that the Episcopal Church of America was headed by a woman, now the ordained Bishop of the American Episcopal Church.

Despite my fatigue, I was filled with gratitude and thanksgiving. It had been a beautiful week of death and dying. And, to the end, Don had made me feel both cherished and protected. His last words to me were the same words he had said to me every day of our marriage: "You have no idea how much I love you, how much I have loved you since the moment we met. I have never loved another as I have loved you. I never knew what love really was until you came into my life." These words also spoke to the nature of my own love and infinitely profound gratitude for Don. For under the umbrella of his love, I had been able to open even further to the blossoming of the *dharma* and my life's divine purpose.

Chapter 27

CLEAR VISION DREAMS

Before the soul can hear
We must become as deaf—
To roarings as to whispers,
to cries of bellowing elephants
As to the silvery buzzing of the golden firefly

Before the soul can comprehend and remember;
She must unto the silent speaker be united
Just as the form to which the clay is molded
Is first united with the potter's mind

For there the soul will hear and will remember
And then the inner ear will speak
The voice of silence
Can't be heard while insistent demands of
False personality clamor for recognition

—H. P. BLAVATSKY,
The Voice of the Silence

I N 2013 I MARKED the twenty-sixth anniversary of meeting HE Chagdud Tulku Rinpoche in the Oakville hills. For me, the past quarter century had been a breathtakingly expansive journey in which I had tasted the sacred nectar of timeless love, traveled in the far reaches of mystical realms, and dived into the dark, radiant depths of loss. In every moment, Light had been my companion. Listening and devotion had been my practice. Learning to follow the noble, esoteric path illuminated by the voice of my Inner Teacher, the Nyingma masters, and my essential Being, the *dakini* Yeshe Tsogyal, had been my sacred journey. It was—it is—an intense and demanding union, an exhilarating and awesome marriage.

Months before meeting HE Chagdud Tulku Rinpoche, I graduated from seminary, completed my ordination requirements, and received a glowing letter of praise from the bishop—who, despite congratulating me on a job well done, informed me that I would not be ordained, that I should go home and create my own church. Not long thereafter, I had a vivid dream that struck me as very unusual. The dream lifted me up in a way I'd not experienced before, and although I would not grasp the significance of this dream for many years, I knew that it was a treasure to protect.

The dream began on a luminous white beach bordering warm ocean waters of turquoise and varying shades of blue. I was frolicking with a tall blonde man who was my age, about thirty-years old. He had an athletic build, blue eyes, and skin tanned a golden bronze. He looked so much like me he could have been my twin brother. We ran and dove into the buoyant, soft ocean waters, laughing and swimming, enjoying the sheer sensual pleasure of floating on our backs under the gentle sun.

Suddenly we heard cries of distress from the depths of the sea. Someone was in danger and needed our help. We dove through shallow, light-blue waters before reaching the ocean's deep, dark depths. The crying intensified as we descended. Suddenly, a large octopus ejected black ink that enveloped and blinded us, then seductively slithered its arms up our legs, intent on sexually arousing us to a point where we would lose control. My twin moaned in deep sexual ecstasy, and I cried out to him, "No! Don't do it! Don't give in! Look up, swim up toward the Light!" My voice did not reach him in the opacity. Fighting for survival, I swam, focusing my eyes upward, until suddenly I sped like a shooting star through different strata of turquoise waters, exploding out of the ocean and up into the sky, where I burst apart into billions of brilliantly colored atoms. I became a Fourth of July celebration showering lively sparks on the earth below.

Then I became a woman, a mother sitting in a warm green field with wildflowers, on a mountain near the sea. A girl was lying next to me, curled in the fetal position, asleep. Her body was bruised, her faded dress torn, and her blonde hair in matted disarray. She was the child we had heard crying at the bottom of the ocean. I spoke to her as she slept and told her she had nothing to fear. I promised we would stay together in that beautiful field until she healed. As time passed, her health improved, and I took her to the beach to play in the sand. While she played, I looked out over the water and thought about my beautiful twin brother, and I knew that the time would come when I'd be called back to the inky depths below the turquoise waters to rescue him.

Within months of this dream, HE Chagdud Tulku Rinpoche appeared in my life. Under his guidance, various elements of this nighttime vision began to unfold. Through the decades of this unfolding process, one of my biggest lessons was learning how to simply be. Western culture does not recognize the necessity of being quiet, of letting go; it values doing over being. We accumulate things. We shop. We feel lonely. We focus on the material world and all its distractions. We seek happiness in external success, fame, recognition, and wealth. We have become unable to sit with our own minds, as we are afraid to meet our true selves. This cycle results in less happiness, more frustration, and eventually a feeling of isolation and separation from our own Truth.

In the years after Lama Gyatso subtly suggested that I was Yeshe Tsogyal, I had no idea how to act. I did not know what was or would be expected of me from either the American community or the Tibetan community. I was deeply relieved that Lama Gyatso segregated me at first from the American community, because the Tibetans did not expect me to do anything. My job was to simply learn to be, to live a secluded life in meditation, prayer, and writing. This is how mystics and visionaries need to live. There are those who tend to the world's soul through meditation, and this has been my path, to heal through union with the compassionate wisdom-mind of the Universal Buddha.

As I have aged, my visionary experiences have only expanded. One series of what I now call Clear Vision dreams occurred over a span of years, and they eventually jumped from the dream world and came to life before my eyes. The first three dreams occurred within three weeks of each other, during the time when Don and I were adjusting to the realities of his cancer, and they were so wondrous that they remain vividly present to this day.

In the first dream, I saw the royal presence of a single, tall, graceful palm tree. In the second dream, there were three palms—all great in height, slim, regal, breathtakingly beautiful. In the third dream, there was again a single palm tree, which appeared to be of a different species; although equally majestic, it was more solid, stouter, and somehow more masculine than the others. In all three dreams, the palm trees rose heavenward into deep blue sky. The beautifully symmetrical, columnar palm trunks were like connections between earth and heaven. Giant fans of fronds like feathered arrows gracefully crowned each tree. Mesmerizing geometric designs were etched on each trunk and each frond, but, most remarkably, an iridescent, illuminating, clear, liquid light radiated from both the interior and exterior of the palm trees. This powerful cosmic light brightened the tree's geometric patterns, the blue sky above, and everything else into an otherworldly brilliance.

In the year following Don's death, I traveled with my children and grandchildren to the Andes in Peru. At the ancient sacred lands of Machu Picchu, on our last night, I once again entered into a Clear Vision dream. The light-filled palm tree was this time embellished with a toucan, a technicolor specimen with a cartoonish, oversized beak. I sensed Don and Lama Gyatso conspiring from the other side to add to my dream an element of humor, some perspective, laughter, a joyful reminder of the magnificent comedy inherent to life. When I awoke, I was overcome with a renewed sense of the play of divinity that transcends both life and death.

The Clear Vision dreams were astounding to behold, rendering me breathless and speechless. All I could do was observe in wonder. Each time one of these dreams began, I would say to myself, "If I pass my hand before my eyes and don't see it and the vision continues, then I must be asleep." This was a difficult feat since my hand was heavy with sleep, but the Clear Vision of the palm trees continued unimpeded by my physical hand. I was indeed asleep. These otherworldly visions however, didn't stay within the confines of my dream world.

One night, shortly after midnight, the doorbell rang at the Family Home. Whoever was ringing at that hour was uninvited. I hid behind my partially closed bedroom door and peered anxiously toward the front atrium. A bright, waxing quarter moon highlighted two strongly built, relatively young, agitated males. They fidgeted about the door. The large, plate-glass windows of the atrium offered no visual protection, so I stood concealed for a moment, chilly in my nightgown, trying to figure out what to do. My mentally rehearsed, forty-year-old escape strategy included a quick exit through one of the bedroom's French doors, which led away from the atrium. In that moment, however, I completely forgot this plan.

The doorbell chimed again. Nervous that the men outside could hear my wildly beating heart, I considered my next move. To get to the front door, I would have to walk down a glassed-in hallway, fully exposed. There was no way that I would walk into the face of danger in my nightgown. On the other hand, it was May 1, my seventy-fourth birthday, and the fact that these burglars thought they could upset my birthday plans irked me. I also grew impatient with my own fear, so I eventually resolved to answer the door. I pulled on a bathrobe and slippers, then marched down the glass hallway, ready to face whatever my future would bring.

Outside the door was Enrique, the son of Francisco, the estate's gardener for twenty-six years. I've known Enrique all his life, but the boy I'd known was now a Marine Special Forces sergeant recently returned home from several tours of duty in Afghanistan. He was looking at me with great concern. He and his friend, a war buddy, quickly explained that there was a dangerous fire on the ranch, not far from the house.

"I don't want to frighten you," he said, "but Tom has told us to prepare the hoses so we can water down your roof if the wind shifts the fire in this direction."

Having already laid out the hoses, the two young men accompanied me out through the atrium to see the hill beyond my house engulfed in tall, leaping flames of orange, red, and ruby. We stood under a giant oak, where quiet hives of honeybees were sleeping through the smoke and heat. The fire raced with the speeding wind across the hillside.

I climbed into the high cab of Enrique's truck, feeling protected between the two Marines. Both had served dangerous, challenging duties in Afghanistan and were now applying for positions with the California Fire Department. They were serious students, not only learning how to fight fires, but also training as EMTs as well. I was in safe hands. We drove to ranch headquarters, and they discussed wind shifts and temperatures. Firetrucks spinning red, white, and blue lights were stationed by historic eighty-year-old barns, the whole scene lit up by the orange light of snapping, spitting flames. Enrique parked, we climbed out, and I strode toward my son Tom, the fire chief, firefighters, the firetrucks, and the raging inferno.

"Happy Birthday, Mom," Tom said. "Those are some amazing Roman Candles you have there for your birthday."

Before us, two burning palm trees rose high into the midnight sky. The trunks' geometrical patterns were outlined in blazing red embers while every frond was an individual fire painting in itself. A giant column of diamond-shaped red sparks erupted from the crowns of the trees, shooting up into the eerie night. This was not a vision, not a dream, not a figment of my imagination. This was happening directly in front of me in a cacophony of sirens, explosions, and clicking cameras, while firefighters in heavy suits directed massive rivers of water at the trees. I was speechless, immobilized, concerned about the messages coming from the other side to mark the advent of my seventy-fourth year.

May 1, my birthday, is what pagans call Beltane, one of the four Gaelic seasonal festivals widely observed throughout Ireland, Scotland, and the Isle of Man. On this day, pagans believed, the May Queen and the Queen of Winter battled one another for supremacy. As I stood before the blaze on May 1, 2013, it appeared that the burning palms were the Queens of Darkness and Light battling it out. The palm trees continued to burn, but not burn. There were no flames, just towers of engulfing red-orange sparks, and embers that delineated the extraordinary geometry of the trunks—a real-life vision of the palm trees in my dreams.

Then the fire careened toward a huge, historic barn. As the flames approached just feet from the structure, I ran over, possessed by the same wrathful energy I'd felt years before, when I told Lama Gyatso, "She wants to be heard!" Standing in the heat of the blaze, filled with inner power, I silently commanded the fire to alter its course. "How dare you!" I raged. "Who do you think you are?" These were not the great lords of fire. They were immature, wild, out-of-control entities about to cause great damage. "Go around the south side of the hill where you will cause no harm!" I commanded.

A lifetime of energy poured into that moment—my childhood desire to create the same magic that the priest symbolically made when he transformed the elements of earth (bread), air and fire (candle flames), and water (wine) into the Body of Christ at my First Communion; the imperative ecstasy of my Good Friday calling at the age of forty-one in the middle of Eucharist when I heard *This is what you will do*; and the powerful accumulation of almost three decades of esoteric mysteries, mystical experiences, visions, and spiritual practice to which I'd devoted myself since taking refuge within the Nyingma school of Tibetan Buddhism. All that energy, practice, and intention poured into and through me, directed at those beings of fire. They were *not* going to claim my barn or my home.

At that very moment the wind shifted and carried the fire away.

Chapter 28

BACK TO THE BEGINNING

O Memory! thou midway world
'Twixt earth and paradise,
Where things decayed and loved ones lost
In dreamy shadows rise,

And, freed from all that's earthly vile,
Seem hallowed, pure, and bright
Like scenes in some enchanted isle,
All bathed in liquid light.

—ABRAHAM LINCOLN,
"My Childhood Home I See Again"

NAPA VALLEY'S ANNUAL grape harvest spawns intense activity, excitement, and exhaustion for the valley's vineyard owners, viticulturists, and winery workers. Prior to harvest and the grape crush, the valley's buckeye trees quietly signal the last days of summer by dropping their leaves, while August's crepe myrtles bloom and pregnant vines explode with the hopes of a standout vintage.

The vibrant autumn equinox of 2013 brought three luncheon guests to the Family Home—Linnea, Lama Gyatso's widow; Anne

Lind, one of his senior students and an Ari Bhöd board member; and Gonajang Semola, a princess in Bhutan's royal family and the wife of HE Gonjang Rinpoche, who had been present in the vegetable garden in 2003, when Yeshe Tsogyal radically emerged from within me. I had never met the vivacious, lovely, and charismatic Gonajang Semola, who was visiting as a close friend of Linnea.

As we lunched under the tulip tree, I asked Gonajang Semola about where she had grown up, envisioning her as a beautiful, dark-haired girl racing her horse through the country's mountainous Himalayan landscape. When I asked about the royal family, she laughed and said, "Come to Bhutan! I will show you my country myself. The four of us women will go and visit the Tiger's Nest."

It is said that Padmasambhava flew to the Tiger's Nest, the most sacred site in Bhutan, to subdue a local demon, then stayed to meditate in a cave for three years, three months, three days, and three hours. Today, the site is a destination for pilgrims and home to a monastery that sits 10,200 feet high and clings to a narrow stone ledge, which drops precipitously to the valley hundreds of feet below. Given my Tiger Mother visions, I was compelled by the term "tiger's nest"—the idea felt mysterious, slipping like a sacred bird through the fingers of time, shaking its wings, opening them wide, and soaring along a trail left by the stars straight to Bhutan.

"Didn't Yeshe Tsogyal fly there on the back of a tiger?" I asked.

"No," Semola corrected me. "It was Padmasambhava who flew on the tiger."

But I had flown on the back of my Tiger Mother, and I remained convinced that it was Yeshe Tsogyal who also flew to that cave. A melodious web of imagination spun around me, and I barely heard the rest of the conversation. A breeze caressed the wind chimes overhead, the inner music grew louder, and my mind became submerged in strong yearnings to go home, back to Bhutan, back to the Tiger's Nest.

Just over a year later, I was once again flying east toward the Himalaya Mountains—although I had barely made it onto the plane. In the year after hosting Semola, I trained for the trek to the Tiger's Nest, but I also injured my hip, required months of physical therapy, and then, having given myself a hernia from an overzealous weight-lifting program, underwent surgery. As if that weren't enough, I also came down with a serious bout of vertigo just weeks before I was scheduled to leave. Medication was helping, but my doctor said that under no circumstances was I to travel. Although my personal divinations supported my travel plans, I couldn't overlook the fact that I often had to lie motionless on the bed to keep the room from spinning, and I was ready to give up. Aimee was insistent, however, and requested a divination from HH Dodrupchen Rinpoche, who gave his blessings for a successful journey. With an ample supply of vertigo medication, trust, and faith, I decided to make my pilgrimage to Bhutan.

Health wasn't the only thing that occupied my time in the months leading up to the trip. Two months before my scheduled departure, Linnea received word that HH Dodrupchen Rinpoche would be making a quiet, private visit to Ari Bhöd–Pema Drawa. For years, Lama Gyatso and our *sangha* prayed that His Holiness would someday visit our retreat lands. Now, five years after Lama Gyatso's passing, this great master of meditation and miracles was actually going to do so. Such a visit required a tremendous amount of preparation. A small group of us set to work. David, an original *sangha* member, dug long, deep trenches for new water pipes, which were installed, quickly covered, and raked clean. We scrubbed floors and windows.

Gonajang Semola arrived early from Sikkim to shop for and prepare suitable menus. On the day of His Holiness's arrival, Lama Lhundrup created elaborate sacred drawings on the dirt road leading into Ari Bhöd for His Holiness's car to cross as he arrived at the new Rinpoche House, where he would stay. When His Holiness finally arrived, we held scarves, bowed, and waved our delighted welcomes. All I could do was throw my head back and laugh with absolute joy.

Unfortunately, during the last days of this momentous visit, a flu also arrived at our retreat lands, and I flew home to recuperate. Just as I was experiencing the worst of the illness, we received word of yet another unexpected visitor: His Holiness Taklung Tsetrul Rinpoche, the Supreme Head of all the Nyingmas and another great meditation master. Ari Bhöd's devoted board members had made annual Losar pilgrimages to Sikkim and Chorten Gonpa for close to a decade. Twice they had also made the rugged journey to the Himalayan hill town of Simla to offer scarves and request a visit from HH Taklung Tsetrul Rinpoche. Though he had agreed to come and to confer his Northern Treasures text, obtaining visas had proved impossible for years. That very week, however, his visa cleared, and he announced that he would arrive in two weeks. This monsoon of unexpected blessings left the *sangha* in a state of exuberant shock. Once again, they undertook a challenging course of preparation, as more than a hundred people signed up for the auspicious Northern Treasure retreat.

Because of my health concerns and the strenuous demands of the retreat, I regretfully missed what felt like a once-in-a-lifetime opportunity. Then, with departure for Bhutan just two weeks away, Aimee phoned to announce that HH Taklung Tsetrul Rinpoche and his entourage would visit Northern California, stay at Aimee's house, then spend a quiet day of rest in the Napa Valley with me. The Family

Home had to be prepared. Tables placed on the lawn were covered with my mother's lace tablecloths, freshly polished silver flatware, and red-and-gold Lenox china. My son Tom delivered his best wine, and we washed the delicate wine glasses we reserved for special occasions. An outside seating arrangement was organized for His Holiness, as Lama Gyatso had taught me to do, with a sofa draped in a red-and-gold brocade cloth I kept for auspicious visitors. Tibetan rugs were placed in front of His Holiness's seat of honor, and green umbrellas were set in place. After this whirlwind of activity, the Family Home, at its best in the fall, was ready to receive our royal visitor.

Students helping with food preparation stopped what they were doing and joined me to greet the black van when it arrived. His Holiness was helped into his wheelchair, and we offered our scarves in greeting. Nothing escaped his notice as he was carried up the steps to the front door. Though eighty-eight years old, His Holiness had a seemingly endless supply of energy. We adjourned to the lawn area for tea and an authentic Tibetan lunch prepared and offered by the owners of our local Tibetan restaurant. His Holiness sat on his special sofa and motioned for me to sit next to him in one of two chairs that had been set up for the lamas and interpreters.

His Holiness's nephew and interpreter, Paljor, sat on the rug by his feet. I leaned back in my wicker chair and let out a long sigh of relief.

"I have waited so long for you to come. So many years! And now you have come!" My words were slow, coming from another dimension, reflecting my deep sense of awe and wonder. "You are here! I am sitting right next to you. It seems like a dream!"

We talked of Dzogchen teachings and the Northern Treasures. When I told him about my upcoming trip to Bhutan and trek to the Tiger's Nest, he emphatically disapproved.

"No!" he said. "Too hard for you, too difficult, too high."

"Your Holiness, I am very strong. I can do this!"

"No! Too high. Too difficult."

I felt unusually stubborn. I was determined to go to Bhutan and had promised myself to at least attempt the hike; I could always turn back if it proved too difficult. A yearning arose, more powerful than ever, urging me to Bhutan, but I decided to hold my tongue. We talked instead about whether America was a good place for *tulkus* to grow up.

"Yes!" HH Taklung Tsetrul Rinpoche's answer was immediate and unequivocal. Two *tulkus*, one of whom had been recognized by Lama Gyatso, lived at his monastery. Though we had been in a three-way conversation, talking thru Paljor, His Holiness now swung his leonine head around and faced me directly. "Whoever Lama Gyatso 'recognizes,' all Nyingmas agree with," he said. "Lama Gyatso very high Nyingma." I felt the intention of his words—that he accepted Lama Gyatso's recognition of me as Yeshe Tsogyal. He fixed me with one of the most penetratingly fierce stares I'd ever experienced. Fascinated, I stared back and heard my Inner Teacher. *Just look deep into his eyes.* Instantly, I was swept into that vast openness between the layers of time and space.

His Holiness turned to Paljor and said, "She can come stay at my monastery!"

Feeling a light-headed joy and familiar waves of love, consumed with wonder at the legend of a man sitting next to me, I leaned back in my chair and looked past the gnarled old oak tree, where thousands of migrating starlings would soon arrive, thickening its foliage and filling it with their babble before lifting up into black avian clouds and spooling away in curling ribbons with perfect timing and precision over the valley.

"Everything is green," His Holiness said, staring out at the valley. "Everywhere you look, you see green."

"Yes," I said. "But different shades of green."

I was moved to offer prostrations to His Holiness. When I had attempted to offer prostrations to HH Dodrupchen Rinpoche several weeks before at Ari Bhöd–Pema Drawa, I had found it almost impossible to rise from the floor. Still, I felt compelled now. I let my body sink down into a place of deep peace, lifted my hands overhead in the prayer pose, and made three prostrations in honor of this great saint who had come to visit me. A youthful, effortless, liquid grace flowed through me each time I touched my head to the ground. Then I resumed my seat beside His Holiness and silently handed him my mala to be blessed. He took the beads in his huge, gnarled hands, blessed them, and spoke to Paljor, who left quickly to retrieve a beautiful *katak*, which His Holiness placed around my neck. We spoke no more.

Now, I thought, *I am ready for the next journey, my pilgrimage to Bhutan.*

Chapter 29

THE TIGER'S NEST

The youthful peacock of East India has returned.
Peacock turn your parasol in the direction of pure Dharma
And we young ones might find the path to liberation.
The sweet sound of the cuckoo bird from the forests of South Bhutan
As he soars along the Empress Spring's chariot of merit
More beautiful than the flutes of those celestial gandharva goddesses
Foretells the auspicious return of a happy summer.
                    —RIGDZIN JIGME LINGPA, *A Song of Realization*

AIMEE AND GREG, ALONG WITH their children Tommy and Cricket joined me for the two-week trip to Bhutan. Our busy itinerary would include visits to the Tiger's Nest and several other sacred sites, some of which we would see together, and some of which I would visit alone. Gonajang Semola was unable to join us as planned, but arranged for her brother, Khenpo Thinley Rinpoche, the celebrated head scholar at Chorten Gonpa, to accompany us throughout the journey. Our flight from Delhi made a short stop in Bagdogra, where we picked up the smiling, youthful Khenpo Thinley for the twenty-minute flight to Paro.

A beaming Aimee escorted Khenpo Thinley to my seat and said, "Mom, this is Khen Rinpoche." As I looked into this young Rinpoche's radiant eyes, I heard an inner voice joyfully exclaim, *So that's the name you are using this time around!* We stared at each other, each sporting ear-to-ear grins. I laughed inwardly thinking that of course I'd go along with the game. "Hello… *Khen Rinpoche,*" I said, thinking to myself, *Don't worry, I won't tell anyone your real name.* Khenpo's presence added an immediate luster to our family group. As he was a member of Bhutan's royal family and a high-ranking rinpoche, I knew he would help us experience magical aspects of Bhutan that would otherwise be inaccessible.

The city of Paro, Bhutan, sits in a beautiful, deep Himalayan valley 1.5 miles above sea level, nestled among mountain peaks that pierce the sky at 18,000 feet. The airport is said to be the most dangerous in the world. The 6,500 foot runway, originally built for helicopters, is one of the few in existence that is shorter than its elevation above sea level. Only eight pilots are qualified to land there. Our Drukair airbus began its swooping descent like one of Bhutan's endangered, sacred black-neck cranes. The plane banked in sharp but graceful turns between steep mountains and came within feet of clipping the houses scattered over the hillsides. Eventually, our pilots leveled out for the short final approach, then glided downward, executing a relatively smooth landing.

The hand-painted terminal, with its forest-green roof, beckoned us as we descended a moveable metal staircase. Looking skyward, I fixated on the azure blue dome. "Look!" I cried, unable to restrain my enthusiasm, and excitedly and pointed toward the sky. "Look at the sky. See how blue it is? Do you see that color blue? And the clouds, look at the clouds!" A virtual garden of translucent white clouds transited the heavens like crowned messengers. In *Blue*'s embracing presence, I felt included in a cosmic congregation and exhilarated by a sense of risk, as though I were jumping into a current of radical aliveness, pioneering another new direction in my life. Greg, already on the tarmac, managed to take a picture that shows the six of us stepping out of our known world through a slit in time under *Blue*'s magical umbrella. We had left behind the problems of the modern world and officially entered Bhutan, the Land of the Thunder Dragon.

Our bags waited in the near-empty terminal. Deeply aware of the blue sky above, I barely restrained laughter as we were quickly escorted through baggage claim and outside to our waiting van. As we pulled out of the airport parking lot, Tsewang Rinchen introduced himself as our head guide. Jigme was his assistant and Tsering our driver. All three were dressed in Bhutan's national costume. These dark-haired, handsome men were striking in their earth-toned, knee-length robes, which were tied with belts in a way that formed pouches in front of their stomachs. These robes, or *ghos*, were set off by ten-inch-wide pristine white cuffs, while knee-length black stockings and Western-style shoes showcased the men's lean, muscled legs. Tall, long-limbed, and slim, Tsewang was in his early thirties and had imposing good looks that radiated competence and intelligence.

"In Bhutan we believe everything and everyone deserves respect, because we are all part of a whole, the trees, the animals, the sky, along with the people," Tsewang informed us, standing in the well next to the van's door. "We believe that no one and no thing exists independent of everything else."

During the short drive to our hotel, the Zhiwa Ling, or "Place of Peace," we learned from Tsewang that Bhutan is governed by a holistic approach to life. This tiny Buddhist kingdom secreted away in the

Himalayas had opened its doors to the outside world just sixty years before. It was quickly emerging from a fourteenth-century culture and catching up to the technological age, and was thus in the midst of a stimulating socioeconomic, religious, spiritual, and radically alive national conversation. Most notably, Bhutan had chosen to define well-being as the primary measure of the country's progress, valuing Gross Domestic Happiness over Gross Domestic Product, the materialistic measure of success that most countries use. The government, which pays for healthcare and education, is jointly run by a monarchy, an elected congress, and religious leaders, all agreeing to enact strict laws protecting the rights of the environment as well as the happiness of all animals, the sky, and people. This was a land where I could speak freely about the spiritual sciences I'd embraced—astrology, meditation, divination, cosmic geometry, and mantric words of power. I wondered if the people actually saw themselves as diamond sparks, part of the dazzling darkness of eternity. During the past year, I had heard what sounded like calls to "come home." Now, as we drove to the Zhiwa Ling, my understanding of home was expanding in all directions.

Two porters pulled at thick ropes to open the heavy front doors of the Zhiwa Ling Hotel, revealing an interior of astonishing beauty. The Bhutanese display their artistic talents in their clothing and in the artwork that decorates their homes and buildings, and here was no exception. The balconied lobby, which rose three stories, was a spectacle of woven textiles, preserved antiquities, and wood columns and lintels carved in colorful, intricate geometries. A wave of *feng shui*, or flow of energy, greeted us inside this handcrafted, living museum filled with ancient sacred memories. Yet it was neither ostentatious nor glitzy. The natural building materials of wood and stone, the warm hues of the artwork, the lovely and humble Bhutanese people all seemed to be offspring of a prolific marriage between the sacred and the secular, between heaven and earth, a sacred conjoining that permeated our entire trip.

Tsewang presided over our midday meal, laying out schedules and answering questions. We were to make the Tiger's Nest trek early the next morning. I had hoped there would be more time to acclimate, and for the first time since I'd decided to make this journey, I began to doubt my skills, strength, and ability. Everyone else at the table looked so young, eager, exuberant, and strong. I fiddled nervously with my rice curry and wistfully imagined myself passing a delightful day alone in this spectacular hotel, reading and gazing at the mountains, two indoor sports I excelled at. None of us would be in Bhutan if it hadn't been for my passionate desire to trek to the Lair of the Tiger. Now all I wanted to do was escape!

I tried to talk my way out of the hike, but was voted down, and before I could voice further objections, we were rushed toward our rooms to gather hiking boots and daypacks. That afternoon, we were undertaking a shorter, less difficult walk, to a ruined fortress that had once been strategic in Bhutan's defense against Tibetan invasion. Although the afternoon hike did turn out to be quite manageable, doubts lingered in my mind. I knew next day's trek would be far more demanding than this one, and my vertigo, though well managed, still caused me to occasionally stumble or wobble. HH Taklung Tsetrul Rinpoche's admonition still echoed as well. But neither old age nor vertigo engendered any sympathy from my travel companions, so I resolved to set aside my fears.

We were the first to arrive at the trailhead the next morning, and true to the family's athletic enthusiasm, we were on the trail in a matter of minutes. Tsering, who was assigned to be my caretaker, accompanied me as I took up my trekking poles and gingerly stepped onto a wide, well-worn path that led gently upward. My family flew around the trail's first curve and then vanished. Tsering followed close behind as I planted my poles on the trail one careful step at a time.

A few moments in the mountain's morning light ignited waves of wondrous joy. Illumined by the sun's first warm rays, I was suddenly struck by where I was and what I was doing. I had done it! I had made it halfway across the world to fulfill my dream in Bhutan. I was still alive and, wonder of wonders, actually on the trail to the Tiger's Nest. Spontaneous laughter bubbled up from within my heart.

An hour passed as we trekked slowly upward. Tsering and I hugged the mountainside to allow for the passage of a string of horses carrying tourists. Two men at different times stopped during that upward climb and asked to photograph me. When I asked why they would want my picture, each said, "Because you look so happy!" And it was true. After another hour, more tourist-laden horses appeared. A young woman leaned over her saddle and said she would be willing to walk if I would prefer to continue the hike on a horse. I must have been some sight. This lovely young woman's kind and generous offer buoyed my spirits, but, to my surprise, I declined the ride. I was determined to complete this trek not only for myself, but for all seventy-five year olds, for the handicapped, for those who wished they could be here but were unable. I felt profoundly fortunate.

This was a pilgrimage, wasn't it? Centuries before, both Padmasambhava and Yeshe Tsogyal had walked this very land, introducing Buddhism to Bhutan. They had meditated here in a series of thirteen caves for three years, three months, three days, and three hours. Entering a state of being beyond words, I sensed delicate, lace-winged visions forming within me, seeking freedom to "declare" themselves. I allowed them to cultivate themselves and concentrated instead on how to climb up the next irregular placement of stones that served as stairs.

The day's hike takes most people three hours up and three hours down, but it took me longer. The last forty minutes were the most difficult, and my fatigue increased as we neared 10,000 feet. Finally, I saw the grandchildren perched on stones under a sign that read "Teahouse," waving and cheering me on. Cricket, gregarious and extroverted at ten years old, grabbed my hand. "I don't want to hike anymore, Nana, so I am staying with you. I have a deck of cards and we can play Uno. Come on!" As Khenpo Thinley vanished with the rest of the family around the next bend in the trail, Cricket led Tsering and me to the teahouse, where she set us up at an outdoor wooden picnic table.

Tiger's Nest Monastery was perched atop a stony ledge just across a narrow green canyon, and I absorbed the magical allure of the mountainous beauty as several cups of strong, sweetened tea refreshed my spirits. Birds hopped about the tables, eating crumbs under the blue sky and pine trees. Subtle forms of energy emanated from the proliferation of colorful prayer flags and from the picturesque, whitewashed monastery itself. It was so close, yet so far. After the teahouse is the final two-hundred feet of trail, but it is challengingly steep, at times with no handrails. When we'd made plans back home, I had been determined to climb to the actual monastery, but now it didn't matter. Nothing mattered other than the fact that I was exactly where I was meant to be.

I lifted my *mala* from around my neck and silently recited mantra, picturing Khenpo Thinley and the family at the Tiger's Nest. As Aimee described later, Khenpo Thinley sat down in the temple and began to chant in his beautiful, polyphonic voice. Spellbound tourists dropped coins at his feet. (Cricket's twin brother, Tommy, thought that was a clever way to earn a living and decided he might become a monk, too.) After chanting, Khenpo Thinley lit and offered a butter lamp, then vanished through a door into the far reaches of the monastery.

Back at the teahouse, I felt included in his prayers. I was euphoric. I couldn't have been taken any "higher" than I already was. I had no visions, but visions didn't matter. The intense peace and jubilation that had filled my being since the moment I stepped onto the mountain were enough. I knew had finally come home, back to the Tiger's Nest.

Chapter 30

REVELATIONS AND ANCIENT TEMPLES

May I take on this suffering for other beings.
May this suffering ripen within me instead of them.
May not even a single sentient being experience this kind of suffering.
May it be so.
May all sentient beings be parted from their suffering.
How fervently I wish this to be so.
May they never experience suffering.
How wonderful it would be if others no longer endured any torment.
I will work hard to eradicate all the suffering of beings.

—COMPASSION MEDITATION OFFERED BY
HIS HOLINESS DODRUPCHEN RINPOCHE,
in Sandra Scales, *Sacred Voices of the Nyingma Masters*

MY EXPERIENCE OF MERGING with no-time had begun at the Paro Airport. During our climb to the Tiger's Nest, ordinary time faded, in the same way that dusk slowly swallows the apparent light of day. The next morning, on a visit to one of Bhutan's oldest temples, yet another dimension of time caught me in its web.

Tsewang explained the history of the Kyichu Lhakhang temple as our tour bus pulled into the parking lot of this ancient site. "This temple was built to pin down part of a giant ogress who was causing a lot of trouble to those who were spreading the Buddhist *dharma*."

This piqued Tommy's interest, and he suddenly sat upright. "An ogress?" he asked. "Did they get her? Is she still alive? Because if she is alive, I'm not getting off this bus!"

"The King of Tibet and Padmasambhava built 108 temples in both Bhutan and Tibet to pin her down. And they succeeded!" Tsewang explained.

Cricket joined with her brother. She also wasn't getting off the bus unless the ogress was dead. She had another concern as well. "Are there tigers or poisonous snakes at this temple?"

The adults smothered their grins. When the children were finally convinced of the temple's safety, we filed out of the bus. I didn't mention to the twins the fact that "the ogress" was likely a series of earthquakes. The mythic terms of the Buddhist legend seemed somehow apropos, more personal and authentic.

Kyichu Lhakhang was originally built in 659 by King Songtsen Gampo, the founder of the seventh-century Tibetan empire. He is also credited for introducing Buddhism to Tibet. His two queens, the Nepalese princess Bhrikuti Devi and the Chinese princess Wencheng, were devout Buddhists and considered to be emanations of the goddess Tara. Tibetans celebrate these women for influencing the king and playing a crucial role in the eventual adoption of Buddhism in Tibet. Some believe their presence explains the two great Indo-Nepali and Chinese influences on Tibetan Buddhism.

Kyichu Lhakhang's whitewashed exterior walls and multi-tiered roofs made it look as if one building folded into another. The highest tier of the inner temple was covered in gold, as was its spire. Elongated niches set in the thick earthen walls, under painted wooden beams, housed handcrafted prayer wheels, which I spun, one after another. I pictured myself standing on the earth, spinning prayers around the sun, as our universe spun through space.

Khenpo Thinley was in conversation with a temple monk when Tsewang and I met him in the inner courtyard. The monk opened a gilded door that led into the inner hall of the main temple. Inside, we stood before a highly revered statue, commissioned in the seventh century, that depicted the original Buddha, known as Buddha Shakyamuni or Jowo Shakyamuni, as a twelve-year-old boy. Grooves shaped like human feet were worn into the wide plank floors before the statue, imprinted by generations of people offering prostrations. Aimee placed her feet into these impressions and did three full-body prostrations. The twins followed suit, but I was unable to perform more than a slight bow. Khenpo Thinley noticed my dizziness and suggested that I do "just a little prostration." I bowed to an unseen congregation that hovered, danced, and spiraled through the aromas of incense and burning butter lamps.

We entered a second temple, in which a five-meter-tall statue of Padmasambhava stood in a great silence. Vertigo prevented me from leaning my head all the way back, so I tilted my head to the side and rolled my eyes upward, but the massive statue was impossible for me to see in its entirety for more than a split second. Another enormous, commanding statue, of the beautiful Kurukulla, or Tara, sat to the side of Padmasambhava. I yearned to see her face, long, flowing black hair, necklaces, her bow and arrows made of flowers, but again dizziness prevailed. I apologized to her for not taking in all the visual blessings I knew pilgrims experienced gazing at her beauty.

I closed my eyes to settle the vertigo and surrendered myself to the energy of the temple, which gently whirled around and through me.

I slipped between the layers of ordinary time-space and into a kind of trance. *Say the Seven Line Prayer!* I heard. According to the great nineteenth-century Tantric scholar Mipham Rinpoche, "This prayer in seven lines is the most majestic of all prayers." It is a celebration of and appeal to Padmasambhava, also known as Guru Rinpoche. I had recited the prayer and its mantra many thousands of times. It is said that if a student calls to Guru Rinpoche in this way, he will come "like a mother who cannot resist the call of her child."

I opened my eyes to see Khenpo Thinley standing across from me. The message felt destined for both of us, so I approached him. "Say the Seven Line Prayer!" I said urgently. He stood rooted to the floor, his eyes large, misting, and round. It felt important that he say the prayer, so I repeated myself again. He remained standing, tall and regal, then shifted his eyes away from mine and stared straight ahead. Khenpo Thinley had indeed heard my message, probably on a more profoundly conscious level than I heard myself.

I needed a respite and stepped into the shadows to close my eyes. Presently, Aimee came to ask for money so that Khenpo Thinley could pay for a butter lamp. "It's important, Mom. He needs to light it."

Still woozy, I unzipped my purse, but its contents blurred before my eyes. I handed it to Aimee. "Just take the purse. I can't see."

Khenpo Thinley stood before an altar. Tsewang ushered me to the altar, too, and instructed me to cover my mouth while lighting the candle to prevent impurities from tarnishing the purified flame. The twins also wanted to light a candle and argued over who would get to do so. All I wanted was to be left alone so I could listen to my Inner Teacher. Being magnetized toward some other realm of consciousness, I struggled between two worlds in the dark interior of the temple, only dimly aware of arguing grandchildren and the counting of money.

Slowly, I took a flaming match from Khenpo Thinley's reverent hands, lit the candle, and handed the still burning match back to Khenpo Thinley. Coordinating my body to perform this simple physical act was cumbersome, heavy, and difficult. I drifted to the side of the altar to collect myself.

Before me was a beautiful gold statue atop a square, gold pedestal. "Who is that?" I asked Khenpo Thinley, who now somehow stood beside me. "His Holiness Dilgo Khyentse Rinpoche," he answered quietly. A powerful energy pulled me forward to the statue. I bowed and rested my forehead on the pedestal. To discover the shining likeness of this great teacher before me was astounding, an unexpected miracle, unleashing a golden expanse of memories, each like a petal bursting open on a lotus blossom. Though I had never actually met HH Dilgo Khyentse Rinpoche, it was as if our hearts and minds had been joined throughout time.

It began when, at the age of ten, I came across a newspaper photograph of a minor movie star and an overwhelming longing riveted my imagination. I was emotionally aroused by his attractive face and powerful physique, but most of all I was drawn to his large hands. The hypnotizing intensity of this attraction convinced me that I would recognize my future husband by his hands, though in fact neither of my husbands had hands similar to those I fell so deeply in love with as a girl.

Instead, sixty years later, in 2009, I sat in my living room paging through Sandra Scales's beautiful book *Sacred Voices of the Nyingma Masters*, when I saw a photograph of a Tibetan Master sitting on a chair, his large hands resting upon his knees. As a seventy-year-old grandmother, I experienced an electrical jolt of arousal erupt from the core of my being—the same experience I had had as a child.

This time, however, it was the explosion of an ancient memory being recognized.

"My God," I whispered aloud. "This is him!" I now realized that the large, passionate hands I had fallen in love with as a girl had triggered the memory of the hands I had *actually* known long ago—those of HH Dilgo Khyentse Rinpoche. In the lightning-bolt moment that I recognized this, I stood rooted in certainty as a jarring stillness possessed me. But upon reading the text that accompanied the photograph, I learned that HH Dilgo Khyentse Rinpoche had passed away seventeen years before.

Standing there in the dappled afternoon light in the living room at the Family Home with HH Dilgo Khyentse Rinpoche's picture laid out before me, I was struck by another memory. In 1992 HE Chagdud Tulku Rinpoche asked me to join a pilgrimage to Asia to attend the cremation ceremonies of one of the twentieth-century's greatest spiritual figures and teachers, HH Dilgo Khyentse Rinpoche. We would have to leave in ten days. HE Chagdud Tulku Rinpoche spoke briefly about this peerless master of the Dzogchen, revealer of Padmasambhava's teachings, who had served as Supreme Head of the Nyingma lineage and as a teacher of the Dalai Lama. In the end, I had not had time to make the necessary arrangements, but HE Chagdud Tulku Rinpoche assured me that I could still receive blessings from His Holiness. Referring to HH Dilgo Khyentse Rinpoche's ongoing legacy, which would survive even when he was gone, HE Chagdud Tulku Rinpoche said, "If healer create medicinal plant, then plant continue to cure people long after healer dead."

Just before I left for Bhutan, HH Taklung Tsetrul Rinpoche and I were discussing my upcoming travel when he said, "Do you know that HH Dilgo Khyentse Rinpoche escaped from Tibet and made Bhutan his home?" Having already felt passionate, powerful, and inexplicable connections with both men, I stared at His Holiness. To be sure I'd heard correctly, I asked, "Did you say HH Dilgo Khyentse Rinpoche?" His Holiness's entire countenance lit up like the sun. Not only had he himself taken many teachings from HH Dilgo Khyentse Rinpoche, but he had in fact succeeded him as Supreme Head of the Tibetan Buddhist Nyingmas.

Now, standing in stunned reverence at the foot of HH Dilgo Khyentse Rinpoche's statue, my head resting on its cool, gold ledge, I felt enveloped in a magically magnetic spin. Eventually I straightened up and backed away from His Holiness's statue to exit the temple. As I passed the burning butter lamp in front of Guru Rinpoche and Tara's altar, I received another clairaudient message: *You are the Palm Tree! You are the Light!* In an instant, the meaning of my Clear Vision dreams, of those exquisitely illuminated, burning palm trees flooded my being: *I was the Light!* The transcendent, clear, liquid Light that pulsed from within and without the trees was not separate from me. It was a projection of the essence of my true Inner Self. The Light was *me!*

The mystery of my palm tree visions and those red burning palms shooting their birthday fireworks heavenward on my seventy-fourth birthday were imbued with special meaning. The Light I saw in my visions was the same Light that connected me to *Blue* and to the rushing river of love from those colorful sunsets so many years ago. It flowed between me, Don, Lama Gyatso, and HH Dilgo Khyentse Rinpoche. Compassion and miracles all came from the same source—the *heart-mind*, the Light! The source from which I emanated is what the Nyingmas call Dharmakaya, the Mother space, where all phenomena manifest, abide, and dissolve. In that strange, sublime, shaky moment, as I reached for the outer door to leave the Kyichu Lhakhang temple, I felt as though I'd received a doctorate in closure.

I stumbled to our waiting white van in a daze, trying to fully absorb the truth before me: the dreams, the visions, the clairaudience, the clairvoyance, the clairsentience, my teachers—all were expressions of the One! For years, I had marveled at the indescribable healing Light I'd seen in my dreams, not realizing, just not realizing, that I am that same Light, the Light that exists in every atom of the universe. That is who I am! A Light Being!

Chapter 31

TOGETHER AGAIN

My head knocks against the stars.
My feet are on the hilltops.
My finger-tips are in the valleys and shores of universal life.
Down in the sounding foam of primal things I reach my hands and play
with the pebbles of destiny.
I have been to hell and back many times.
I know all about heaven, for I have talked with God.
I dabble in the blood and guts of the terrible.
I know the passionate seizure of beauty
And the marvelous rebellion of man at all signs reading "Keep Off.

My name is Truth and I am the most elusive captive in the universe.

—Carl Sandburg, "Who Am I?"

THE DAY I RETURNED HOME from Bhutan, I settled in to read the newspaper. The *New York Times* featured an article by the MIT physics professor David Kaiser, "Is Quantum Entanglement Real?," about experiments to test the possibility of entanglement. "Entanglement concerns the behavior of tiny particles, such as electrons, that have interacted in the past and then moved apart," the article reads. "Tickle one particle here, by measuring one of its properties—its position, momentum or 'spin'—and its partner should dance, instantaneously, no matter how far away the second particle has traveled. The key word is 'instantaneously.' The entangled particles could be separated across the galaxy, and somehow, according to quantum theory, measurements on one particle should affect the behavior of the far-off twin faster than light could have traveled between them."

I am neither scholar nor scientist, and I would never be able to "do the math" on the quantum theory of entanglement, but I've never heard or read anything that describes so well what I have encountered with HH Dilgo Khyentse Rinpoche and other great Nyingma masters as does the quantum theory of entanglement. The word *entanglement*, however, strikes me as incompatible with the felt experiences I have had. In these enlightened moments, I have never felt trapped, knotted, snared, or entangled. What the theory omits is the overwhelming spiritual experience and understanding of unity and the compassionate love that floods my being when magnetized by either the physical or spiritual presence of these great teachers, even those who lived centuries ago. I have found, in fact, that what certifies the purity of my visionary episodes is the accompanying passion, the sense of "falling deeply in love." Intellectual understanding of this love is impossible, but the emotional wisdom of these experiences is woven into my *heart-mind* at the cellular level. It is indelible.

In August 2015, the Venerable Gonjang Rinpoche return to Ari Bhöd, along with our dear Khenpo Thinley Rinpoche, on his first American tour. It was a nostalgic, high-spirited, powerful reunion filled with teachings. Yeshe Tsogyal and Red Tara empowerments were offered to students who arrived from all over the world, including thirty from mainland China. Between teachings, Khenpo and I found time to discuss many things—my being a living incarnation of Yeshe Tsogyal, the nature of a Buddha, and My Yogi, whom I was disappointed not to have met in person. "After all these years, I still don't know who he is," I lamented.

"I can't finish my memoir, because something is missing, but I don't know what. It's like a jigsaw puzzle. Almost all the pieces are joined together, except the last few."

After the retreat concluded, the rinpoches visited the Family Home. We walked the gardens, reminisced, ate ripe figs from trees. There were riotous ATV rides around the property. The Family Home was decorated with colorful Indian corn from the vegetable garden and bright orange volunteer pumpkins. The four-year drought had much reduced the vegetable garden, however, so there were none of the giant pumpkins that Gonjang Rinpoche remembered so vividly from his visit in 2003. We still enjoyed a sense of abundance as mouth-watering aromas of lamb stew, steamed rice, and fresh apple cobbler lured us into the kitchen for our last lunch together.

At the table, Gonjang Rinpoche flipped through the working draft of my manuscript, offering silent prayers and blessings, while Khenpo and I again turned to the subject of My Yogi. "I understand that My Yogi is me but also someone I knew in a past life, someone I shared a profound love with, but I also know he is here in my present life," I said. "I *know* that because I can *feel* him, but why can't I figure out who he is? Why can't I find him?" As these words left my mouth, I wondered if I somehow meant that he was here in my kitchen with us. Could he be right here in my home?

During our time together in Bhutan, Khenpo had offered me teachings and guidance concerning my spiritual practices. With folded hands, he had fervently requested that I increase my Guru Yoga practice, which involved specific prayers and repeated visualizations of Padmasambhava. I knew that this instruction, combined with the clairaudient message I'd received in the Kyichu Lhakhang Temple—*Say the Seven Line Prayer*—was significant. Now it dawned on me that perhaps Khenpo had been suggesting practices specifically to awaken me to the possibility that Padmasambhava was My Yogi. This seemed doubtful.

"Khenpo," I said sadly, "My Yogi isn't Padmasambhava."

"Why? How can you say that?" Khenpo's eyes bore into mine, demanding an explanation. Khenpo has a great deal of what we astrologers call Mars energy, the energy of the spiritual warrior. His concise words can slice through obscurations like diamond swords.

"Because My Yogi is ancient," I said, resigned. "He is *very* old, and Padmasambhava never grew old, so the two cannot be the same." There was another reason as well, which I was unable to articulate in that moment: when I visualized Padmasambhava, I experienced his genuine and receptive compassion, but those visualizations were more static than the warm, engaging visions I had of My Yogi.

Khenpo can be playful, full of laughter, extremely observant, and compassionate. In an instant he can also become a determined, highly focused teacher. My words launched him into a teaching about how a Buddha can manifest in any form they choose. "They can be human or nonhuman. Light Beings like your yogi can be male or female, old or young. They can manifest themselves in this world or in alternative or parallel universes. They can move instantaneously from one realm to the next. They choose appearances that speak most directly to the individual."

Something about the word *move* captured my attention. It activated something within me, and a vision emerged. I saw a limitless ocean of enlightened beings. I was one of them. My Yogi was one of them.

All of us were *moving* from one manifestation to another, as Khenpo described. I did not see my physical self, yet I was undeniably part of the vast undulating expanse from which everything emerges. My Yogi and I, along with the enlightened beings, traveled faster than the speed of light between various realms, sometimes unseen, sometimes appearing either as Light Beings or as human beings.

Khenpo continued to describe how Buddhas manifest, and I observed as his silvery, silent words enter my self.

When it was at last time for final goodbyes, Khenpo approached me with a smile. I was profoundly happy to have seen both rinpoches again and indescribably grateful they had come to visit. Yet in saying goodbye to Khenpo, and for reasons that are still mysterious to me, I shifted "personas" in the blink of an eye.

"I did not know if I would ever see you again, so I am quite pleased you came to visit me, Khenpo," I said, my voice flat, loud, and mechanical, my body rigid, my words distant, polite, and detached.

Aimee protested, "Mom! What are you doing? Why are you using that tone with Khenpo? Please stop it!"

I turned toward Gonjang Rinpoche, vaguely aware that I was going to issue a similarly mechanical speech of farewell. At this moment, HE Gonjang Rinpoche took me firmly by the shoulders and placed his forehead against mine, as Tibetans often do. A thunderbolt of energy poured into my head and rigid body, which I met with a corresponding surge of diamond-like energy until I heard an inner voice say, *Just relax.* We stood in the driveway in this profound field of Light for timeless moments. When Rinpoche finally stepped back, the state of my body normalized, and I realized that my friends were leaving. Rinpoche danced toward the car, laughing and waving.

Dazed, I watched as the rinpoche's pulled out of the driveway, circling past the small garden statue of the fat-bellied Laughing Buddha.

Once they were out of sight, I rushed to my bedroom. *Please don't let me behave like this! I cried inside myself. Don't let these feelings be negative. Don't let me create negative karma. Don't let me be hurtful. Don't let me have hurt Khenpo!* What had begun as a normal exchange of farewells had turned into distress and confusion. My eyes locked onto my Longchen Nyingthig practice book, which I picked up in desperation. It fell open to a pen-and-ink line drawing of Padmasambhava.

In an instant my Inner Being flew like a meteor into the arms of Padmasambhava, and the two of us merged as One. Electric volts of passion streamed from our hearts as I once again fell ardently in love with my consort from 1,200 years ago. Everything within and around me seemed to be in motion, and I now understood that it was true: My Yogi *was* Padmasambhava! He had been so many things to me over the course of my life. He was the grandfather, and I was the child. He was the teacher, and I the student. He was the twin brother in my dream of diving to oceanic depths in response to a child's cry for help. In that dream, however, he stayed immersed in the darkness of the ocean, while I rose forth to the Light. Now, in my bedroom at the Family Home, held in Padmasambhava's embrace, I was a woman and he the Beloved.

As I gazed at his image, I thought, *He is not two-dimensional. He is not a black-and-white line drawing. He is color. This is red and that is blue, and white goes here, and over here is yellow. Weren't the flowers more pastel, less primary in color?* The luminescence that illuminated this vision, the vivid moving colors and blooming flowers surrounding him were a bold and dynamic display. *He is real!*

He is a dance of multidimensional movement! He is a field of vibrating flowers and light!

Of course Padmasambhava had been with me, around me, *within me* my entire life! As I merged with him, becoming one with my twin, with myself, the vision shifted into a rainbow-colored multitude of flower-lights giving birth to a new woman: an enlightened being ready to share her journey of discovery.

APPENDICES

Acknowledgments

BUDDHIST LUMINARIES

Through the Venerable Chödak Gyatso Nubpa, I met many renowned Nyingma adepts and spiritual masters with whom I experienced the vast richness of the true nature of my mind. In profound gratitude, I offer them my autobiography, which materialized due to their auspicious blessings, in both this and past lives.

HIS HOLINESS THE FOURTH DODRUPCHEN RINPOCHE
Known to Nyingma practitioners as our Sun and Moon, HH Dodrupchen Rinpoche offered his blessings to my book, which empowered a long writing process. His Holiness is the Supreme Head of the Nyingma School of Tibetan Buddhism, abbot of Chorten Gonpa, and the principal lineage holder of the Longchen Nyingthig Treasure known as Heart Essence of the Vast Expanse. His Holiness is the spiritual grandfather of Lama Gyatso's son, Tulku Rigzin.

HIS EMINENCE CHAGDUD TULKU RINPOCHE (1930–2002)
Born in Eastern Tibet, Rinpoche was an advanced master recognized as the Fourteenth Chagdud (iron knot) incarnation. As my beloved Root Master, he recognized me as Yeshe Tsoygal's living incarnation and introduced me to Lama Gyatso. Chagdud Rinpoche's wife, Khadro, and his son, Jigme Tromge Rinpoche, have been my friends and supporters for many years.

HIS HOLINESS CHATRAL SANGYE DORJE RINPOCHE (1913–2015)
His Holiness, whose name translates as "Enlightened Indestructible Freedom from Activity," was a world-famous reclusive yogi known for his great realization. His early recognition empowered my life for many years.

HIS EMINENCE NAMKHA DRIMED RINPOCHE
His Eminence is the Supreme Head of Tibetan Buddhism's Rigpa lineage and a *tertön* who revealed one of Yeshe Tsoygal's *termas*. He led Yeshe Tsoygal

retreats at Ari Bhöd–Pema Drawa for ten years. He has supported my long spiritual journey and a mentor and invaluable guide.

THE VENERABLE TULKU THONDUP RINPOCHE

Tulku Thondup Rinpoche is a celebrated scholar, spiritual adept, and prolific writer affiliated with HH Dodrupchen Rinpoche's monastery and Harvard University. His early and invaluable critique of my book, along with our subsequent friendship, remains a transforming and unforgettable experience.

THE VENERABLE GELONG KALSANG RINPOCHE

A fully ordained Bhikshu monk and longtime Vajra Master to HH Chatral Sangje Dorje Rinpoche, Gelong Kalsang Rinpoche officially recognized me as a living Buddha. He is a major spiritual force and retreat master at Ari Bhöd–Pema Drawa and is the founding abbot of Kunkhap Yoesal Thonkdol Chöling Monastery ("Every Wish to See the Village of Light"), in Nepal.

THE VENERABLE LAMA NAWANG THOGMED RINPOCHE

Raised by His Holiness Trulshik Rinpoche, Lama Thogmed Rinpoche is the abbot of Thupten Chöling's Solokumbu–Nepal monastery, home to three hundred nuns, two hundred monks, and fifty homeless boys. A renowned master temple and mandala artist, his artwork glorifies Ari Bhöd–Pema Drawa's retreat lands. With Gelong Kalsang Rinpoche, he has led Ari Bhöd–Pema Drawa's powerful annual retreats for many years. Lama Thogmed Rinpoche gifted me with the Tiger Mother paintings that protect my book.

KHENPO THINLEY RINPOCHE

Khenpo Thinley is the head scholar for His Holiness the Fourth Dodrupchen Rinpoche and founding abbot of the Bhutanese monastery school Zangkhar Tashi Chöling Institute. He served as guide during my pilgrimage to Bhutan and the Tiger Nest in 2015, ushering in a more public chapter in my life as Yeshe Tsoygal.

WESTERN SUPPORT TEAM

STEVEN FORREST

Steve is the founder of Evolutionary Astrology, a psychological mode of astrology that emphasizes free will and compassion. His writing, which offers a far-reaching introduction to the pageant of the universe, led me directly into an exploration of the mystery beyond the cosmos.

PATRICIA MICKELBERRY

From the book's early days, Patricia illuminated for me the difference between keeping a journal and writing a book. A gifted developmental and line editor, Patricia has helped transform my manuscript. The editor-writer relationship is unique and in this case cherished.

KRISTIN KAYE

Having two very capable editors has been my good fortune. Kristin is a talented developmental editor whose flair for reorganizing the book and establishing a narrative arc will always amaze me. During our time together, Kristin came to be a student of Tibetan Buddhism and dear friend.

AIMEE GAMBLE PRICE

My beloved daughter, Aimee, has been an indispensable support and *dharma* sister since 1991, when she met her "surrogate father" Lama Gyatso, who in turn considered Aimee his American sister. Her husband, Greg, and her four children have been instrumental in bringing Tibetan Buddhism to America and the building of Ari Bhöd–Pema Drawa.

LINNEA NAN NUBPA

Since Linnea's marriage to Lama Gyatso, our lives have been substantially woven together in a relationship of genuine love and care. Becoming widows at the same time deepened our bond, as we strove to preserve Lama Gyatso's vision of Ari Bhöd–Pema Drawa. She was present when Lama Gyatso and I first began visualizing this book, in 2008, and introduced me to the book's designer, Daniel Tesser, eleven years later.

LISA SLATTERY, OFFICE ASSISTANT

Lisa organizes my day-to-day business schedule, handles countless other tasks, and reminds me of everything I've forgotten, thus freeing me to write.

FRANCISCO MORALES

Francisco has maintained the exquisite grounds of the Family Home for twenty-five years, fielding countless emergencies and greeting every visitor with a smile and gifts from his gardens.

Glossary

anni-la: grandmother

Ari Bhöd–Pema Drawa: Ari Bhöd is a nonprofit foundation founded by the Venerable Lama Chödak Gyatso Nubpa Rinpoche to preserve the ancient Nyingma wisdom tradition of Tibet. Pema Drawa is the retreat land at the heart of all Ari Bhöd's activity.

bardo: intermediate state of existence between life and death

chorten: a monument reflecting the perfect proportions of the Buddha's body

Chorten Gonpa: His Holiness the Fourth Dodrupchen Rinpoche's monastery in Sikkim, a Himalayan state of India. Located on the outskirts of the capital city of Gangtok, this monastery has become the main seat of the Longchen Nyingthig tradition.

chuba: an earth-colored, woolen, ankle-length wrap

delog: one who has crossed the threshold of death, traveled to unseen realms, and returned to tell of what they have discovered

dharma: Buddhist teachings about the nature of reality

Dharmadhatu: the realm of all phenomena

Dharmakaya: the unmanifest aspect of a Buddha, encompassing qualities such as wisdom, compassion, fortitude, and patience

dorje: literally, "thunderbolt"; a ritual tool that symbolizes spiritual power

Dzogchen: a tradition of "Great Perfection" teachings aimed at realizing the innermost nature of mind, the primordial state of being. It is central to the Nyingma school of Tibetan Buddhism.

Glossary

gonpa: a center for spiritual practice and learning

Thupten Chöling: a retreat community and monastery established by His Holiness Trulshik Rinpoche in northeastern Nepal. It is home to more than 700 monks and nuns, the majority of whom are Tibetan refugees.

khenpo: a title awarded for completion of intensive higher Buddhist studies

Kyichu Lhakhang: an important Himalayan Buddhist temple in Bhutan. In the eighth century, Padmasambhava visited the Jowo Temple of Kyichu, where he is believed to have concealed many spiritual treasures.

lama: title for a teacher of the *dharma*

Longchen Nyingthig: a *terma*, or revealed scripture, of the Nyingma school of Tibetan Buddhism, which gives a systematic explanation of Dzogchen. It was revealed by the *tertön* Jigme Lingpa.

mala: a string of prayer beads

mindstream: the continuity of awareness between moments and lifetimes

p'howa: practices to prepare for dying and death

Pure Land: celestial realm of a buddha

Rigdzin Drub-Pai Ghatsal: the retreat center of His Holiness Chatral Rinpoche in Pharping, Nepal, where the Venerable Gelong Kalsang Rinpoche served as Vajra Master

Rigdzin Ling: a retreat center for Chagdud Gonpa, an international Tibetan Buddhist organization founded by Chagdud Tulku Rinpoche to promote and preserve the arts, philosophy, and meditation practices of the Nyingma school

rinpoche: literally, "precious one"; honorific used to demonstrate respect for reincarnated, notable, learned, and/or accomplished lamas

samsara: the cycle of death and rebirth

sangha: spiritual community

siddha: one who has achieved spiritual enlightenment

siddhi: spiritual powers

stupa: mound-like structures that serve to house relics and facilitate meditation

terma: various forms of hidden teachings

tertön: a person who discovers a terma

thangka: Tibetan Buddhist spiritual painting

Thondup Ling: a practice group for Chagdud Gonpa, an international Tibetan Buddhist organization founded by Chagdud Tulku Rinpoche to promote and preserves the arts, philosophy, and meditation practices of the Nyingma school. The group provides for the study and practice of Tibetan Buddhism in the Los Angeles area.

tonglen: practice of transforming the pain of others by visualizing inhaling their pain and exhaling blessings

tulku: reincarnate custodian of a specific lineage of teachings

vajra: a club with a ribbed spherical head that is used as a ritual object; it symbolizes the properties of both diamond (indestructibility) and thunderbolt (irresistible force)

Plates

Tiger protectors, painted and gifted by the Venerable Lama Nawang Thogmed Rinpoche, a master artist and abbot at the high-altitude Thupten Chöling Monastery in Nepal

PAGE 129
Upper left: Mary Ann's mother, University of California at Berkeley (1929)

Lower left: Mary Ann, two years old, Piedmont, California (1941)

Upper right: Mary Ann with her father at Christmas (1939)

Lower right: Mary Ann at her high school graduation, Sacred Heart Convent, Menlo Park, California (1957)

PAGE 130
Upper: Mary Ann's children Tom, Jim, and Aimee at Christmas (1965)

Lower: Mary Ann and her father traveling to China, Taiwan, and Hong Kong as part of a research trip (she was reporting on the Vietnamese and Cambodian refugee problem for the *Napa Register*) (1980)

PAGE 131
Upper: Mary Ann hosting one of many large family dinners

Lower: Mary Ann graduating with a dual masters degree from the Church Divinity School of the Pacific, Berkeley, California

PAGE 238
Upper: Wedding portrait with Don (1997)

Middle: Wedding portrait with Don and Mary Ann's mother, her children, their spouses, and her granddaughter Sarah (1997)

Lower: Wedding portrait of the combined family (1997)

Plates

PAGE 239
Upper: Chagdud Tulku Rinpoche and Mary Ann officiating at the wedding of Lama Gyatso and Linnea at the Family Home. Also present are their son, Rigzin Norbu, and Lama Gyatso's mother and sister. (2001)
Lower left: Mary Ann's grandchildren David and Sarah helping her bless the grape harvest at the vineyard of their parents, Jim and Stephanie Gamble (2003)
Lower right: Don, Chair of the Board of Trustees, Queen of Valley Hospital, Napa, California (2002)

PAGE 240
Upper Left: Don and Patches, Easter (2002)
Upper Right: Lama Gyatso holding Tommy, who was born while Mary Ann was visiting the Guru Rinpoche statue in Sikkim (2004)
Lower Left: Mary Ann and her granddaughter Cricket (2007)
Lower Right: Khenpo Thinley Rinpoche and HE Gonjang Rinpoche at the Family Home (2015)

PAGE 241
Upper: Rinpoches and lamas with the *sangha*, Ari Bhöd–Pema Drawa (2016)
Lower: Mary Ann and Tom during the grape harvest (2017)

PAGE 242
Upper: Mary Ann and her grandchildren on the family trip to Machu Picchu after Don's passing. Left to right: Cricket Price, Tommy Price, Jonathan Gamble, Mary Ann, Emma Price, Olivia Price, David Gamble, Sarah Gamble
Lower: The Venerable Lama Nawang Thogmed Rinpoche, abbot and master temple artist (1995)

PAGE 243
Upper: The Tibetan spiritual adept Gelong Kalsang Rinpoche, abbot of the Kunkhap Yoesal Thonkdol Chöling Monastery in Nepal and spiritual leader at Ari Bhöd–Pema Drawa (1995)
Lower: In Ari Bhöd–Pema Drawa's magnificent handcrafted temple (2018) hand crafted temple and Aimee Price 2018

About the Author

MARY ANN MCGUIRE has dedicated her life to the uplift of humankind through her spiritual and philanthropic pursuits, both public and private. In addition to offering guidance to those in need as an ecumenical chaplain, Mary Ann has played an active role in establishing and sustaining charitable organizations that promote spiritual study, the integration of Eastern and Western healing modalities, the arts, education, and the advancement of underprivileged youth. She has traveled the world not only as a seeker, but also as an advocate for positive change and the empowerment of all.